50

KINGDOM OR I

British History in Perspective
General Editor: Jeremy Black

KINGDOM OR PROVINCE? SCOTLAND AND THE REGAL UNION, 1603–1715

KEITH M. BROWN

MACMILLAN

First published 1992 by
THE MACMILLAN PRESS LTD
Houndmills, Basingstoke, Hampshire RG21 2XS
and London
Companies and representatives
throughout the world

ISBN 0–333–52334–2 hardcover
ISBN 0–333–52335–0 paperback

A catalogue record for this book is available
from the British Library

Copy-edited and typeset by Cairns Craig Editorial, Edinburgh

Printed in Hong Kong

I will make them one nation in the land
on the mountains of Israel.
There will be one king over all of them
and they will never again be two nations
or be divided into two kingdoms
Ezekiel 37, v. 22 (NIV)

Can a country be born in a day
or a nation be brought forth in a moment?
Isaiah 66, v. 8 (NIV)

CONTENTS

ACKNOWLEDGEMENTS

I am especially grateful to Dr Roger Mason not only for reading and making helpful corrections to the typescript, but also for engaging in many useful discussions during over-long morning coffees in St Andrews. A similar debt is owed to Dr Jenny Wormald and Dr John Morrill for reading and commenting on the typescript. The fact that all three of these scholars are such distinguished and effective ambassadors for a British approach to the early modern period also makes one hopeful that a book on Scottish History will be more widely read than might have been the case only a decade ago.

I wish to thank B. T. Batsford Ltd for use of a map from I. Donnachie and C. Hewitt, *A Companion to Scottish History*, Map 16, 1989. Every effort has been made to trace all the copyright holders, but if any have been inadvertently overlooked the publishers will be pleased to make the necessaary arrangement at the first opportunity.

Thanks are also due to all mentioned in the bibliography at the end of this book. We all see the landscape of the past on the shoulders of others. I am grateful to the British Academy and to the Royal Society of Edinburgh who each sustained my research career at the outset of this inquiry into the nature of the regal union. Finally, thank-you to my wife, Janice, for tolerating my neglect of things present for things past, and to my children, Michelle and Mark, for agreeing occasionally to turn down the volume on the television set.

PREFACE

A book of this nature relies very much on the work of a great many scholars, and my own own role simply has been to try and bring together recent research in a format which is accessible. I owe, therefore, a considerable debt to many colleagues who have greatly expanded our knowledge of seventeenth century Scotland, even in the relatively short time since I was an undergraduate.

However, there remain surprising gaps, and one would have little difficulty suggesting topics for research students in this period. Here and there I have tried to fill in some of those gaps, but it would require a very different type of book to do that task properly. On the whole the first half of the century and the post-1689 years are better researched than the restoration era. I suspect that the 1688–9 revolution in Scotland is the least understood of the major events of this remarkable century. Generally, we know more about political ideas than about how government operated, especially the post-1660 privy councils, while the whole area of government finance is very sketchy. The picture we have of burgh elites and the clergy is more complete than that of the landed aristocracy. Individuals like Montrose and Claverhouse have been the subject of a surfeit of biographies while the likes of Argyll, Lauderdale and Queensberry are crying out for revision. Surprisingly, a region like the highlands has been more written about than the south-west, and on the whole rural local studies are non-existent. I suppose what this is leading up to is an excuse for the patchy nature of this present work. It is also a plea for scholars and their research students to take up some of the above topics.

Preface

Seventeenth-century historiography has been something of a battleground over the years. Scottish historians have been, on the whole, less combative than their English colleagues in recent times, although there are a few notable exceptions. It has been difficult to write this book without treading on some toes, and especially at a time of such national uncertainty over the future of the union, it is particularly difficult to be dispassionate. I have tried to reflect the state of the current literature rather than to imprint my own interpretation in too partisan a way. Needless to say there is no such thing as objective history and, since prejudices make their appearance, perhaps I should declare them. The views expressed here, therefore, are those of a lowland, protestant Scot with little sympathy for Gaelic culture, for Stewart romanticism, or for bishops. I also have a deep distrust of London while remaining ambivalent about the English and the union. Very probably I would have agonised before voting for the union in 1707, and then spent years worrying over whether the Scots had made a dreadful mistake. If any of that baggage gets in the way I apologise, and hope this cautionary note helps the reader see past my own inadequacies.

One other point. I am sure some colleagues will disagree with my treatment of the aristocracy, but I remain unimpressed by any arguments which suggest even a relative decline in aristocratic power in the early modern period.

Since this is essentially a history of Scottish politics I have retained the Scottish spelling of the Stewart dynasty, and the Scottish designation of monarchs, namely James VI, James VII and William II. At all times £ are £ Scots unless £ sterling are specifically stated. £1 sterling was the equivalent of £12 Scots.

There are no notes to the text, but an extensive bibliography of secondary works can be found at the end. In using the bibliography readers should be aware that works are only cited once where I think they might be most useful. However, this does not mean that they cannot be used in the context of another topic or chapter.

KEITH M. BROWN

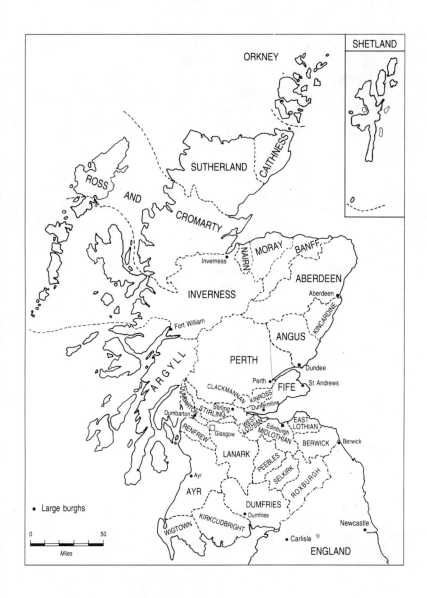

Scotland; counties and major burghs

From I. Donnachie and G. Hewitt, *A Companion to Scottish History* (Batsford, 1989), map 16.

INTRODUCTION

When is a kingdom not a kingdom? One answer to that riddle is when it does not have a king. Seventeenth century Scotland had kings and queens, but after 1603 they were absentee, and all but one of them had no sustained experience of Scotland. Furthermore, only James VI can reasonably be described as a Scot. Charles I was born in Dunfermline but migrated to England as an infant, and the remaining monarchs who ruled the country until the arrival of the German George I in 1714 were English with the exception of the Dutchman, William II. Yet multiple monarchies were not uncommon in early modern Europe, and the Spanish, Danish and Polish monarchies all experienced problems arising from this phenomenon. The seventeenth century saw a succession of crises in states like Bohemia, Portugal and Ireland which were bound to supranational sovereign powers. The Anglo-Scottish regal union, therefore, was only one among a number of troubled unions. What made it peculiar was that in 1707 the union between them was freely strengthened. What was it about the regal union that persuaded the Scots in particular to seek an even closer relationship with their partner kingdom? Was the regal union so benevolent and were the English so reasonable that a parliamentary union was the natural step on the road to British state formation? Or was the regal union so damaging to Scottish interests, and the partnership so unequal, that the country was squeezed into a corner from which there appeared to be no escape except into the arms of the English state which offered protection on terms of its own choosing?

The purpose of this book is to try and answer the above questions by analysing Scottish politics and government throughout the regal union. However, as far as possible the emphasis is on the workings of the regal union, not on the road to parliamentary union. Too much interest in the latter gives the impresssion that the regal union never was anything more than a halfway house to 1707, and that union was an all-consuming issue of the period. In fact, there was very little interest in union except at periodic intervals and among a very small number of politicians. For most of the time most people accepted the regal union as a form of government which was far from satisfactory and perhaps needed some fine tuning, but was tolerable and was likely to endure. Therefore, while there is a very important British dimension to Scottish politics in the seventeenth century, it is important not to overstate the case. Much of the time the Scots worked out their own solutions to their own set of problems, and the local, regional and national agendas were equally important in defining the course Scottish politics followed in this period. It is the interplay of politics at these other levels within a British context which provides an answer to the theme of this book, revealing the extent to which Scotland's legal rights as an independent sovereign state were or were not compromised, and her politics reduced to a *de facto* provincialism by regal union or retaining a life and momentum of their own.

Because this is a book about politics in a world very different from our own, and different too from many other seventeenth century states, it is necessary to begin with an analysis of that world rather than with the political narrative. The first three chapters of the book therefore set out the parameters in terms of institutions, personnel and ideas within which Scottish politics operated. Even more than in most other early modern societies, political institutions in Scotland were small-scale, flexible and highly localised. The absence of the king and his court removed one major institution, parliament was an occasional event, the royal administration was rudimentary, the central courts were very limited in their competence, taxation was low, the coercive powers of the state were minimal, and the country was divided into a mosaic of private and ecclesiastical courts which ensured that for most people most of the time government was a very local concern. Only the church provided an approximation to a permanent national institution which, though not political in intent, was highly politicised. The men who presided over the affairs of this world were overwhelmingly aristocrats. The Scottish nobility were among the most powerful in Europe, and they emerged even stronger in the early eighteenth century, having brushed aside challenges from the crown and the church to curtail that power. Occasionally lesser men rose to positions of prominence, and other status groups or professions could apply political pressure very effectively over issues which interested them. However, only noblemen were born to rule, and this they did, dominating the court, parliament, the privy council, the law courts, the army, and the countryside. Aristocratic colonisation of the state undoubtedly added to their authority, but it was their overwhelming economic, legal and social power in the localities which was the foundation of their success. While Scotland enjoyed considerable social cohesion – the social hierarchy was only briefly challenged in the late 1640s – Scottish politics were infused with heated debate about fundamental ideas which reflected very differing world views. At the risk of grossly oversimplifying these issues, divine right kingship, an episcopal church subject to the crown and an imperial British vision contrasted with ideas of popular sovereignty, a presbyterian church from which the crown was excluded and an intense sense of Scottish identity and exclusiveness. The issue of sovereign power and of the limits of royal authority rumbled on throughout the seventeenth century, and was at the heart of most of the major political events of the period. Connected to that concern were issues affecting religion; the question of toleration, the nature of church-state relations, and the argument over the form of church government. Finally, there was the important debate over the idea of Britain, the exact form of the regal union, and the desirability or otherwise of parliamentary, ecclesiastical, legal or economic union.

In tackling the above topics first it is hoped to provide a map of seventeenth century Scottish politics which will make the subsequent narrative more accessible. Some might prefer to read the narrative chapters first, and certainly it would not be impossible to approach the book in this way. However, for those wholly unfamiliar with this subject a very concise summary of the chronology, charting the course of Scottish politics, might be helpful. A starting date of 1603 is obvious as this marked the beginning of the regal union when James VI of Scotland succeeded Elizabeth I to the crowns of England and Ireland. The terminal date of 1715 is less obvious since the regal union ended in 1707 with the union of the parliaments. However, it was the defeat of the jacobite rebellion in 1715 which shut the door firmly on a Stewart restoration, or on any renegotiation of the act of union. Within these dates the chronological divisions imposed by the last four chapters are traditional to Scottish historiography, there being no reason to remove or confuse familiar landmarks. The revolution of 1637 marked the end of an experiment in imperial monarchy which enjoyed modest success in creating the regal union and governing Scotland from London until c.1615, but already James VI was running into trouble before the end of his long reign in 1625. Distance learning proved disastrous for Charles I in his efforts to fulfil the job of a Scottish king, and his policies and personality intensified the problems which had surfaced in the later years of his father's reign, inciting a national revolution.

The period bounded by the revolution in 1637 and the restoration of the monarchy in 1660 is more confusing and difficult to understand than any other. The war of the three kingdoms best describes this clash which brought the monarchy and all three British kingdoms into a complex power struggle in which national interests competed with international political and religious loyalties. The signing of the national covenant in 1638 was the focal point of a constitutional and religious revolution between 1637–41 which overthrew the power of the king, the bishops and realigned Scottish power in Britain. Increasing Scottish involvement in the affairs of England and Ireland was formally marked by the solemn league and covenant in 1643, leading to an intensification and spread of war throughout Britain, and to the defeat of Charles I by 1646. A second phase of fighting was initiated by the engagement in which the Scots switched support to the king in 1648, but were defeated. Charles I was executed by the English in 1649, the Scots gave their backing to Charles II, and the war was ended finally by the English republican conquest of Scotland in 1651. The military occupation of Scotland by the English endured from 1651–60 and marks the final phase of this violent period. The restoration era of 1660–88 saw the return of the monarchy, the episcopal church, the aristocracy and the very loose regal union of the early seventeenth century. However, the crown lacked the imperial ideology which rendered the earlier experiment unstable, and while events and developments in the two kingdoms were not unconnected there was less political interaction than during any other period of the regal union. Although a restoration was effected peacefully in 1660 it was 1666 before the failure of the Pentland rising underlined the security of the monarchy. Royal power grew over the succeeding years, but the failure to settle the religious problem forced another clash with presbyterian dissenters in 1678. The decade 1678–88 saw the creation of an arbitrary government which rode out further rebellion in 1685 before succumbing to a more dangerous and lucky challenge in England in 1688. The revolutions of 1688–9 followed different courses in the British kingdoms, that in Scotland being the most radical, but each was linked by common causes and military considerations. It was this political diversity at a time of major involvement in European war which generated English strategic concerns and Scotland's economic crisis, itself a product of the war. The solution to both in 1707 was the union of the parliaments. Finally, the years 1707–15 saw the Scots wrestling with the consequences of their decision, but the steadily mounting grievances against Westminster were insufficient to arouse the kind of rebellions seen in 1637–8 or 1688–9, and when jacobitism offered an alternative to union in 1715 it was rejected.

1
POLITICAL INSTITUTIONS

The Monarchy and the Court

In a period when Charles I was stripped of all but ceremonial power and executed by his English subjects, James VII's Scottish crown was forfeited, and George I was chosen as Anne's successor by parliament, it is clear that British kingship was an uncertain and insecure business. In spite of the ideological support for the idea of monarchy and the legal undergirding of royal authority, kings had to be good politicians, and personality was a vital ingredient to their success or failure. This was especially true in a kingdom where the institutions of royal government were under-developed and the exact limits of royal authority were undefined. The king could not choose his own successor, the choice being made by God and nature, and from 1689 by parliament. The king could not make law by prerogative, but he could employ privy council proclamations which had the force of law. He had enormous influence over the legislative procedure, being able to summon, prorogue and dissolve parliament at will, although from 1689 the annual sitting of parliament was required. The king made war and peace, signed alliances, and conducted diplomacy without consulting parliament, and after 1603 he did so overwhelmingly with English policy considerations in mind. It was the unpopular

1702 declaration of war against France which led, in 1705, to the act anent peace and war in which parliament attacked this particular prerogative. He could raise an army and command it, but the common host was an anachronism at the end of the sixteenth century, and subjects were not obliged to pay for professional troops. Even when Charles II and James VII had an army, its use against dissent was less a demonstration of power than a sign of the erosion of an authority which required consent and co-operation in order to be effective. Monarchs appointed officers of state and privy councillors, but had difficulty sacking office holders, and could not interfere with hereditary offices. Between 1609–38 and 1669–89 the king was supreme head of the church with the power to appoint and dismiss bishops or lesser clergy, and to preside over ecclesiastical affairs. Yet this authority was challenged repeatedly and rested on parliamentary statute. Monarchs lacked a universal pardoning power and had only a circumscribed appeal jurisdiction over public or private courts, but the king could order arrests, imprisonment and torture without trial, redirect juries, and appoint judges in the central courts. The royal writ extended from the borders to the Shetland Isles, but much of the highlands and islands lay outside effective control. The meagre royal income was supplemented by raising customs tariffs, or by managing the supply and content of the coinage, but the king could not raise taxation by prerogative power, and had to ask his subjects for extraordinary revenue. It was outside the king's powers to surrender the sovereignty of the kingdom, but James VI ceased styling himself King of Scotland and declared himself King of Great Britain by prerogative power. However, he could not create a union of England and Scotland by prerogative, and on this issue was defeated by his parliaments.

After 1603 Scottish kings faced a new problem in operating an unstable system of multiple monarchy. As rulers of three different kingdoms with three parliaments, privy councils, churches and three national aristocracies to manage, seventeenth century kings had a difficult job. England was so much more powerful than the other two kingdoms that an imbalance in the political geography of Great Britain was unavoidable. Ireland was legally subject to the English crown, but the native Irish resented their subjection to English law and to British colonists. Scotland was a kingdom on equal terms with England only in legal theory, and the king now resided in London and shared in a world view which saw Scotland as an unimportant adjunct of England. The Scots were sensitive to Anglicising policies, although very often the intent behind royal policies had less to do with Anglicisation than with the rationalisation of the state. Yet the Scots were equally offended if they were ignored. Being king of three kingdoms made Scottish kings more powerful in that they had greater international prestige, an enormously expanded range of patronage, a physically more secure base from which to conduct government, potentially more military force to command, and the freedom to play off one kingdom against the other. Yet there were disadvantages in multiple monarchy, and the greatest danger lay in allowing discontent in one kingdom to infect the others as occurred in 1637–42 when Charles I lost control of all three kingdoms. Scottish kings now found themselves distanced from events and people in Scotland, and therefore less able to give government the personal attention on which successful kingship was founded. James VI had sufficient residual knowledge of Scotland to make the system work after 1603, although even he was less sensitive to his Scottish public by the time of his visit in 1617. Every one of his successors failed to do a satisfactory job. It simply was not possible to govern Scotland effectively from London in the seventeenth century.

The absence of the monarchy after 1603 was permanent. James VI reneged on his promise to return every three years, apart from a few weeks holiday in Scotland in the summer of 1617. Charles I belatedly came to Scotland in 1633 to be crowned, and returned in 1641 when he was stripped of power, and when parliament demanded more frequent royal residence in the kingdom. Charles II was in Scotland only to fight for his throne in 1650–1, and was crowned at Scone. James, duke of York set up court in Edinburgh throughout most of his exile in 1679–81, but did not visit as a reigning monarch. William

II never went to Scotland, and was reluctant even to spend time in England, while Anne never strayed out of the home counties. Charles I and Charles II were crowned in Scotland, but William (and Mary) and Anne made do with a coronation oath at Whitehall, and James VII even failed to take the oath. After Charles I, who was born at Dunfermline, all royal births were in England, and the royal family was buried in Westminster abbey.

This emigration of the dynasty deprived Scotland of the important ritual and ceremonial aspects of monarchy which scarcely were compensated for in the celebration of the king's birthday after 1660. There also was a running down of architectural patronage, although there were bursts of expensive repair work in 1617 (£100,000 was spent) and 1633, and Holyrood palace was renovated in the 1670s. The political impact of this absentee kingship was that the centre of royal decision making and patronage moved to London, but the fact that the institutions of central government remained in Edinburgh created a clumsy arrangement. The king and his secretary of state, who usually resided at court, conducted a correspondence with Edinburgh, but this could never compensate for personal appearances in the council or at parliament. At certain times, usually during a crisis, kings spent a considerable amount of time on Scottish business with their court advisors, but always the line of communication was unsatisfactory. The absence of a formal Scottish committee in London was a disadvantage, leading to the appearance of an informal lobby of Scots, and some Englishmen, at court who often represented different or conflicting interests from those in Edinburgh.

In 1603 James VI and I created a hybrid British court. The influx of personnel from Scotland, the institution of the Scottish bedchamber in London, the adoption of the less formal Franco-Scottish court etiquette, and the impact of a Scottish king all brought about changes at London. For the Scots this meant that their king now was surrounded by a household staff some fifteen times bigger than in Scotland, in the midst of a much larger court in which the king was less accessible. Yet James proved to be a loyal master, sticking by his old, familiar servants and deliberately using the court to bring the English and Scottish aristocracies together. This meant employing the Scots at court, and even under Charles I they had a disproportionate share of court offices. In James's court two out of every five of those offices acceptable to a gentleman were held by Scots, and the share increased the closer one got to the king's person. English courtiers and members of parliament complained it was impossible to gain access except through the Scots, especially those servants of the bedchamber. The officers and gentlemen of the bedchamber were the most privileged of all courtiers, having the readiest access to the king and the greatest opportunities for acting as patronage brokers with a key role in court faction. In 1614 six of the seven gentlemen of the bedchamber and all ten of the grooms were Scots, and fifteen out of the total of twenty appointed between 1603–25 were Scots. In addition, the bedchamber offices of chamberlain, groom of the stool and privy purse were in Scottish hands. Bedchamber men like Sir George Hume, first earl of Dunbar and Sir William Alexander, first earl of Stirling acquired important offices of state and were key advisors to James VI and Charles I respectively. Scots were appointed as steward of the household, master of the horse, captain of the guard, master of the household, master of the wardrobe and gentleman of the robes. Charles's master of the horse, James Hamilton, third marquis of Hamilton, was the pre-eminent courtier of the 1630s. Half of the forty-eight gentlemen of the privy chamber appointed in 1603 were Scottish, while the important offices in the lesser households of Queen Anne, Prince Henry and Prince Charles were staffed by a large number of Scots. This predominance in offices was reflected in other forms of patronage, and Scots made huge fortunes out of English gifts and pensions, inciting an English reaction against what they perceived as unscrupulous carpet baggers. The remarkable profiteering of the first two decades of union was never repeated, but the court continued to attract Scots who recognised its crucial role in patronage and political faction.

Charles I's defeat marked a watershed in the influence of the Scots at court. The Protectorate court of Oliver Cromwell was a pale shadow of the Caroline court, and was staffed entirely by Englishmen. Scots were almost as scarce in Charles II's exiled court, and only six Scots reached the bedchamber after 1660. While the bedchamber was less significant than earlier in the century it remained a useful means of access to the king's ear for the likes of Lauderdale under Charles II or Queensberry under William II. No other significant court office fell into Scottish hands after the restoration, and the court was much more thoroughly English than it had been before the wars. Yet the brief Holyrood court presided over by the duke of York in the opening years of the 1680s indicated a wealth of untapped Scottish enthusiasm for court life. There was a slight increase in the number of influential Scots in the 1680s, largely because of the association of men like the second earl of Middleton and John Drummond, earl of Melfort, with James VII, but also because John Maitland, second earl of Lauderdale's twenty year monopoly of Scottish affairs at court had excluded rivals. Unfortunately, the cost of living in London and the fierce competition from the English tory aristocracy in a period of severe retrenchment in expenditure made it difficult for Scots to establish themselves in the south. Nor did the revolution of 1688–9 greatly help, as William had his own Dutch servants and the English whigs to reward. Anne largely reverted to employing traditional court families. Her own Anglocentrism and the difficult financial restraints imposed by Treasurer Godolphin left little room for favouring Scots, and in a household employing just under a thousand people there were only two Scots, both doctors.

Between 1603–25 the court was more Scottish than English in personnel and style. Before 1603, James VI's household servants established a powerful position in court and government, one marked in 1597 by their defeat of the Octavians, a team of eight royal officials who were entrusted with reorganising royal finances. Once removed to London the courtiers' influence with the king became greater, making it essential for the administrators in Edinburgh to have good and direct lines of communication with the king, and friends at court. James's open style of government, and his refusal to allow one faction to dominate his government until the end of the reign allowed for a fluid political situation in which men like the earls of Dunfermline and Haddington in Edinburgh retained a degree of independence from the courtiers. Dunbar almost established a hegemony over Scottish affairs between 1603–11, but his successor as court favourite, Robert Ker, earl of Somerset, enjoyed only nominal recognition from the men who actually ran the country. The same could not be said of the duke of Buckingham who by 1621 had established a monopoly of royal patronage which threatened the stability of English politics, and made the Scots dependent on an English court favourite. Buckingham, like Somerset, had other priorities, but Scottish politicians sought his favour, allowing him to build up a Scottish clientage. It was during Buckingham's dominance from 1621–8 that the relationship between the court and the administration changed, partly as a result of Buckingham's personal influence, but also as a consequence of Charles I's preference for the counsel of London-based courtiers. Surprisingly, Hamilton, the leading courtier of the 1630s, remained uninterested in Scottish politics until 1638. Charles II permitted Lauderdale to use his position as the only Scot in the bedchamber in conjunction with the office of secretary to attain a prominence in British politics between 1663–79 which had not been enjoyed by a Scot since Dunbar. It was Lauderdale's presence at court in 1660–3 which ensured his triumph over his rival, the earl of Middleton.

Like Dunbar, Lauderdale had no successor, but James VII's preference for closet government favoured courtier-Scots like the earl of Melfort. After 1689 the need to manage parliament and to co-operate with English party leaders became the major factors in deciding royal favour. Scottish courtiers were scarce, but Queensberry's rise to dominate the court party during the 1690s rested on a secure court base. The role of courtiers like the Dutch favourite, William Bentinck, earl of Portland, and the Scottish clergyman, William Carstairs, in deciding Scottish policy was also founded on personal relations with the king. The disappearance of influential Scottish courtiers during Queen Anne's reign, and the decline in the importance of the household under a female monarch, meant that Scottish politicians dealt directly with English ministers.

Parliament

Until the last few years of its existence, from 1689–1707, and possibly during the covenanting period of 1638–51, the Scottish parliament was less of an institution than an an irregular and short-lived event which brought together the political leaders of the kingdom to grant taxation, pass new legislation and adjudicate on disputes between its members. The irregularity of parliamentary sessions and the short duration of sittings supports this idea. There were seventeen parliaments and a further twelve conventions of the estates during the period of the regal union, which compares favourably with England where there were twenty-seven parliaments (including the 1689 convention). However, this evidence disguises important differences. The English parliament sat for longer and longer sessions, reflecting the huge growth in business and a tendency among the members to talk too much. On the other hand, throughout 1689–1707 when it was at the height of its activity, the Scottish parliament only was in session for 123 weeks, or seven or eight weeks a year. Before 1689 when annual parliaments were instituted there were long periods when it never sat at all. Furthermore, it was not until after 1689 that business was conducted for more than a couple of days in the week. Parliament also lacked any permanent officers, and had no fixed residence until the completion of Parliament House in 1639. As an event, however, parliament was colourful and impressive. James VI deliberately encouraged a more formal and staged public image from 1587, drawing up dress requirements for the members at the 'Red Parliament' at Perth in 1606. Similarly Charles I's coronation parliament in 1633 was turned into a platform for the display of royal pageantry and power. In the later seventeenth century the riding of the parliament, when the great procession of members made their way from Holyrood up to Parliament

House, remained a visual lesson in the dignity and authority of the three estates.

Parliament was also an occasion in another sense, providing an opportunity for the scattered political elite to meet. Edinburgh was filled to overflowing with noblemen and their attendants, taverns and coffee houses became impromptu debating chambers, covert literature circulated, merchants did profitable business, and crowds were drawn to the spectacle. From the fencing of parliament, its formal opening, special laws and regulations were in operation to facilitate its business and ensure good order. Parliament was an event which temporarily heightened political awareness, and it was essential that government remained in control of proceedings. Yet the most stringent efforts to stage-manage parliament could be frustrated. Even in 1633, when Charles I's presence was intended to intimidate the members, there were protests, votes against the crown, and the occasion provided a setting for dissident noblemen to discuss their grievances. Parliament therefore was a potentially dangerous fixture in the political calendar. The November 1641 session almost provided the stage for a royalist coup, and the 1706 session of parliament brought huge, angry crowds into Edinburgh to oppose the union and created an ugly, threatening atmosphere in which the debates took place.

Yet public interest in parliament was low throughout most of the century, and the many fines imposed on its members for non-attendance suggests a general apathy towards parliamentary business. Attendance ranged from a mere twenty-nine in April 1641 to 232 in June 1705, although averages were approximately 100–150 in the first half of the century and 150–180 after 1660. Membership of parliament was unevenly divided among the aristocracy (the peerage and shire commissioners), burgesses, bishops and officers of state, all of whom sat in the same chamber and voted together. Since peers were individually summoned, the doubling of the peerage between 1603–1707 represented a significant shift in voting power and only minorities, illness and laziness prevented this group forming a larger body in parliaments. Shire commissioners (it was 1681 before all thirty-three shires were represented) were elected annually (after 1660 annual elections became less common) from among the barons of the shire, those holding forty shillings worth of land in freehold from the king. The local aristocracy showed little interest in these elections, and even the sixty to seventy contested elections ajudicated by parliament between 1669–1706 suggests a low level of competitiveness among the lesser nobility of the shire. The two commissioners for each shire had a composite vote, but in 1640 they were granted one vote each, a further increase in the voting strength of the landed aristocracy. In 1690 a further twenty-six new commissioners were distributed among the shires. Not surprisingly, parliament reflected the political views of the landed elite, and was protective of their economic interests. Only excessive crown management allowed the parliaments of 1621 and 1633 to attack aristocratic interests successfully, but this was followed by a failure to implement legislation locally, and the subsequent reform of parliament after 1638. At the beginning of the century the burghs were also unwilling to spend time and money in attendance at parliament, and in 1608 the convention of royal burghs drew attention to the damaging effect this had on the interests of its members. Each of the royal burghs also had a commissioner, and in the case of Edinburgh two commissioners. In 1603 there were fifty royal burghs with a seat in parliament, and this rose to sixty-seven by 1707, an insignificant change in the size of burgh representation in relation to the growth in the size of the aristocratic presence. The burghs could not halt this erosion of their influence, and governments appreciated the political mileage in shifting the tax burden away from the nobility and onto the towns. James VI's ministers did this with the tax on annual rents in 1621, and Lauderdale punished the burghs in 1672 in order to retain aristocratic support for religious and foreign policy. However, the burghs benefited from their preparedness and mutual co-operation, agreeing policies before parliament in the convention of royal burghs, and from their complicity in crown policy. Burgh councils and burgh commissioners to parliament were often crown clients, especially before 1638 and between 1660–89, and in return for providing crown voting fodder the burghs often got their own business enacted. The presence of a clerical estate in parliament virtually disappeared after the reformation, but was resuscitated by James VI by 1608. Thereafter, the fourteen bishops acted as compliant supporters of the crown, a factor which influenced their abolition in 1640 and again in 1690 after their reinstatement in 1661. Officers of state, nominated by the crown and numbering between one and eight, had the right to sit and vote in parliament. They were excluded from parliament by the covenanters, only to return in 1660, and surprisingly they survived the 1689 revolution. However, dismissed crown ministers, particularly peers, often made a nuisance of themselves, and in 1704–5 the former commissioner, Queensberry, helped undermine the Tweedale ministry. Yet it would be a mistake to think that members of parliament voted primarily as status groups. The bishops and the officers of state supported crown policies, but the remainder divided along lines drawn by ideology, geography, status, clientage, and management techniques which ranged from physical threats to patronage.

Parliament could not be ignored, and even the most authoritarian of kings, Charles I and James VII, legitimated their government by seeking the support of the estates. Successive kings tried to treat parliament as an instrument of government, but a sense of self-preservation and constitutional conservatism ensured there was strong support among the political elite for the idea that parliament, including the king, was the sovereign power in the state. Consequently, kings relied on intense management of parliament in order to get their way. The underlying vulnerability of parliament to this pressure was constitutional. The early seventeenth-century parliament did not enjoy a monopoly over the making of laws or the granting of taxation. Laws could be enacted by a proclamation of the privy council, or by a convention of the estates, or a convention of the nobility. It was desirable that formal statutory authority be sought from parliament, but government could carry on for an indeterminate length of time enforcing laws to which parliament had not assented. Taxation, too, could be granted by a convention. For example, Charles I received a substantial tax in

1630 from a convention of the estates. Conventions were more easily managed, although taxes were refused by conventions in 1599 and 1600, while that of 1616 unenthusiastically granted a good deal less than the king demanded. The constitutional changes of 1638–41 gave parliament a stronger role in the making of law and the granting of tax, and the committee of the estates ensured an executive role for parliament in 1640–1 and again 1643–51. After the restoration, conventions were no longer as common and they ceased altogether after 1689. However, it was only with the 1689–90 reforms that parliament acquired an unchallenged supremacy in the realms of law and taxation. There were two other institutions which acted as rivals to parliament. The convention of royal burghs decided on most legislation affecting the burghs, but only as a preparatory stage to parliamentary enactment. Besides, the increasing interference of the privy council in burgh politics and economic affairs resulted in a decline in the convention's political independence and influence. More importantly, the general assembly of the church remained a powerful institution with a widely recognised right to decide on ecclesiastical matters, until it fell into a long abeyance after 1618. It assumed a quasi-parliamentary role in the 1640s, and again after 1690, when the complete separation of church and state was recognised.

Crown ministers had to show great skill and expend enormous effort in getting what the king wanted from parliament, but while compromise often was necessary the crown had considerable advantages. The regal union reduced the importance of parliament to a king whose income from Scotland was relatively insignificant, and even when the crown lost control of parliament, as occurred in 1702–5, Queen Anne's government was not paralysed. Similarly, in 1687 James VII could afford to dismiss parliament when he did not get the religious toleration he wanted. Only in the parliaments between 1638–41 was the inability of a Scottish king to exercise control politically fatal, but this was preceded by the collapse of royal government in the country, and was accompanied by a simultaneous political crisis in all three British kingdoms. The second factor which gave the crown leverage over parliament was its prerogative powers. Only the king could summon parliament, being under no obligation so to do, and he could prorogue or disolve it whenever he wished. There was no sitting of either parliament or a convention at all on twenty-three years between 1603–38, and parliament sat only in 1604, 1606–09, 1612, 1617, 1621 and 1633. After the restoration there was no parliament on fifteen of the years between 1661–89 – none at all on 1674–7 or 1682–4 – and while it sat annually from 1689–1707 there was no election between 1689 and 1702. The crown also enjoyed an array of procedural and tactical mechanisms and ploys of which the most important means of control was the lords of the articles. This committee was elected by parliament at the beginning of a session to sift through proposed legislation, most of which had been screened by the privy council. It then prepared a package of approved bills to present to the full parliament for its approval, often by voting on the entire programme. In 1612 James VI secured effective control of the selection procedure of the lords of the articles, and that control was made water-tight in 1633. The full committee was composed of eight members each from the bishops, peers, shire and burgh commissioners, and between six and ten officers of state. This body of privy councillors and royal clients ensured that no legislation came before parliament unless it was approved by the crown, debate was curtailed to a minimum, and opposition to any one measure was difficult without opposing the entire legislative programme. The committee was abolished in 1640, but between 1661 and 1663 the crown restored it to its former role. When the lords of the articles finally were abolished in 1690 ministers had to resort much more to persuasion and patronage to retain the initiative in parliament. However, the crown had other weapons in its armoury. Charles I's presence in 1633 did something to stifle dissent, although in 1641 his presence merely underlined the extent of his defeat. Officers of state, privy councillors and bishops ensured a core of crown supporters, while newly created peers often owed a debt of loyalty to the king, at least in the short term. Interference in burgh elections produced commissioners amenable to royal control, but managing shire elections was more difficult. For example, in 1629 the barons of both Ayrshire and Roxburghshire ignored instructions from the crown to elect its nominees. Other forms of patronage ranging from pensions to military offices and royal support in passing a private bill were exploited by crown managers. Absent members were encouraged to give proxy votes to the crown, a practice which aroused particular anger in 1633 when Englishmen who had been created Scottish peers employed their proxies in support of the king, leading in 1640 to the introduction of minimum property qualifications for peers, effectively disenfranchising these English noblemen. Yet even with a minority of votes the crown could retain the legislative initiative as in 1705 when ministers exploited the lack of a revising chamber or a second reading of bills to hurry through a motion recommending that the queen nominate commissioners of union. Even after 1689–90 the power of the crown in parliament remained great, hence Andrew Fletcher of Saltoun's unsuccessful efforts to introduce further limitations.

Yet the level of constant parliamentary management underlines the crown's difficulties in getting its way when the Scottish political elite gathered, and there is no evidence to suggest that the powerful and independent aristocracy became subservient on taking their seats in parliament. Had this been the case crown ministers from Chancellor Dunfermline to Chancellor Seafield would not have expended such effort on management. It was the Scottish parliament along with the English parliament which sank the union project in 1604. The 1621 tightening up of the lords of the articles was introduced precisely because of the difficulties James VI had in getting his nominations accepted in 1617. Opposition to taxation occurred in all James's parliaments, including that of 1621 when the combination of high and new taxes with the five articles of Perth induced 51 of 129 members to vote against the crown. There was vocal dissent in each of Charles I's parliaments and conventions in 1625, 1630 and 1633 in spite of his presence in the last of these. The new parliamentary constitution of 1641 demonstrated a desire within the political community for a parliament which debated issues and counselled the king, and while the covenanters did proscribe intransigent royalists and manage elections, the parliaments of the 1640s were open to persuasion. After the restoration the crown sought to reimpose control, but in spite of the act rescissory which abolished all legislation passed since 1633, it was impossible completely to turn back the clock. The 1641 orders of the house, regulating debate, were retained, parliamentary sessions were longer, and even the reimposition of the lords of the articles did not lead to the same repressive atmosphere of pre-covenanting days. The 1661 session saw open opposition to the oath of allegiance and the act rescissory; only the king's strenuous efforts prevented the introduction of secret balloting of parliament in 1662; while in 1673 the third duke of Hamilton's attack on Lauderdale succeeded in holding up the crown's entire legislative programme. Throughout the 1680s ministers withdrew unpopular bills, like the 1681 bill for modifying the usury laws, or the 1686 excise bill. In 1689 the convention of the estates avoided any dithering over how to justify the revolution, simply forfeiting James VII's crown. Thereafter the idea of a loyal opposition was recognised tacitly. It was the opposition club in parliament which abolished the articles in 1690; the outcry over the massacre of Glencoe in 1692 resulted in a parliamentary inquiry and in time led to the dismissal of the secretary, John Dalrymple, master of Stair; and the 1703–4 sessions were a disaster for the crown, which was unable to prevent the passing in 1704 of the act of security. Throughout the century parliament acted as a guarantor of Scottish interests and liberties which were being eroded by a British imperial monarchy. It was parliament's increasing success in regulating its own affairs and in acting as a watchdog on the nation's rights which persuaded crown ministers in the early eighteenth century that parliament was unmanageable and had to go.

The Administrative Structure

Seventeenth century Europe experienced a marked expansion of government institutions and capabilities, chiefly in the closely linked functions of tax gathering and warfare. The absence of war in Scotland deprived government of a major catalyst for change until the 1640s, but the effectiveness and efficiency of Scottish government showed signs of recovering in the 1580s and 1590s. Evidence was seen in tax gathering, improved law and order, and witch-hunting. This qualitative enhancement of government did not indicate a fundamental shift in power from the localities to the centre, but there was more interference in the localities by royal government, an interference which reached its greatest extent in the 1630s. When domestic war did arise in the following decade it forced the covenanters, who began as rebels against meddling from the centre, to become exponents of the most intrusive and dynamic government of the century. After 1660 the restored royal government made little further effort to extend its parameters, and if anything the frontiers of the state were rolled back. The revolution in 1689 confirmed aristocratic suspicions of government, and the strains imposed on the system by King William's unpopular foreign wars exposed the limitations of a creaking adminis-tration not designed to meet the demands being made of it. The continuance of war after 1702, and the introduction of new customs and excise officers after 1707 suggested a heightened degree of governmental activity would follow, but in Scotland the eighteenth century state remained unobtrusive and undemanding.

At the centre of administration was the privy council in Edinburgh. The fact that the king now was in London com-promised the council's effectiveness as an arm of the executive, since its ability to react quickly to unfolding events was reduced in proportion to the extent of personal control exercised by the king. James VI tolerated disagreement from his councillors, but Charles I discouraged dissent and by 1637 the privy council temperamentally was incapable of showing initiative, hence its sluggish response to the anti-prayer book riots in Edinburgh. Councillors facing hard choices were likely to pass the buck to London in order to avoid responsibility. Thus the Worces-ter affair of 1705 arose because politicians in Edinburgh and London refused to take difficult decisions. On the other hand councillors could exploit the king's lack of interest to push ahead with their own schemes, the 1661 act rescissory or the massacre of Glencoe in 1692 being good examples. Distance from London also gave the privy council a different perception of events to that of the court. In 1637 Charles I did not believe his government was collapsing in Edinburgh, and again the rebellion in 1679 was a much greater surprise to London than it was to harassed councillors in Edinburgh. By contrast, the privy council's relaxed attitude to the Aberdeen assembly in 1605 or the jacobite plot in 1708 evoked alarm in London. A further factor influencing decision-making was the division between court and council which was exacerbated by distance after 1603. Many officers of state rarely ever saw the king, and therefore council policy and the positions of individual councillors could be undermined at court by rival factions. The switch to a more tolerant religious policy after 1667 was made because of Lauderdale's ascendancy at court, and against the inclinations of the administration in Edinburgh. Chancellor Aberdeen was destroyed in 1684 by his enemies in London irrespective of his power base in the privy council. However, it was unusual for factions to split along a court-council axis, it being more common for a powerful councillor like Chancellor Dunfermline to cultivate courtiers like the earl of Kellie, or a powerful courtier like Lauderdale to ensure he had agents in Edinburgh to dominate the council.

From 1603 King James's new British empire was governed through three national privy councils in England, Ireland and Scotland. The Irish privy council took its orders from London and was composed largely of English civil servants and colonists. However, except for some overlap of personnel, the English and Scottish councils were wholly distinct bodies, a situation which suited successive monarchs who saw advantages in divide and rule. Yet in 1603 James VI intended that there should be a British administration, and appointed six Scots to the English privy council before the end of the year. In addition, Sir George Hume was appointed chancellor of the exchequer and Lord Kinloss became master of the rolls. The failure of his union scheme destroyed this idea, and only on the joint border commission was there close co-operation between Scottish and

English officials. However, Scottish officers of state and courtiers continued to be appointed to the English privy council, reaching a peak in the 1630s when over twenty per cent of the English privy council was composed of Scots. However, these men appear to have had little influence in steering policy. By contrast both James VI and Charles I excluded English officials from Scottish business, although Buckingham did play a role in the revocation scheme, and Archbishop Laud clearly influenced religious policy in the 1630s. Sir Thomas Wentworth, the lord president of Ireland, later criticised this conciliar division precisely bcause it kept English councillors ignorant of Scottish affairs, and his solution was to go down the same road as Ireland, subordinating the Scots to the English crown and English law. However, even Charles I was not that provocative, and it was over two years from the outbreak of the crisis in Scotland in 1637 before he appointed a mixed committee for Scottish affairs.

The one experiment in conciliar union, the committee of both kingdoms which was established by the English parliament and the covenanters in 1644 to conduct joint operations against Charles I, demonstrated the difficulties in pursuing policies advantageous to both nations. At the restoration Charles II returned to a clear division of powers, against the advice of the earl of Clarendon who was suspicious of an independent political interest in Scotland. Clarendon persuaded Charles to establish a council for Scottish affairs at Whitehall composed of a few resident Scottish and six English councillors, but Lauderdale ensured it was swept away when Clarendon fell from power in 1667. There were occasions when government in the two kingdoms was co-ordinated, as in 1667 when both treasuries were put into commission in an effort to ensure more efficient financial management. In wartime too there naturally was a greater level of co-operation, and while distinct military establishments were maintained, Scottish regiments were being paid by the English treasury in the 1690s and 1700s. A handful of Scots like Lauderdale continued to be admitted to the English privy council, while the emigré second earl of Middleton acquired high office in the English government in the 1680s, being appointed successively to each of the two secretaryships of state. However, during the 1690s English ministers achieved a more dominant role over their Scottish counterparts, and the idea that there ought to be some form of Scottish council in London was floated by Lord Godolphin in 1702 in response to criticisms that he knew little of Scotland. Nothing came of this scheme, and following the union of parliaments the Scottish privy council was in 1708 swallowed up in the privy council of Great Britain.

Within Scotland the privy council wielded extensive powers. Except during the period 1638–41 and 1643–51 when it was superseded by the committee of the estates, and 1651–60 when it was abolished altogether by the occupying English regime, the council provided Scotland with national government. Its authority was circumscribed only by the need to rely on the aristocracy for local enforcement and by their entrenched heritable jurisdictions. However, the council was free from interference either by parliament or the central courts, and the small number of specialised committees preserved its omnicompetence. It handled the most sensitive of political issues. For example, it was expected to get the five articles of Perth onto the statute books in 1621, to implement Charles I's 1625 revocation, to snuff out conventicling in the 1670s and 1680s, and to defuse the uproar which followed the collapse of the Darien scheme in 1700. The privy council's nerve and astuteness in crisis management was often the difference between the fall or survival of the government. The contrast between the self-preserving paralysis of Charles I's councillors in 1637–8, or James VII's in 1688–9, and the much more determined response of ministers in dealing with rebellion in 1685, or in brazening out a tide of unpopularity in 1706 was crucial to the outcome of events.

One consequence of the council's omnicompetence was that it was burdened by a mass of private and peripheral business. Most business was initiated as complaints by individuals or corporate bodies who petitioned the council, mostly about law and order issues. In such cases the council worked alongside the court of judiciary or the court of session in forcing parties to seek or accept a judicial settlement. The public side of its business concerned virtually every aspect of royal government.

Some of the ordinary business of government was handled in small departments, that of the lord treasurer being the most independent, but most matters fell within the council's competence. There were specialised committees such as the committee of grievance in 1623, or the highland committee established in 1664. The privy council enforced laws, passed enabling measures when necessary, and issued proclamations which had the force of law. It directed policing operations, and quelled outbreaks of disorder ranging from petty feuds between neighbouring noblemen to major outbreaks of violence in highland localities. However, mediation remained the most effective means of restoring local peace, for example in 1665 the council settled a feud between the burgh of Inverness and a branch of the Macdonalds. In wartime the council organised the raising and provisioning of troops and military supplies, although in the 1620s a specialist committee of war was created. The council supervised a range of economic regulations including the operation of monopolies, the quality of the coinage, the oversight of foreign trade and the level of grain prices. It had responsibility for the collection of taxation, customs and the king's other revenues, and its interests extended to forms of social control like organising emergency relief in times of dearth, limiting the spread of disease, and restricting the movement of the unemployed.

In size the Scottish privy council varied between fifty and thirty-five members, with a working core of around twelve. The profile of the councillors as a whole changed little over the course of the century. The most variable factor was the bishops who formed a cohesive and reliable group in the council by the 1630s, were swept aside in 1638, and made a limited return between 1661–88. The majority of councillors continued to be noblemen, and kings recognised the 'right' of peers to a place on the council, but many of these were nominal members. The remainder were career officials, most of whom had a legal training and whose family roots were in the lesser nobility. The prospect that the privy council would become the preserve of bishops and lawyers dependent on the king briefly arose in the 1630s, but disappeared at the covenanting revolution. After the restoration the dominance of the landed aristocracy was unquestioned. The strong element of continuity on the privy council was in part due to the fact that office was a form of real property which could not be taken away unless treasonable grounds were demonstrated. That continuity extended down to the largely apolitical secretaries, clerks, notaries and messengers who constituted the small government bureaucracy.

The seventeenth century did see a growing trend for the work of the council to be done by a smaller, inner group of councillors, and as early as 1621 King James recognised the *de facto* existence of a cabinet as distinct from the bloated 'grite counsell'. The issue of cabinet government in Scotland was tied up with the court-council tussle and never became as constitutionally contentious as it did in England. The need for small working committees was accepted, and the more sinister aspects of this development only became apparent in something like the committee for public affairs which evolved in the later 1670s to deal with dissent, or the 'secret committee' formed in January 1686 to administer the test act. The curbing of the council's power by parliament at the 1689 revolution encouraged the trend towards its dominance by a small body of politicians who could straddle court and parliament, and were prepared to work within the political parameters set by the English ministers. After the union the privy council of Great Britain grew to an unmanageable eighty-two in 1712, but the actual business was done in the cabinet with real power being wielded by an even smaller preparatory working party, the lords of committee, of whom the only Scot, until his death in 1711, was Queensberry.

The close working relationship between the privy council, the court of session and the court of judiciary ensured that the courts did not become rival centres of power as was the case with the parlements in France, or the common law courts in England. Scots law was not arbitrary, but while sixteenth-century jurists had sought to provide protection to individual liberties, the best guarantor of freedom was good lordship. With the decline of the latter, both parliament and the church began to assume a greater responsibility in curbing the drift towards an arbitrary use of the law. Scots law was greatly influenced by Roman law which was inherently sympathetic to a strong executive, while the political relationship between the crown and the courts made them amenable to royal control. Until the 1701 act for preventing wrongous imprisonment, there was no equivalent of *habeas corpus* in Scotland, prisoners could be tortured by order of the privy council, juries had little freedom to interpret the law and could be charged for returning 'wilful' verdicts as happened with the trial in 1606 of the six ministers who held an unlicenced general assembly at Aberdeen, and the judiciary was subservient to the crown. The oppressive aspect of the Scottish legal system allowed successive regimes to crush dissent through the courts with relative ease, the scandalous conviction of Lord Balmerino for treason in 1634 being the most notable example. However, it was equally typical of the crown's use of the law in Scotland that the sentence of execution imposed on Balmerino was not implemented and he was allowed to retire to his estate. The covenanters sought to reduce the crown's arbitrary and partial manipulation of the courts, although their own political interference in the courts grew throughout the 1640s. It was the systematisation of Scots law by Stair, and the appalling treatment of religious dissidents by the government and courts in the 1680s which inspired the revolutionaries of 1689 to demand the abolition of the more arbitrary aspects of the judicial system, especially the use of torture. The Articles of Grievance also addressed the question of the appointment and control of judges. At the beginning of the century the head of the court of justiciary, the justice general, was the earl of Argyll who had hereditary possession of the office, but in 1628 Lord Lorne, Argyll's son and heir, resigned the justice generalship into the king's hands. By 1633 real responsibility for the court was handled by the lord justice clerk. The remaining criminal judges all were crown appointments, and the restructuring of 1672, including the revival of the idea of circuit courts, probably tightened up the crown's political control. Prosecutions on behalf of the king were undertaken by the lord advocate, while the solicitar general provided yet another office of state concerned with the law. The reform of the court of session in 1592–3 nominally reduced the king's influence in the appointment of the fifteen ordinary judges, restricting him to the presentation of a short-list of three from which the existing judges made their choice, the election being for life. But James VI repeatedly bullied the court into accepting his nominees, and Charles I simply nominated the lord president in 1633. A large number of judges also served as privy councillors, and the president of the court of session was recognised as an office of state. In 1625–6 Charles I broke this connection in order to weaken the political autonomy of the court of session, making it more responsive to his direct control. By altering the tenure of judges to appointment during the king's pleasure he further eroded the court's independence. The presence of four extraordinary lords, usually non-professional aristocrats, allowed the king further patronage. In 1638 the judges proved less pliant than Charles expected, but sufficiently loyal to be purged by the covenanters. The crown's political control was revived after 1660, and it was Lauderdale's blatant packing of the court which led in 1674 to demands for reform which nevertheless left the crown's patronage intact. While Lord President Stair chose exile in 1681 rather than take the test oath, the bench remained relatively subservient, and the chief guarantor of its independence was the high social status of the judges.

In the early seventeenth century the belief persisted that the king should not need taxation and should live off his own income. However, his income was inadequate, and even after reforms and the introduction of more effective management, in the exchequer in 1626, Charles I's ordinary income remained £196,500 in 1628–9. This was a fraction of the income of the English crown, and much less than that of the crown in Ireland. The royal coffers therefore were dependent on good trade since so much of its income came from customs revenue or the wine impost. In spite of improvements to the tax system in the later sixteenth century, and an increase in the frequency of taxation, annual taxation only became effective from 1621 when parliament granted a tax for four years. Thereafter, succeeding parliaments and conventions made further grants for fixed periods. The sums granted also became greater, new taxes were introduced from 1621 on a variety of consumer goods and on investments, and in 1633 the basic rate at which the land tax was calculated was raised and the tax net widened. By the 1620s and 1630s the crown could raise some £300,000 per annum in taxation. Yet the business of collecting taxes remained in the hands of tax farmers like the consortium of merchants who paid £54,000 for the tack of the customs for fifteen years in 1628. The crown was assured of an agreed income which was smaller than the full taxation, and the tax farmers hoped to make a profit by collecting more than they paid the king. The system was notoriously corrupt and inefficient, and all that could be said in its favour was that it was more effective than leaving the job to the sheriffs. At the 1673 parliament the third duke of Hamilton was still trying to recover some of the massive debt owing to his family since 1633 when the third marquis of Hamilton was collector of the taxes. It was the covenanters who made the most important advances in tax management with a national taxation in 1640, a new excise in 1644, and the very effective cess in 1645 which taxed the valued rental income of land rather than its capital value. Local government was placed under more direct control through the shire committees of war, ensuring efficient collection.

In spite of the improvements in raising revenue, the covenanters resorted to borrowing more heavily than Charles I on the strength of debts owed to them by the English parliament. In fact creditors on both sides of the war were ruined. The very heavy cost of maintaining the covenanters' military machine, and the punitive taxation of the 1650s which paid for the English occupying army, left the Scots unenthusiastic about paying high taxes after 1660. This was offset by the enthusiasm for the return of the monarchy, and in 1661 Charles II was granted £480,000 per annum for the rest of his reign, a sum far in excess of Charles I's ordinary income. A similar rush of enthusiasm led parliament to grant James VII the excise in perpetuity in 1685. Yet Charles soon found his income inadequate, and the disbanding of the army in 1667 was in part due to the need to economise. In order to increase income the cess was revived in 1665, being gathered on a monthly basis by the commissioners of supply, locally elected officials drawn from the lesser nobility. The growth in the financial side of government led to repeated attempts to manage crown finances by a commission, and after 1667 the treasury evolved as a separate department of government. Except for 1682–6 when the first duke of Queensberry was treasurer, it was managed by a treasury commission of the chancellor and between five and eight privy councillors who worked directly with the king and were not subordinate to the privy council. Accounting procedures also improved, and while corruption continued, the massive scandals which had been a feature of earlier administrations ceased. After 1689, parliament kept the crown on much tighter reins financially, necessitating annual requests for money. Surprisingly, the huge British involvement in European war had little impact on tax-management in Scotland where the revenue barely supported the Edinburgh administration. After 1706 the imposition of English treasury practices and of new tax agents in the form of customs and excise officials made little impression on the tax-resistant Scots, and it was the attempt to impose the new malt tax in 1713 which created popular anti-union resentment.

Royal government operated relatively effectively at the centre, but in the localities it scarcely existed. The plethora of overlapping heritable private courts and ecclesiastical courts created an irrational patchwork of justice. For example, in Stirlinghire, an area of 451 square miles (the population was 37,014 in 1755), there were two large regalian courts, a sheriff court, a royal burgh court, nine burghs of barony each with their own courts, a scattering of justices of the peace, an unknown number of barony courts, five presbyteries each of which extended into neighbouring shires, and twenty-four kirk sessions. The privy council and the justiciary court's circuits also exercised jurisdiction depending on the crime or the particular rights of the local court. What gave order to this mesh of jurisdictions was not institutional authority, but the patronage networks of noblemen like the marquis of Montrose or the earl of Callendar who controlled the regality courts and who provided the nexus between government and locality. Repeated attempts from 1587

to revamp local justice under direct royal control made no headway against entrenched privileges and traditional patterns of
deference. Similarly, a new initiative to introduce commissioners of the peace in 1609 made very little impact on local justice.
In the lowlands there was a greater willingness on the part of
the nobility to concede jurisdictional rights to the crown for a
price, but even in the 1700s the crown had less influence in the
localities than the nobility who generally administered justice
effectively and fairly. Even the occupation government of the
1650s found that its abolition of private franchise courts in 1652
was impractical. Government dependence on the co-operation
of local noblemen and the need to authenticate local power
structures was reflected in policies like the general band of
1587, the statutes of Iona in 1609, and the 1692 commission
for securing the peace of the highlands. The crown also had less
local influence than the church, hence the determination on
the part of kings to control it. Even with an episcopalian polity
the devolved workings of the church ensured that responsibility
for education, poor relief and moral discipline was parish based.
Here there was no real disagreement with the crown, and on
most matters of social control, king, nobleman and minister
were agreed. Both baronial courts and kirk sessions did get the
state's business done, and left to themselves local communities
had a good record of maintaining order and raising taxes. They
could also be frighteningly efficient as the witch-craft trials of the
period demonstrated. Excessive interference from the centre,
however, was unwise, and when Charles I attempted to buy up
the regalian courts and to turn kirk sessions into government
agencies in the 1630s he precipitated the collapse of his regime.
Similarly the 1679 rebellion was aroused by the combination of
heavy-handed interference from the centre and the withdrawel
of local co-operation in enforcing the crown's religious policy.

When disorder did threaten, the crown's weakness at a local
level was exposed, as was its lack of coercive authority. Powerful
citadels existed at Edinburgh, Stirling and Dumbarton, but
these proved unable to prevent revolution in 1637–8 or 1688–9.
Neither James VI nor Charles I could afford an army, and while
both the covenanters and the English army in the 1650s proved

that the localities could be quelled by force, it was at massive political and financial cost. The small standing army established in 1660 reinforced popular antagonism to the idea of professional troops, and was disbanded in 1667 to save money. The militia was more acceptable and more effective in policing, but it was controlled by the local aristocracy, not by the king, and the aggressive deployment of the 'highland host' in 1678 was a provocative and counter-productive use of the militia. Similarly, in the highlands the crown granted authority to privately run independent companies to gather taxation and quell disorder since the few available troops were needed in the south for action against covenanters. The vast increase in Britain's military commitment in the 1690s and 1700s was reflected in the raising of more Scottish regiments which were, in effect, integrated into a British army and paid by the English establishment. Of course the union of 1707 made the deployment of English forces on Scottish soil more likely, giving the crown a greater measure of force in the case of rebellion, although in 1715 the limitations of the British army in responding to domestic crisis were exposed. As for using troops to enforce local government, or even to put down disorder, the Scottish elites remained distrustful of soldiers. The localities of eighteenth century Scotland would prove just as able as those of the seventeenth century in keeping government at a distance and running their own affairs.

2

POLITICAL ELITES

The Aristocracy

Only a very few people in Scotland were involved in politics, and an even smaller number belonged to the political elite, or elites, those who directly influenced and had a hand in decision making. Perhaps around 2,000 heads of aristocratic families dominated the political life of a nation of three-quarters of a million people, and among these less than 100, chiefly peers, could command a voice in national affairs. In addition were a handful of crown officials and judges most of whom had some connection with the landed aristocracy, or who had ambitions to join its ranks. The only areas of public life not dominated by the aristocracy were the church, where bishops and the more articulate and ambitious ministers provided political leadership, and the towns, where oligarchies of merchant burgesses controlled the burgh councils. In both church and burghs, however, clientage of one form or another often bound ministers and merchants to the nobility. It is possible to make tentative suggestions about shifts in political power such as the rise of the lairds, the challenge to the existing order from the presbyterian clergy, or the growing confidence of the merchant burgesses. It is also the case that lordship had to adapt to different ideological and social conditions, that the moving of the centre of political power to London raised the spectre of provincialisation, and that individual families waxed and waned. Yet it is doubtful if there was any significant change in the underlying structure of political power, or its social distribution throughout the entire early modern period. The 1640s provides the closest Scotland came to alternative forms of political power and political structures prior to the nineteenth century, but the brief experiment horrified the aristocracy which thereafter kept a very firm grip on its power. In 1700 Scottish political life was every bit as hierarchical and exclusive as it had been in 1600. Even the names did not greatly alter, and the Campbells, Douglases, Hamiltons and Gordons are repeatedly found at the centre of political history between the fifteenth and eighteenth centuries.

Nobility was not only enjoyed by the peerage, which was a relatively recent creation of the late middle ages, but peers did form the top layer of the aristocracy. However, the distinguishing characteristics of a heritable title, the right to an individual summons to parliament, personal access to the king, and pre-eminence in precedence were marks of status within the aristocracy, not proofs of nobility. Arguments about the true nature of nobility were commonplace in medieval Europe, and answers to the question varied according to the value placed on blood, honour, jurisdictions, property and titles. The Scottish nobility comprised a broad and shifting population of landowners, most easily identified as the baronage, or tenants in chief to the crown. While a small number of these noblemen were peers, the vast majority were untitled, although some were distinguished by hereditary baronetcies, first introduced in 1625, knighthoods, and clan chieftaincies. There is some reason to believe that nobility extended beyond the baronage to all their male descendants, a fact demonstrated by their right to display a coat of arms. These arms, regarded as outward symbols of nobility, were popular, and when the court of the lord lyon decided to create a public register of arms free of charge in 1672 such was the volume of business generated by real and spurious claims that it took five years to complete the register, and even after 1677 the court remained busy confirming claims.

These lairds, to give them their most common appellation, formed a landowning community estimated to be in excess of 10,000 houses. Such an open-ended definition for nobility is too wide, and wealth acted as a practical limitation on aristocratic pretentions so that an impoverished peer like the ninth Lord Sommerville stopped using his title, while poor lairds had no serious claim to nobility. Because in Scotland there were no economic advantages in nobility, unlike France where various tax concessions and privileges were available, the pressure to maintain aristocratic status was reduced. The Scottish aristocracy was an open elite, blurred at the edges by impoverished peers, younger sons of noblemen, army officers, and upwardly mobile lairds who merged with a wider landowning community of bonnet lairds and heritors to form a parish elite with no aristocratic credentials.

Political leadership of the aristocracy lay with the peerage. In 1603 there were fifty-seven peers; one duke, two marquises, twenty-one earls, and thirty-three lords of parliament. Over the previous twenty years the peerage had already experienced a modest expansion from a base of forty-nine as James rewarded his friends; there had also been a large number of promotions within the existing peerage. After 1603 James and Charles I accelerated the expansion dramatically. Between 1603–25 there was a fifty-one per cent increase and between 1625–49 a further thirty-eight per cent increase, the single biggest group being men who had acquired former church lands, the lords of erection. At the time of Charles I's death there were two dukes, four marquises, fifty-six earls, eight viscounts and forty-nine lords of parliament, a total of 119 and a doubling of the peerage since 1603. Thereafter the rate of increase slowed considerably to twelve per cent between 1649–88, and three per cent between 1688–1714. In 1714, prior to the jacobite forfeitures, the total number of peers stood at 137: nine dukes, four marquises, sixty-five earls, sixteen viscounts and forty-three lords of parliament. Over the entire period 1603–1714 the peerage expanded by one hundred and forty per cent, and sixty-four per cent of the families who held peerages in 1714 had been untitled in 1603. While the rate of increase in the first half of the century was excessive (at the 1633 coronation alone Charles elevated ten peers, created nine more and dubbed fifty-four knights), prompting some concern among the 'ancient' nobility that their order was being diluted, but it was inevitable that the peerage had to 'recruit' if it did not want to die out. Among the peerage families of 1603 almost one in five were extinct by 1714, but these families had a better chance of remaining ahead of their newer rivals, and of the thirteen dukes and marquises in 1714, eight had been peerage families before 1603 and one duke was descended from a bastard of Charles II. The remaining four, the dukes of Atholl, Queensberry and Buccleuch and the marquis of Annandale all had reached the peerage by 1633 and all were drawn from powerful noble families with extensive estates and large kindreds. Some eighteen per cent of the new peers were men who experienced rapid social acceleration, younger sons of lairds or sons of royal officials, courtiers or soldiers, who were granted or bought land with the money they earned in royal service, and finally were granted a title. Without exception they aspired to an aristocratic lifestyle, building a country house, defending noble privileges, and often encouraging a family myth which disguised their relatively humble origins. Around ten per cent of the new peers were Englishmen who held Scottish titles and never acquired land or any other interest in Scotland. Of the remainder, twenty-one per cent were younger sons of peers and fifty-one per cent were men who inherited landed estates from their fathers. The great majority of new peers were recruited from within the aristocracy, from among men whose power already was based on land and local clientage, who held some form of local jurisdiction, who took pride in a noble ancestry, and shared similar ideas on honour.

A great deal of the authority exercised by noblemen was jurisdictional. Even at the end of a century which saw considerable progress in the development of Scots law, the legal profession and the crown's powers to enforce justice, the aristocracy retained their heritable jurisdictions. These jurisdictions ranged from baronial courts in which the baron or his deputy judged cases largely related to the economic and social management of the barony, to huge regality courts such as that of the duke of Argyll within which neither royal sheriffs nor justice ayres had any legal competence. Regality courts had the right to repledge cases from royal courts, could try rape, murder, arson and robbery, the four pleas of the crown, and could execute criminals on the lord's own gallows. While jurisdiction over these capital crimes declined in lowland regality courts over the seventeenth century, many highland lords retained their full regalian authority. Naturally these powers conferred huge political power in a locality, and one of the most effective means of coercion in the later seventeenth century was to exploit hereditary courts in the manipulation of debt. Not every nobleman enjoyed such authority and not all localities were subject to regalian authority, but even where the sheriff was appointed by the crown it was usual to chose a local nobleman. In fact the majority of sheriffdoms were hereditary, and in the early eighteenth century twenty-one of the thirty-three sheriffdoms were still in private hands. James VI recommended the abolition of heritable jurisdictions in *Basilikon Doron*, but was forced to live with them while Charles I tried unsuccessfully to buy them out. In 1652 all heritable jurisdictions were abolished by the occupying regime, but they were restored after 1660, were guaranteed by the treaty of union in 1707, and survived until 1747.

Economic power rested above all else on the extent of landholding. The widespread use in the sixteenth century of feuing – a form of landholding in which the tenant acquired hereditary ownership of the land in return for annual feus paid to the feudal superior in perpetuity – together with the secularisation of church lands and temporalities combined to increase the number of landowners as well as the global landholding of the nobility. The vigorous landmarket of the early seventeenth century was a consequence of this great turnover in land which saw a number of spectacular collapses among old magnate families like the earls of Crawford as well as some of the newly-titled noble houses like that of Newbattle. Charles I's interference in the structure of landholding with his revocation scheme was intended to impose order on the confusion arising from the reformation land grab. Instead it aroused aristocratic fury at what was perceived as an attack on fundamental property rights. By the 1650s aristocratic economic dominance of the countryside appeared to be threatened by catastrophic debts and political defeat, which resulted in massive wadsetting or mortgaging. However, the reluctance to sell land or alienate jurisdictions ensured that the underlying power structure remained intact, and it is unsurprising that the post-restoration era saw political conservatism allied to a determined effort to rebuild encumbered estates. The possibility of a larger and more egalitarian landed community, stimulated by extensive feuing and wadsetting, receded in the later seventeenth century when economic conditions changed to suit the larger landowners, and the nobility squeezed out many of the smaller lairds. The consolidation of the great estates and subsequent contraction of the landed elite which was a feature of the later seventeenth and eighteenth centuries was encouraged by the parliamentary legislation of 1685, which made provision for the strict entail, curtailing the freedom of landowners to dispose of their heritable property. One result of this volatile land market was a massive increase in litigation, and by the early eighteenth century the court of session was popularly known as the land mercat club.

The progressive use of their estates also ensured economic success for the aristocracy who could best afford improvements. Landlords always had adopted commercial attitudes towards their lands, but before c.1600 political instability often qualified estate management with the need for military service from tenants. Long leases, and a strong emphasis on kindness (the cultivation of paternalistic relationships on the estate) remained a feature of landlords' thinking, and military tenures survived in parts of the highlands into the eighteenth century. However, even in localities like Balquidder in upper Perthshire, the latter half of the seventeenth century saw improving landlords like the marquis of Atholl introducing more commercial estate management, while John Campbell of Glenorchy applied new farming methods and longer leases further west in Breadalbane. Rents rose over the century, especially throughout the first quarter, and particularly in the lowlands, landlords desirous of money commuted services and rents in kind for cash payments. Progressive landlords also founded new baronial markets, built enclosures, expanded land under cultivation and introduced liming, while in parliament the landed majority passed legislation to facilitate improvements, such as the enclosure of common lands. In all this the nobility led the way, as it did in the expansion of the cattle trade with England, the most dynamic sector of the late seventeenth century economy. Low grain prices in the latter half of the century persuaded noblemen to take the lead in exploiting estate resources like salt and coal. The second earl of Kincardine was the biggest salt producer in the country in the 1670s, while the fourth duke of Hamilton owned the lucrative Bo'ness coal mines on his Kinneil estate in West Lothian. During the first four decades of the century, and again in the period from about 1680, the aristocracy spent huge sums of money remodelling castles like Carlaverock or Glamis and in building luxurious country houses like Hopetoun which was constructed between 1699 and 1703, monuments to conspicuous consumption which acted as physical evidence of the aristocracy's confidence and ongoing economic dominance.

Until the first decade of the seventeenth century the most virile demonstration of political muscle among the nobility was the fighting power of their kindred and dependants. The ability to summon armed supporters was crucial in a feuding society where disputes were often settled by trials of strength rather than at law, and the private armies of the magnates regularly intervened in national politics. The deliberate pursuit of policies designed to eradicate feuding, the pacification of the borders after 1603, the growth of church influence, and changing patterns of loyalty imposed by the commercialisation of landed relationships reduced the military dimension, at least in the lowlands. In the highlands lordship remained potent and chiefs continued to raise small private armies, bonds of friendship were exchanged, local politics were territorial, and private wars, cattle raiding and blackmail racketeering continued to be a feature of the region into the eighteenth century. In the western highlands political conflicts and disputes were shaped by the ambitions of the house of Argyll and by the efforts of smaller clans to escape from Campbell domination. However, it is easy to exaggerate highland distinctiveness. Undoubtedly there was greater resistance to external influences, and indebtedness, for example, was kept within the clan, but commercial and political pressures increasingly forced clan chiefs to adapt such that they undermined the traditional culture of raiding, feuding and feasting by which they had expressed their power. Most clan disputes were settled at law by the latter half of the century, and few chiefs pursued careers as bandits or warlords. Nevertheless, the military power of the chiefs was a factor in national politics in the 1640s, 1680s and in 1715, reorientating Gaelic society away from Ireland towards lowland Scotland. Even in the lowlands the Bishops Wars of 1639–40 demonstrated that while the trend was towards a national army and new allegiances, lords still were able to raise large forces owing personal loyalty to themselves. Yet while the idea of granting bonds of manrent and doing homage to lords grew unfashionable in the lowlands after 1600, claims of kinship remained potent, and even in the late seventeenth century the scramble to seek the patronage of magnates like the dukes of Hamilton or Queensberry was feverish. At a local level the jurisdictional and economic power of the nobility gave them great influence, which lesser men cultivated in the pursuit of local offices, in the hope of support against rivals in disputes, or in exchange for help in arranging marriage alliances, or in marketing their estate produce. For their part noblemen wanted their kinsmen and clients in local offices like the justices of the peace or holding commissions in the militia. The latter was formed in 1668 with the precise objective of ensuring local aristocratic control of the military, and the privy council often appointed joint command by rival magnates rather than risk offending one of them and rendering the militia impotent. The election of shire commissioners to parliament could also become a trial of strength between the leading local noblemen. The extent of local dominance by the aristocracy was especially important in a society where power was highly centrifugal. Attempts to impose control from the centre through the church in the 1630s, or through the army in the 1680s, failed, and it was the loss of aristocratic confidence

in government which led to the collapse in the localities of
Charles I's and James VII's regimes. It also was the inability to
govern the localities effectively which persuaded the English
occupation forces to seek the co-operation of the nobility in
the 1650s, while in 1715 the Hanoverian government came
close to defeat by forces raised on the estates of the northern
aristocracy. However, attempts to rebel or pressurise the central
government in 1666, 1679, 1685, 1689 and 1707 failed miserably
because of insufficient aristocratic support.

Discussion of the patronage relationships which connected
localities to the centre usually focuses on the use of patronage by the crown to control the nobility. Certainly the
increase in resources available to kings after 1603 impacted
on political behaviour, and James VI's scattering of patronage
before his Scottish nobility was more than wanton waste. The
desperate need for crown patronage explains much about the
unadventurous aristocratic politics of the 1660s and 1670s, and
patronage did persuade some noblemen to back a parliamentary union in 1707. However, instead of seeing noblemen
only as passive clients of the state, the point which often
is overlooked is that kings had to cultivate their nobilities.
Kings needed aristocratic support and got it at the price of
pensions and offices for noblemen and their constituencies
of kinsmen, friends and clients. There is little evidence to
suggest that patronage persuaded noblemen to damage their
own interests, or to support policies of which they disapproved
fundamentally. What is more significant is the high political
cost government faced when it neglected to cultivate the
aristocracy, as increasingly was the case in the 1630s, 1680s
and the early 1700s. In terms of their own importance as
brokers in the patronage scramble the moving of the court
to London increased the bargaining influence of the higher
nobility since access to the king was reduced. Deprived of
access to a court in Edinburgh, and unable to afford the cost
of living in London, most noblemen had to seek the help of
magnates and courtiers. The court embodied aristocratic ideals,
manners and lifestyles, and it was here, at the very centre of
political power, that aristocratic influence over their rivals was

at its greatest. It was at the court too that the pre-eminence of the peerage was most evident, and there existed a court aristocracy comprising, for example, successive heads of the house of Hamilton, whose access to the king made them natural leaders of political factions whatever their personal qualities.

The necessity of involving noblemen in government while at the same time preventing noble factions from controlling royal institutions was a familiar problem for Scottish kings. James VI could not overcome the unwillingness of the higher nobility to take seriously their role in the routine of central adminstration, and the fact that some noblemen sought royal office did not mean the emergence of a new service nobility, but was evidence of aristocratic colonisation of the state apparatus. This process was a consequence of the self-exclusion of the clergy from government after the reformation, and the attempt to reintroduce clerics to government in the 1630s was resented deeply. After 1660 this colonisation accelerated, and the revolution of 1689 guaranteed that the aristocratic take-over of state institutions could not be reversed. The tedious nature of much administrative work and the legal specialisation required in certain offices meant that many noblemen were disinclined to serve or were unsuitable. However, with the exception of Charles I who excluded the magnates from government, and the later covenanting governments which had a smaller contingent of peers, most seventeenth-century governments were aristocratic. Certainly among the more important offices of state the nobility predominated. The chancellorship was held by eleven peers and one archbishop, the latter being sufficiently unusual to outrage public opinion. Only one of the eight treasurers appointed were non-peers and the exception, Sir George Hume of Spott, was created earl of Dunbar while in office. Most of the secretaries of state appointed before 1640 were members of the lesser nobility, but between 1640–1714 fifteen of the eighteen secretaries were peers. The office of justice general was in the hereditary hands of the earls of Argyll until 1628, and apart from a few years between 1635–43 and 1676–8 it remained the preserve of the peerage, returning to the Campbell family in 1710. Both the lord president of the session and the lord advocate were legal offices and neither was filled by a peer throughout the seventeenth century, but both offices were dominated by men drawn from the lesser nobility who had received a legal training. Even the mundane clerk register's office attracted aristocratic incumbents in the latter half of the century.

These offices only were the tip of the privy council which continued to be dominated by aristocratic appointments. In the 1610 reconstruction James VI appointed eighteen peers among the thirty-five members, and a number of the others were lesser noblemen. Only Charles I sought to break aristocratic influence in the royal administration, and the number of bishops on his privy council became a grievance against him. Of the 110 councillors who attended at least one sitting of Charles II's privy council sixty-eight were peers prior to their appointment, including the earls of Rothes and Linlithgow who headed the councillors in frequency of attendance. Most of the remaining councillors were lesser nobility, and some of these were created peers after their council career commenced. On the court of session and within the faculty of advocates the landed aristocracy and their clients provided the largest share of the places. Of the twenty-two ordinary judges appointed between the reforms of 1605 and 1626, twelve were members of the aristocracy (including four peers or their heirs), seven were younger sons of lesser noble families, and the remaining five were made up of an archbishop and his son and three advocates. Between 1689–1707 the new appointments to the court included nineteen noblemen or their heirs of whom seven were peers, and eleven younger sons of landed families. Thirteen of these men were trained advocates, but only one advocate reached the bench who did not have a landed background. Finally, the small size of the army during most of the century provided few opportunitiies for the aristocracy to pursue what remained the most attractive form of state service. However, they dominated high command from the marquis of Hamilton in Germany in 1631–2 to the duke of Argyll at Sheriffmuir in 1715. War always provided the most rapid route into the nobility, and the growth in military professionalism certainly saw a number of men like the earls of Leven, Middleton and

Portmore rise from fairly ordinary origins to the peerage. However, as the aristocracy came to accept the need for a disciplined army in which ability mattered as much as status, the officer class of the early eighteenth century was filled up by noblemen.

Only in parliament was there a formal distinction between the peerage and the lesser nobility, who were represented by the commissioners for the barons or shire commissioners. The latter were elected annually by the forty shilling freeholders of the shire, two commissioners being allowed for each shire. Peers were excluded from participating or even observing the elections, and since 1587 peers' heirs had been disqualified from being elected to parliament. However, this effort to prevent the shires becoming sinecures of the peerage was only partially successful, and shire commissioners often were elected as clients of a local magnate. While electoral competitiveness did heat up in the later seventeenth century, the landed community was on the whole content to leave the business of parliament to a handful of rich and powerful local leaders. Shire elections were notoriously apathetic affairs, and even allowing for the fact that the electorate was small, averaging perhaps fifty to eighty freeholders, there was a general reluctance to be burdened with the responsibility and cost of attending parliament. In Aberdeenshire in 1616 only twenty-two barons turned up to elect the commissioner, and this was one of the more populous shires. Peers too could be unenthusiastic about parliament, but every peer had the right to a personal summons to parliament and on average over one third of parliament were peers. Except for the 1640s when the peerage lost influence – their share of the vote was as low as fourteen per cent in 1649 – their voting strength fell below thirty per cent only in 1617 and 1690. The peerage vote rose as high as forty-one per cent in 1633, reflecting the recent increase in titles, the thirty-eight per cent in 1661 was the highest post-restoration representation, and in 1706 thirty-three per cent of the members of parliament were peers. The office of commissioner to parliament was also conferred on leading peers and between 1661–1707 all of the fourteen men who filled the office held the rank of earl or duke. The presence of the lesser nobility further swelled the aristocratic presence in parliament, and with the exception of 1617 and 1649 the aristocracy always had a majority in parliament. The aristocratic share of votes was on the whole greater after 1660, and was as high as seventy per cent in 1706. The doubling of the votes of the lesser nobility in 1640 and the elimination of the bishops in 1690 saw a progressive increase in the power of the nobility at the expense of the crown and the burghs. Above all else parliament was a meeting of the landed aristocracy, and the attempts by kings to turn it into an instrument of state required enormous political effort. The relative success of James VI and Charles I in 1621 and 1633 was bought at the price of an aristocratic reaction in the 1641 constitution, and James VII's disregard for parliament led to a similar revolution which increased the influence of the nobility. It was, of course, the magnates' dominance of parliament after 1690 which led the crown to seek its abolition in 1707. The removal to Westminster reduced the independence of the nobility in parliament, but the reduction in the number of members of parliament increased the aristocratic stranglehold over parliamentary representation.

The nobility dominated the Scottish state, but how Scottish was the nobility? The transfer of the king and the court to London in 1603 confronted the nobility with the dilemma of slipping into provincial insignificance, or of submitting to Anglicisation. In fact only a few Scots rushed to court and whole-heartedly embraced England, particularly Jacobean courtiers like the earls of Somerset and Carlisle. One or two aristocratic families emigrated to England; the dukes of Lennox only had superficial Scottish connections, the earls of Elgin settled in the south in the early 1600s, the earls of Stirling and Kinnoul were transplanted to England over more than one generation. Scots who were born after James VI and I's succession to the English throne in 1603 had rights of citizenship in England, but a few noblemen were born in England, most of these to English mothers. The second earl of Ancram, for example, was the son of Sir Robert Ker, gentleman of the bedchamber to Charles I, and his second wife, Anne Stanley, a daughter of the earl of Derby. While Ancram and the second earl of Newburgh, who shared a similar background, pursued English careers, both the second duke of Argyll and the first duke of Atholl were not prevented from involvement in Scottish affairs by their English maternal parentage. The low number of peers with English mothers does not reflect the rate of marriages between the English and Scottish aristocracies, and there were a little under a hundred marriages between Scottish peers or their sons and English women, these being spread evenly throughout the period. The chief reason for contracting an English marriage was likely to be financial. Thus John Campbell, younger of Glenorchy, made a net profit of £54,000 from his marriage in 1654 to Mary Rich, daughter of the earl of Holland. However, a large proportion of English marriages were second marriages, and when looking for a first wife noblemen concentrated their efforts closer to their political and economic interests in Scotland. This marital conservatism was enhanced by the reluctance among English noblemen to encourage Scottish marriages, and only a handful of English peers married a Scottish wife, all in the early years of the union.

In their education the nobility continued to attend school and university at home, following this with a continental tour and possibly some time at a European university. There was little interest in attending Oxford or Cambridge where the religious test oath prevented most Scots from gaining entrance. A court education meant greater exposure to English ideas and culture, but there is no evidence of aristocratic parents seeking out English schooling for their children until the last quarter of the seventeenth century when one or two cases do appear. Apart from the growing use of English in writing there is little reason to believe that the nobility were uncomfortable with Scottish culture, and they continued to speak Scots or Gaelic (at the very least to their wives, children, friends and servants), to operate through Scottish institutions like parliament and the law courts, to embrace Scottish education, and to patronise native artistic and architectural styles and forms. Nor was there any great pressure for English honours which were sparingly handed out, especially after the death of James VI. Ten Scots were granted English peerages during the regal union, but the second duke of Argyll was the only Scot holding an English peerage – he was duke of Greenwich – in 1707. Sixteen Scots were honoured with the order of the garter, but only four of these were awarded after 1660. Economically the interests of the nobility also remained in Scotland, and only a very few noblemen became significant English landowners, the fourth duke of Hamilton for example had large estates in Lancashire. A minority of nobles acquired English property, a London house or a manor in the home counties, and many more looked to the court, or the English military establishment for financial opportunities. Naturally absenteeism was more common after 1603 because London was much further away than Edinburgh, but also because of the growing fashion throughout Europe for living in urban-based royal courts. Yet the interest most noblemen took in improving and enlarging their Scottish estates, the energy and money they poured into building new and improved residences in Scotland, their involvement in local politics, and their many trips back and forward between London and their homes, all suggest a determination not to sacrifice their Scottish identity. When Patrick Maule, first earl of Panmure, retired to his Scottish estates in the later 1640s after four decades of service in the royal household in England, he expressed his patriotism by writing a history of William Wallace. In the early eighteenth century the Scottish aristocracy remained an essentially native aristocracy. There was in Scotland no equivalent of the Anglicized Welsh nobility, or the colonial English aristocracy of Ireland. James VI's hopes that the aristocracies of England and Scotland would be at the van of a British melting pot were unfulfilled.

The Clerical Elite

The political role of the clergy in Scotland was dominated by the issue of crown control of the church. A church with bishops meant a high political profile for clerical leaders, but subordination to the crown. Until 1638, and again between 1661–89, the church was governed by the archbishops of

St Andrews and Glasgow and twelve bishops. Unlike the pre-reformation bishops these men were not quasi-secular lords with aristocratic backgrounds and they lacked the wealth and independent political power of their catholic predecessors. Their backgrounds were modest, and all had trained and served as parish ministers. Of Charles II's 1661 appointments the only bishop with aristocratic connections was Robert Wallace, bishop of the Isles, a distant kinsman of Chancellor Glencairn, while Archbishop Burnet married his daughter to Lord Elphinstone's heir. Nevertheless, as archbishop of Glasgow from 1603–15, John Spottiswoode had precedence over a lord of parliament, he lived in a palace, owned a house in Edinburgh and tower houses elsewhere, controlled the lordship of Glasgow, was chancellor of the University of Glasgow, sat on the privy council and the court of session, and held a number of other civil and ecclesiastical appointments.

Yet the very point of having bishops was to ensure the church's obedience to the state. Bishops therefore lacked political independence, being appointed and dismissed by the king, and constrained by the obedience they owed under the royal supremacy. It was the obsequiousness which flowed from this relationship which made bishops useful to the king, not only in ensuring the church was co-operative, but as royal servants in national and local government. The church was given a voice in parliament, each of the bishops having his seat there, but the principal advantage of their presence to the king was in increasing the crown's votes. James VI altered the mechanisms for electing the lords of the articles in such a way that it was the bishops, acting as his most pliant servants, who ensured his control of the process. The two archbishoprics effectively became offices of state with a place on the privy council, and Archbishop Spottiswoode of St Andrews was appointed chancellor in 1635. It was Charles I who went furthest in packing his privy council with bishops, much to the resentment of the nobility, and neither Charles II or James VII was so rash. No attempt was made to restore bishops to the court of session, but the court of high commission was rejuvenated under both episcopal regimes, giving the archbishops judicial autonomy largely over matters pertinent to the discipline of the clergy but also over the religious life of the laity. The bishops also managed the appointment of ministers and the regulation of church affairs through synods and presbyteries over which they presided. A few bishops occupied offices of political significance, but their lack of independence and their devotion to ideas of non-resistance and divine right monarchy allowed little room to manouevre. When the bishops tried to oppose the five articles of Perth in 1617 James VI bullied them into obedience, and Charles II simply removed Archbishop Burnet of Glasgow when he objected to the drift of royal policy in 1669. A few bishops did carve out a degree of political autonomy within the constraints imposed by the supremacy. Archbishop Spottiswoode had some success under James VI, and in the 1660s Archbishop Sharp of St Andrews almost emerged as an independent power broker before Lauderdale intervened and turned him into a state functionary. As long as the bishops did not threaten aristocratic power they were tolerated, but when in the 1630s they were seen to support policies antagonistic to the nobility they were eliminated politically. Ingrained with the habits of obedience, the bishops found themselves tied to the fortunes of unpopular regimes in 1637–8 and 1688–9, and on both occasions their loyalty to the crown ensured their defeat.

A presbyterian church sought independence from the state and lacked any formal role in government. Furthermore because of the parity of ministers and the sharing of church government with the laity, power was diffuse and localised. It is more difficult therefore to evaluate the political role of the parish ministers, who acquired a remarkably powerful position in parish administration and as opinion formers in local society. In 1596 there were 539 ministers in over a thousand parishes, by the 1620s there was a graduate ministry throughout the lowlands, and by mid-century there were 838 ministers whose social and educational backgrounds set them apart from the great majority of the population. In 1649 over half of those ministers whose origins are known came from manse families and another twenty-six per cent had modest landed backgrounds. These were men who did not lack in social confidence. The status of the minister rose along with minimum stipends which were increased to £333 in 1617 and hiked up to £533 in 1627, but could be much higher among a profession who were better paid than their English counterparts. At the top a minister like Alexander Henderson acted as a creditor to his landed neighbours in the 1640s, while Archbishop Burnet left an estate worth £41,470 in 1684. In 1649 the parish minister at Erroll in Perthshire had an income of £912 while the ministers of Edinburgh had stipends of £1,200. Even the more average stipend of £569 enjoyed by the Scone parish minister was exceeded by only around one hundred landowners in the whole of Perthshire. However, it was their role in local education (the clergy also dominated university teaching), poor relief, the control of vagrancy, moral discipline and pastoral oversight which made the minister the most important figure in the parish community next to the landlord. Their dominance of the presbyteries, where the laity were discouraged from attending, extended the influence of more assertive ministers beyond the boundaries of individual parishes. The political significance of this influence was demonstrated most effectively under pressure. In the 1620s and 1630s conventicling arose in response to popular opposition to liturgical reform, while in the 1650s the English military found it impossible to exert social control without leaving the kirk sessions undisturbed. Between 1660–88 the ministers' effectiveness as political organisers and enthusiasts kept alive a cause which was ground down by the state with the connivance of the greater part of the political elite. Such tenacious defiance of the state by people operating outside hierarchic power structures would have been impossible before the reformation, or even before 1600, and was due both to the spread of protestant ideas and to the leadership provided by a confident, articulate and ideologically inspired parish ministry. However, these virtues were not exclusive to the presbyterians and after 1688–9 episcopalian clergy, particularly in the north-east, maintained a defiance of the Church of Scotland, although from 1713 their position was eased by toleration.

Beyond their role as parish ministers the presbyterian clergy claimed neither political office nor responsibility, ostentatiously rejecting both. They preferred to exert indirect pressure through the general assembly, or from their own pulpits where they brought God's word to bear on any shortcomings they identified. Only between 1638–51 did the parish clergy take a more direct role in politics and government, and their skills in organisation, propaganda and negotiation provided much of the dynamic to the covenanters' success. Not surprisingly a core of political activists quickly developed, dominating the office of moderator of the general assembly, while of the 296 ministers who sat on the commission of the assembly between 1642–51 only an elite of eighteen sat on more than four commissions. Following the defeat of the engagers in 1648, the general assembly siezed the political initiative, and while the period of quasi-clerical government was brief, the ministers showed they were capable of governing the kingdom. It was precisely because the minister proved a threat to the established political order that the king and aristocracy insisted on the return of the bishops in 1661 and on keeping the clergy out of politics. The church leaders of post-1690 were prepared to leave the laity to get on with the business of government as long as the crown kept its distance and allowed the general assembly and its ministers to run their churches and parishes. William II was forced to accept this by 1694, but politicians had no illusions about the power of the clergy. In 1706 grumblings from the church about the terms of the treaty of union sent government officials scurrying off to draft a new clause guaranteeing presbyterian supremacy and the independence of the Church of Scotland from England. Clerical opposition was not to union, but to a union which threatened presbyterianism, and the crown's response ensured that the church became a vehicle for the expression of Scottish national consciousness after 1707.

Urban Elites

Within the towns economic and political power was concentrated in a small elite of rich and powerful merchant burgesses. Admission as a burgess varied from burgh to burgh but was relatively easy, and even entrance to the merchant guilds was possible for enterprising and hard-working craftsmen. Although there was a strong tradition of recruiting from the sons of merchants or their sons-in-law, a surprisingly high number of merchants came from outside the burgh. In Edinburgh between 1666–1700 thirty-four per cent of merchant apprentices were recruited from landowning families whose younger sons were squeezed off the land by primogeniture and the strict entail. Of course there was movement in the opposite direction as successful merchant families acquired estates close to the town, but the numbers of merchants who bought land as opposed to holding wadset land as debt security was small. In the 1690s, for example, only seven of Aberdeen's 239 merchant burgesses owned landed estates. Naturally, there were enormous disparities in wealth among merchants like William Dick of Braid, the Edinburgh merchant and financier who acquired a massive fortune prior to 1637, and the provincial merchants of Dumfries who mostly involved themselves in local trade and farming. In the 'boom town' of Glasgow there were some 400–500 merchant burgesses, but only between 100–200 were involved in international trade, and perhaps around thirty constituted a fluid political elite.

The political power that the merchant burgesses enjoyed was based on tight control of the town councils where elections of new councils by outgoing councils ensured a self-perpetuating oligarchy. It was these councils, varying in size from seven to thirty-three members, which in turn elected burgh commissioners to parliament so that the urban electorate for Scotland was perhaps a little in excess of two thousand men. There was little threat within the burghs to this merchant power. While Glasgow experienced a high level of craft participation in burgh government before 1637, any challenge to merchant pre-eminence from the crafts had disappeared in most towns by the early 1600s, and the entrenched position of the merchants on burgh councils was unshakable. There was no threat to the urban elite from popular revolt, and even during the turmoils of the 1640s burgh society retained internal discipline. To some extent the relaxation by the 1680s of entrance requirements to burgessship or to merchant guilds in burghs like Stirling reflected an ease about urban social relations which rested on the self-confidence of the merchants during a period of commercial expansion. Insofar as there was conflict within burghs it was between merchant factions.

It was more difficult to resist external pressures. Obviously larger burghs like Aberdeen, Dundee, Edinburgh amd Glasgow were more able to repel local interference, but many smaller burghs found it politic to submit to the informal clientage of neighbouring magnates. However, the kind of political dominance of the burghs by lords which had been a feature of the sixteenth century was less apparent, and on the whole burgh commissioners to parliament continued to be resident merchants. In many cases it was noblemen who found themselves becoming economically dependent on rich merchants, particularly the Edinburgh merchants who, between the 1600s and 1630s, acquired extensive landholdings as security against the enormous debts of their aristocratic clients. Throughout the covenanting revolution the organisational skills, the financial power, and the political confidence of the merchants was placed at the disposal of the covenanters, and Glasgow alone provided £20,000 in 1639–40. However, in spite of the considerable increase in their political influence, the merchants were content to accept aristocratic leadership, and had to acquiesce in the relative diminution of their parliamentary representation in 1640. Only in 1649–50 did they appear to consider overturning the accepted hierarchic order in their support for the radical covenanters. But the cost of such intense political commitment was the collapse of their economic power, and William Dick's massive lending to the covenanter government brought about his ruin. The impact in the 1640s and 1650s of war, plague and conquest resulted in a political retreat which lasted until the later eighteenth century. Furthermore, the renewed urban patronage the nobility enjoyed in the eighteenth century began its revival in 1660. The landed aristocracy was forbidden from holding burgh office in 1609, but after the restoration the nobility ignored this prohibition. Royal burghs, too, were confronted by the growing economic challenge from burghs of barony, essentially local markets under the control of noblemen. In 1619 the convention of royal burghs protested against a development which threatened to undercut their monopolies, but the creation of new baronial aristocratic markets continued. By the later seventeenth century the erosion of the privileges of royal burghs was more marked, their formal monopoly of foreign trade being breached in 1672. In the long term, competition did not particularly damage the royal burghs, but at the time merchants were concerned. The general economic difficulties experienced by international traders in the later seventeenth century also undermined political confidence among merchants whose economic conservatism – the principal reason for the burghs opposing the union – was in contrast to entrepreneurial aristocrats.

The most insidious threat to the independence of the burghs came not from noblemen but from the crown. The obvious reason for this development was the growing fiscal importance of the burghs. Already by c.1600 royal burghs were paying a sixth of the standard taxation, and from the late sixteenth century a succession of new taxes were levied on burghs and their trade. The parliament of 1621 marked another sharp increase in burgh taxation with the new, levy on annual rents which left merchants as the most heavily taxed sector of the economy. The deterioration in economic independence accelerated in the latter half of the century with the privy council taking over more of the responsibilities of the convention of royal burghs. The latter was for much of the century a highly effective lobby for urban interests, and it was common for the burghs to vote in parliament as a block, having decided already at a convention what policy to adopt. On the whole merchants were interested in narrow sectional matters, but in parliament they had a national role to fulfil. As early as the 1580s the crown's interference in council elections was intrusive, and it became normal for burgh councils to elect magistrates approved by the king. Control of the burghs was important in itself, but because burgh councils elected burgh commissioners to parliament the crown had an additional incentive for interfering in urban politics. The lord provost of Edinburgh became a crown nominee, usually with a seat on the privy council, and political tests were demanded of burgh magistrates, for example support for the five articles of Perth in 1621, a denunciation of the covenants in 1661, or the taking of the test oath in 1681. By the reign of James VII the crown was determined to control burgh politics, and in 1688 John Graham of Claverhouse was appointed constable of Dundee much against the burgh council's wishes. Not surprisingly burgh elites were at the fore of opposition to the crown both in the years after 1637 and in 1688–9, and popular riots in Edinburgh accompanied the early stages of both revolts. In the former case Edinburgh merchants were outraged by the multiplying of taxes, the additional civic costs imposed by royal policies such as the new bishopric and the Parliament House, by blatant manipulation of the burgh elections, and by religious changes. Like the clergy, the merchants were politicized during the 1630s to an extent unseen since the 1590s, and they suffered for their commitment to the covenants. The restoration brought a return to crown manipulation of burgh politics, and the merchant community was too financially depressed until the 1680s to play any role in national politics other than to protect their sectional interests. However, James VII's attempts to nominate all town councils added a political grievance to the widespread religious dissatisfaction with his catholic policies. The severe treatment with which James VI had threatened Edinburgh in 1596 following a civic riot had demonstrated the dangers of misjudging the political climate, and both in 1637 and 1688 the burghs followed an aristocratic lead. While the mob took to the streets in Edinburgh, Glasgow and Dumfries in 1706 to oppose the union, and the burghs campaigned hard against union, neither the extra-legal politics of the riot or the loyal petitioning had any effect without aristocratic leadership.

The Legal Profession

Unlike the aristocracy, clergy or merchants, lawyers cannot be identified with one of the traditional three estates of the medieval political community, and it was only from the middle of the sixteenth century that lay lawyers became common. After 1560 the clergy withdrew altogether from the law, and with the growth in litigation among the landed elite and the proliferation of legislation by parliament, the profession boomed. As a profession it had no distinct political role or independent power, and the lords of session had no right to a seat in parliament. However, the usefulness of lawyers to the crown and aristocracy ensured that individual lawyers often fulfilled a political role. Over the course of the seventeenth century the number of lawyers increased, professional standards and practices were encouraged by the high calibre of teaching in Scottish universities, by the foundation of the advocates library in Edinburgh in 1680, and by the publication of both James Dalrymple of Stair's and Sir George Mackenzie of Rosehaugh's *Institutes.*

By the early seventeenth century the social background of most lawyers was landed. In 1605 James VI agreed that the judges on the court of session should be appointed either from experienced advocates, or peers, their sons or knights worth £2,000 per annum. In fact few advocates became judges, and the court was dominated by noblemen. The sixteenth century had seen the emergence of a few legal dynasties, but the prohibitive costs of a legal training, and the social contacts required to succeed in a business which derived most of its income from servicing the landed aristocracy made it difficult for those with a less privileged background even to enter the profession. The landed presence in the faculty of advocates grew from sixty per cent to ninety-one per cent between 1660–1705, and one conservative estimate has calculated the share of advocates with aristocratic backgrounds to have increased from twenty-three per cent in 1660 to fifty-four per cent in 1705. In 1701–11 all but two of the forty-eight admissions to the faculty of advocates were recruited from landed families, and three-quarters of the new advocates were from aristocratic families. Here too was an emphatic aristocratic colonisation made all the more dramatic by the fact that the faculty of advocates itself increased in size by fifty-four per cent between 1660 and 1690. The attraction for those lesser noblemen who constituted the majority of lawyers was a career which provided additional income to preserve the ancestral estate from indebtedness. The standards of living of judges appear to have risen in the early seventeenth century, and they were often involved in money lending and financial speculation, but the law also could provide a modestly comfortable living for a professional advocate. In the 1630s there is evidence to suggest that advocates were three times better off than the average Edinburgh householder, but very few lawyers became rich simply on the proceeds of their legal practices. In addition to financial considerations, it was important for a family to have a voice in the law courts, particularly on the court of session, providing a powerful political tool in an age when litigation increasingly was the means of resolving disputes over land.

The possibilities a legal career opened up of service to the crown or as the agent of a magnate were more likely to lead to the making of a fortune or to political prominence than the practise of law itself. By the early seventeenth century men with a legal training were a common sight at the privy council table, and while the latter half of the century saw a reduction in the number of lawyers attaining prominence, the law was a useful springboard to a political career. Thomas Hamilton, first earl of Haddington, provides the most dramatic case of a man with relatively lowly social origins rising to the peerage through service to James VI, but this was unusual. Legal dynasties among the lesser nobility, like the Hopes and Dalrymples, were more typical in taking their time to reach the heights of a peerage. It required four generations of judges on the court of session before Sir James MacGill of Cranstounriddell was created Viscount Oxfuird in 1651. The distinction that has to be made is between lawyers as a profession making relatively little impact on politics, far less than ministers, and a number of individual lawyers who operated within the political elite. As a body, lawyers formed no organised lobby, and the faculty of advocates never had any political programme. Certainly lawyers were able to use their skills and contacts to ensure that as a profession their privileges were protected and their status enhanced, but none of this impinged on politics except in a very general sense.

On the whole judges and advocates supported the interests of the landed aristocracy from which most of them were drawn and which supplied most of their business. It is possible that lawyers were predisposed to a political philosophy which placed greater emphasis on statute than the prerogative. It does seem significant that one of the principal architects of the national covenant was Archibald Johnston of Warriston, a lawyer, that there was little enthusiasm on the court of session for the king's covenant, and that even the king's own lord advocate, Sir Thomas Hope, clandestinely backed the king's enemies. Again in 1689 lawyers like Stair were among the leading proponents of contractual monarchy. Of course, another lord advocate, Mackenzie of Rosehaugh, was the principal apologist for royal absolutism in the 1680s, and a succession of lawyers from Sir Thomas Hamilton to Sir John Dalrymple were prepared to work for kings who expected them to find ways around the law, and even to ride roughshod over it.

In their attitude to England and to the threat of Anglicisation, the legal profession was antagonistic. The exclusive claims of the English common law, so ruthlessly imposed on Ireland in the sixteenth and early seventeenth century, were viewed with suspicion by the Scots who had a cosmopolitan and eclectic attitude towards law, although they too appreciated its imperial uses, for example in Orkney and Shetland. There was a strong body of opinion in both kingdoms in the early seventeenth century which felt that the two legal systems were incompatible, and the legal conference of 1607–8 failed to break the deadlock. Succeeding developments, especially in Scotland where the law was progressively systematised, increased the determination of the lawyers not to support legal union. On the whole critics of integration had the better of the argument, for the two systems were very different, especially in the realm of private law, and the contrasts were enhanced by mutual ignorance. Englishmen had no interest whatsoever in Scots law, and while as many as forty per cent of admissions to the faculty of advocates in 1661–1750 had studied in Dutch universities, few Scots were ever found in the English inns of court. Of course, there was no reason why Scots should be found there as plenty of opportunites for aspiring lawyers were available within Scotland. Sir Thomas Craig tried to demonstrate the common origins of the two legal systems in *Jus feudale* (1603), but later retreated on this issue, and as time passed the likelihood of legal union receded with most lawyers remaining unconvinced of its merits. In 1670 prominent lawyers like Sir John Nisbet, the lord advocate, and Sir George Mackenzie opposed legal union, while in 1705–6 lawyers used their influence in parliament to ensure that the act of union contained a clause protecting Scots law, and of course their own professional interests.

3
POLITICAL IDEAS

The Dissemination and Control of Ideas

Ideas are commonly associated with words, but in an age when
the mass of the Scottish population remained illiterate, or at
best semi-literate, the propagation of visual ideas was important.
The crown's unionist ideas were popularised in the early
seventeenth century through a number of different media,
for example the coinage and flags. Religious disputes centred
on issues like clerical dress and the simplicity or ornateness of
church decoration. Aristocratic domination of the countryside
was expressed in the building of castles and country houses,
and the conservative values of the aristocracy were reflected
in their architectural styles. The rotting heads and quarters of
traitors were left in public places to demonstrate the penalties
of rebellion. These visual messages conveyed powerful political
ideas which reached a wide audience. More exclusive visual
ideas were directed at the aristocracy by the crown through its
artistic patronage. The loss of the court to London in 1603 gave
the king access to greater artistic and financial resources, but
the number of Scots subjected to the royalist propaganda was
diminished. The court masques of the Jacobean and Caroline
courts, in which Ben Jonson and Inigo Jones employed ever
more elaborate means to demonstrate the virtues of royal

government, were seen only by a handful of noblemen. Of course the projection of Charles and his queen, Henrietta Maria, as idealised lovers presiding over a paradisical kingdom did not make it so, and not even the court fell for the illusion. Royal portraits were another medium for expressing political ideas. James VI and I is the British Solomon on the Banqueting hall ceiling at Whitehall. While this image of 'The judgement of Solomon' was inaccessible even to many of the Scottish aristocracy, a nobleman could hang a copy of Geoffrey Kneller's painting of William II in a hall, impressing his family, friends and clients by the association with his imperial majesty. In 1684 Charles II was persuaded by his brother, James, duke of York, to commission Jacob de Wet to paint 110 portraits of his Scottish ancestors to be hung in Holyrood palace. The repetition on a grander scale of George Jamesone's 1633 Edinburgh mural demonstrated the continuity of royal power through hereditary succession, and identified the Stewart dynasty with the nation. Specially struck medals encouraged popular association with the monarchy, and by the end of the century these and other artefacts were being produced for a large market. While public ceremonial after 1603 was largely confined to London, the most notable exception was Charles I's 1633 entry and coronation at Edinburgh. The king's success in visually presenting his autocratic ideas to a shocked Scottish public instigated the first steps in organised opposition to his policies. After the restoration observance of a royal calendar became more common, and from 1661 bells, bonfires and loyal toasts marked the annual celebration of the king's birthday in Edinburgh and other major towns.

The means of influencing ideas by word of mouth were meagre. Royal proclamations were published, distributed and both read and posted in the market crosses of royal burghs by sheriffs and king's messengers in what was a rudimentary means of informing the public. By far the most effective medium was the parish pulpits established throughout the lowlands by c.1600. Control of what ministers said therefore was crucial to the government, and in the 1630s Charles I even pushed the clergy towards read lessons instead of sermons and extempore prayers.

Prayers for the king were seen as a communal affirmation of loyalty, and the English occupation forces went to considerable efforts to persuade the resolutioners to give up praying for Charles II and his family in 1657. Imposing an oath of loyalty on the clergy, such as that introduced in 1690 was intended to weed out dissidents, in this case the jacobite clergy who continued to teach the principles of divine right monarchy. Far more than in published works, sermons provided the political education of the mass of the population, and contributed significantly to the opinions of the political elite. As late as 1706 Queen Anne's government foresaw the wreckage of the treaty of union if the church actively campaigned against it, and consequently the presbyterian settlement was guaranteed.

Universities had a more exclusive role to play in educating the aristocracy and the professions, and their sensitive position as opinion formers was recognised by successive governments. Purges of unacceptable professors followed political change in 1637–8, 1660–1 and 1688–90. In the last instance there was a wholesale clean out of the academic community at the University of St Andrews, and the purge was carried down to the grammar school teachers. The political significance of the academic community was never great, but the opposition the Aberdeen Doctors put up to the national covenant in 1638 was some indication of their mischief making potential.

The absence of the court and the influence of the church ensured that seventeenth century Scotland had no political theatre. There only was one theatre in the kingdom, the Tennis Court at Holyroodhouse, and Scottish theatre goers had to rely on English touring companies performing non-controversial productions. As yet there existed only a very nascent country house culture, and the emerging professional culture of Edinburgh remained closely dependent on royal patronage until the early eighteenth century. There is some evidence to suggest that masonic lodges had a political dimension to them. Those at Edinburgh and Kilwinning attracted the support and patronage of the duke of Lauderdale's enemies, while the lodge founded at Dunkeld in 1696 had a jacobite membership. The first coffee house was opened in Edinburgh in 1673, although it was the 1690s before these places became meeting places for the chattering classes. Jacobite subversion, however, was more likely to be talked over in taverns well known for their political affiliation. At a more popular level the ballad or tavern song could be a means of expressing political ideas. Rival whig and jacobite ballad traditions were spawned after 1689, each sustaining their versions of recent history. In the highlands Gaelic poets composed panegyrics for a royalist hero like the marquis of Montrose, and celebrated the social order over which their chiefs presided. There was also polemic from the likes of Iain Lom who lamented the intrusion of lowland values and criticized the powerful house of Argyll, while political poems like 'An Cobhernandori' was a highland peace protest song against the folly of the engagement in 1648.

Among the political elite literacy was universal, and even on the fringes of political activity, among tenant farmers and craftsmen, levels of literacy were high and were growing with the spread of parish schools. The availability of books, pamphlets and newssheets grew with the reading public and the development of an expanding printing industry. In the 1630s and 1640s and again from the 1680s heightened political activity spawned a large body of controversial literature. The covenanters appreciated the value of propaganda far more than the royalists, and made good use of the Edinburgh printing presses throughout their revolution, and evidence that all governments were concerned at what people were reading is obvious from the efforts to impose censorship. Throughout the seventeenth century the crown supervised the printing trade, and both authors and printers faced severe physical and financial punishments for unlicensed publishing. As early as 1584 James VI banned the works of George Buchanan, while many subversive presbyterian books written in the 1620s and 1630s remained unpublished for years. In the 1630s even the possession of a manuscript protestation implying criticism of Charles I was enough to see Lord Balmerino sentenced to death. The notorious catch-all law against leasing-making, the uttering of falsehoods against the king or his councillors, made it treasonable to criticise the king or even to fail to report such criticism. In September

1660 the changed political circumstances of the restoration were signalled by the privy council's proscription of Samuel Rutherford's *Lex Rex* and the public burning of his works. The first newspaper published in Scotland, the anti-clerical and royalist *Mercurius Caledonius* was closed down in March 1661 after only four months because Charles II thought it would alienate moderate presbyterians, and because its ironic style offended leading politicians. In the mid-1680s a paranoid government executed people for refusing to condemn James Renwick's *Apologetical Declaration*. However, it was not only the crown which exercised censorship, and Archibald Pitcairne's 1695 play, *The Assembly*, was not performed during his lifetime because of church opposition. Yet a surprising amount of dissenting literature was in circulation, chiefly as a result of publication in other countries like the Netherlands or for a royalist like John Maxwell in the 1640s, in England. After 1689 censorship was just as tight even if the penalties imposed were less rigorous. Jacobite publications remained covert, but ironically it was the government's own efforts at disinformation which stimulated interest in the jacobites and exaggerated their importance.

The Idea of Monarchy

The Scottish fixation with monarchy might seem surprising in a country which experienced a popular reformation in 1560 and the enforced abdication of Queen Mary in 1567. Yet neither the revolutionary heritage of the reformation, the resistance ideas of calvinism, or association with English or Dutch republicanism led to a rejection of monarchy. Even the successful revolutions of 1637–41 and 1688–90 adhered to a notion of monarchy which was underpinned by social conservatism and the historic role of the Stewart dynasty. It was the very antiquity of the Scottish monarchy, expressed in the ancient king lists, that defined the nation's historic roots. Yet while kingship itself never was in question, there was great disagreement over the distribution of sovereign power, or over the nature and extent of royal authority. The high ground for monarchy was claimed by James VI who felt the need to embark on a public defence of royal power. His *The Trew Law of Free Monarchies* (1598) was an absolutist manifesto asserting that royal power was based on conquest, although the commonsense approach of *Basilikon Doron* (1599) presented a less autocratic view of kingship. The Stewart monarchy always had been inclined towards despotism, but it was James who provided the theoretical basis for the idea that God entrusted sovereign power solely to the king's person. His view of monarchy was mystical, expressed in images of kings as fathers of their people and even as lesser gods. For James, absolute kings were not tyrants, and a wise king listened to counsel, not least because of the terrible punishment God reserved for tyrants. In practice his kingship was relatively tolerant and pragmatic, but even if the king was a tyrant, James believed rebellion was not an option for Christian subjects, particularly as the king also was head of the church. Unionist ideology enhanced James's exalted view of monarchy, turning a mere King of Scots into the emperor of the whole of Great Britain and Ireland. His ideas were less unwelcome in post-Tudor England where natural law theories claiming a divine origin for sovereignty were common, and where patriarchalists claimed that the king's power over his people was similar to that of the first fathers who enjoyed kingly authority over their children. This intellectual atmosphere was conducive to James's thinking, and court culture promoted the idea of a new golden age at the centre of which was the divine majesty. However, the absence of a royal court in Scotland meant that royalist ideas were less effectively disseminated there. In spite of their British dimension, the sophisticated Caroline court masques, extolling royal power and the divine godliness of the monarchy, lacked a Scottish perspective and were irrelevant to the kingdom's public culture. Poets like Sir William Alexander at court and William Drummond of Hawthornden in Scotland did constitute a small royalist circle, but even they were not uncritical of Charles I, a king who firmly believed in divine right kingship and who ignored Drummond's advice that he should listen to good counsel.

The dearth of royalist propaganda in Scotland immediately after 1637 demonstrated the superficiality of absolutist ideas in the kingdom. Like Drummond, many royalists were embarrassed by the king's policies, and Sir James Balfour of Denmilne, the lord lyon king of arms, took refuge in blaming the evil counsel of the bishops. The marquis of Hamilton's effort in 1638 to steal the covenanters' clothes in the unsuccessful king's covenant, a petition in the form of the national covenant which attempted to identify the king's cause with the protestant church, was an admission that the debate was being conducted on enemy territory. It was 1639 before Walter Balcanquhall made a robust defence of royalist ideas in *A Large Declaration Concerning the Late Tumults in Scotland,* claiming that the covenanters represented an ambitious faction who cloaked their designs in the garb of popular sovereignty. Attacks on the covenanters came in 1639 from Henry Peacham in London and John Corbert in Dublin, underlining the threat covenanting thinking posed for royalists throughout Britain, but the covenanters' success created a need to redefine a royalist ideology within a native Scottish tradition. In 1640 fear of anarchy led Lord Napier in his draft 'Letter on sovereign power' to take refuge in Jean Bodin's state absolutism. Napier made no excuses for a bad ruler, but said that tyranny must be endured, predicting rightly that the aristocracy would lose control of events. Yet his conclusions found little favour even with the earl of Montrose who agreed it was wrong to attempt to restrain the king or to govern through parliament, but insisted that the king rule within the law. A more extreme case for the restoration of royal authority, *Sacro-sancta Regum Majestas* (1644) was written by the Laudian bishop of Ross, John Maxwell who drew heavily on Jean Bodin and on English patriarchal ideas. However, a more persuasive argument for the restoration of royal power arose in the 1640s when those prophecies by Drummond and Napier that the people would be subjected to the tyranny of powerful subjects like the marquis of Argyll, and that the aristocracy would be overwhelmed by popular anarchy, appeared to be fulfilled.

While the royal prerogative was restored fully by 1669 with the act of supremacy, the monarchy's ideology was less assertive than in pre-covenant days. The cult of the 'Divine Martyr' (Charles I), the orchestrated hagiography surrounding Montrose, and the duke of York's careful cultivation of Scottish enthusiasm for the Stewart dynasty all signalled a growing confidence in the royalist armoury of ideas which finally flowered in the 1680s. However, unlike the 1630s it was contained within an indigenous tradition in which returning Scottish self-confidence was harnassed to the monarchy. The formation of the Order of the Thistle, the rebuilding of Holyrood palace, and even Sir Robert Sibbald's natural history of Scotland, *Scotia Illustrata* (1684), reflected an ordered, peaceful country under a beneficient king. Against this background Sir George Mackenzie of Rosehaugh published his *Jus Regium: or the Just and Solid Foundation of Monarchy* (1684). Mackenzie was less extreme in his royalism than the English tory Sir Robert Filmer, the publication of whose *Patriarcha* in 1680 (but written c.1640) heralded a renewal of absolutist philosophy. Essentially Rosehaugh followed James VI's notions of conquest. He argued that government was a form of property, and that just as the king could not interfere in the private property of his subjects, so the subjects could not dictate government to the king. Nothing here was new, and such ideas were popular among the aristocracy only for so long as the crown could provide stability. Few noblemen countenanced the full blown divine right monarchy which James VII tried to revive, and even among the post 1689 jacobites there was a majority in favour of a constitutional settlement which distinguished between a powerful crown with extensive prerogatives, and a king who governed by prerogative. Supporters of divine right monarchy with its emphasis on indefeasible hereditary rights were nurtured by the non-juring episcopalian clergy well into the eighteenth century, but after 1689 they were associated with Roman catholicism and French absolutism. Queen Anne's attraction to the cult of monarchy and the mythology of her family had minor political significance in encouraging tory ideas of non-resistance, but ritual already had become little more than an exercise in ceremonial.

The roots of the alternative view of shared sovereignty lay in the early sixteenth century with John Mair, and found expression in the conservative idea of the commonweal by which John Knox and his colleagues justified the reformation. Much more radical was George Buchanan who drew from a potent mixture of humanist and conciliar ideas, calvinist resistance theory and possibly Celtic traditions concerning the obligations of chiefs. Buchanan defended the revolution which removed Queen Mary in 1566–7 in his shocking *De Jure Regni apud Scotos* (1579) and the polemical *Rerum Scoticarum Historia* (1582). His ideas had enormous influence among the new wave of presbyterian ministers who clustered around Andrew Melville during the subsequent twenty-five years. Sovereignty, according to Buchanan, did not lie with the king, but with the people who entrusted kings with certain prescribed authority to rule over them. Like Knox before him, Buchanan did not suggest that political rights were enjoyed by the common mass, but by the nobility who were responsive to the welfare of the nation. However, his most controversial assertion was that a legally denounced tyrant could be killed by any private individual. James VI's proscribing of Buchanan's works was followed by similar action in England, and there was an ongoing campaign throughout the seventeenth century to suppress his ideas. His books and those of Knox were burned by the University of Oxford in 1683, Queen Anne blocked efforts to republish them, and as late as 1715 Thomas Ruddiman's edition of Buchanan's collected works, *Opera Omnia*, managed to raise a political storm. Ideologically the Stewart monarchy in Scotland never recovered from Buchanan's onslaught, and the entire seventeenth century can be seen as a struggle between his ideas and those of his pupil, James VI.

The crown's suppression of the Knox-Buchanan-Melville legacy was ineffective, since their ideas had been imbibed by a generation of protestant noblemen and clergy who nurtured them in the presbyterian underground. Presbyterian preaching ensured that resistance ideas were disseminated among a lowland population which combined millenariam expectation with a sense of divinely inspired moral disapproval of royal authority.

The constitutional revolution of the 1640s drew on this resevoir of ideas to advocate the limitation of royal power by God, parliament and the law. The national covenant's roots in tradition, federal theology, natural law and statute is eloquent evidence of the eclectic nature of covenanting thought, but there was an underlying commitment to a form of contractual monarchy. The essentially radical thought of the covenanters was expressed more clearly in, for example, Alexander Henderson's 1639 *Instructions for Defensive Arms* which was read in pulpits throughout Scotland. Henderson rejected patriarchalism, arguing that resistance to an ungodly ruler was a Christian duty. The most formidable case for popular sovereignty and a mixed monarchy was made in 1644 by Samuel Rutherford in his *Lex Rex: the Law and the Prince*, a specific attack on John Maxwell. Rutherford believed royal power was fiduciary, or held in trust for the people, arguing that absolute sovereignty was tyranny and would lead to insecurity among subjects, the reverse of good government. In common with other covenanting thinkers, Rutherford believed government was instituted for the good of the people not for the good of the king, and that monarchy was a product of positive law not natural law, being only one among a number of legitimate forms of government. He too denied that royal power could be likened to paternal power. But the problem the covenanters never resolved was the source of sovereignty. Rutherford struggled to hold in tension the rights of the people and the rights of the king in what was a more moderate version of popular sovereignty than Buchanan's. Sovereignty lay with God who instituted government in the first instance, but the people constituted power in a particular ruler whom they must obey except in the case of tyranny.

The problem of defining godliness or tyranny, and therefore the limits of obedience, came to a head when parliament and the general assembly divided over the engagement in 1648. Deepening splits in 1649–50 over the issue of forcing Charles II to take the covenants as a price for support against his enemies in England led to the development of rival political ideologies expressed in theological language. The implications of the *Western Remonstrance* of 1650 led in the direction of private citizens responding to government according to their individual consciences and under the guidance of their ministers. This relationship, which always had existed between political rights and religious conformity, was emphasised by Hugh Binning in *An Usefull Case of Conscience*, which was written in 1651 but remained unpublished for over forty years. For the mainstream resolutioners the contractual principle was overtly applied in 1651 when Charles II was crowned after swearing to uphold the covenants and to respect the 1641 constitutional settlement. The covenanters unequivocally condemned Charles I's execution, but Robert Douglas's coronation sermon informed Charles II that he held his throne on condition that he met the expectations of a godly king. Military defeat filled the remonstrants with guilt that they had enforced the covenants on an unwilling and ungodly king, this being the case made in James Guthrie's *Causes of the Lord's Wrath against Scotland* (1653).

At the restoration radical ideas again were forced underground, and Rutherford's books were publicly burned by royal command. However, the political ideas of the covenanters proved tenacious. In 1665 John Brown, a deposed minister, circulated his *An Apologetical Relation of the Particular Sufferings of the Faithful Ministers and Professours of the Church of Scotland since 1660*, scorning compromise with the royalist regime. When a covenanting rebellion broke out in the south-west in 1666 justification was offered in *Jus Populi Vindicatum*, probably written by James Stewart of Goodtrees. The latter was closer to the recently executed Guthrie than to Henderson or Rutherford, upholding the covenants and asserting that divine law took precedence over civil authority. Stewart argued that the people must judge the actions of government, kings or parliaments by their consciences according to their knowledge of God's will. He co-operated with John Stirling in an equally popular covenanting work, *Naphtali, or the Wrestlings of the Church of Scotland* (1667), and the sense of identification between a presbyterian church and personal liberty was enhanced by the long awaited and posthumous publication in 1678 of David Calderwood's massive *History of the Kirk of Scotland*. Defeat in 1679 led radical covenanters like Richard Cameron and James Renwick to more radical positions. In the *Rutherglen Declaration* (1679), the *Queensferry Paper* (1680) and the *Sanquhar Declaration* (1680), and in Renwick's *Apologetical Declaration and Admonitory Vindication of the True Presbyterians of the Church of Scotland* (1684) the cameronians renounced their allegiance to Charles II, formally deposed the king, declared they were at war with him, and placed themselves under direct allegiance to Christ, rejecting any dependence on the lesser magistrate. Even passive obedience to an ungodly regime was attacked by Robert Macward in *The Banders Disbanded* (1681). Brutal persecution failed to crush these ideas, and in 1687 Alexander Shield published *A Hind Let Loose*, demonstrating that there had been no diminution in the desire for a monarchy subject to godly rule. Shield followed Buchanan in advocating the duty of individuals to kill tyrants, accusing the catholic James VII of usurpation, and of murdering the equally tyrannical Charles II, and of failing to take the coronation oath.

The breach between the political elite and popular covenanting in the late 1640s led to the neglect of a secular language of dissent. Yet the publication in 1681 of Sir James Dalrymple of Stair's *Institutes of the Laws of Scotland* with its emphasis on the rational and divine basis of law marked the beginnings of a new political agenda. Stair was president of the court of session and his concern was to codify Scots law, but he advanced the authority of law against that of the prerogative, and endured exile for refusing to take the test oath. Lawyers did not supersede ministers as critics of arbitrary government, but the codification of the law, and Dutch influence among Scottish lawyers encouraged reforming ideas. Scotland might not have produced an Algernon Sidney or a John Locke, but the Scottish contribution to whig principles is understated. It was Monmouth's Scottish secretary, Robert Ferguson, who wrote the radical 'Taunton declaration' of 1685. Another Scot, Gilbert Burnet, was a political advisor to William of Orange and became the most memorable apologist for the 'Glorious revolution'. Robert Fleming, a Scottish minister resident in London published *Redidivum, or the Divine Right of the Revolution* in 1706, infuriating the English tories with his espousal of populist claim that the voice of the people was the voice of God. In Scotland, concern with the rule of law permeated the 1689 convention of estates, and both the Claim of Right and the Articles of Grievance demanded that kings rule according to the law. The Scots were less timid than the English whigs, and James VII was forfeited as an arbitrary despot who had broken the contract entered into at his accession, failing even to take the coronation oath. As in 1651 with Charles II, William and Mary were offered the crown conditionally in 1689, and in 1702 Queen Anne followed this precedent in a ceremony at Whitehall. Within the club, the whiggish caucus which broke the crown's institutional control of parliament by 1690, there was a commitment to ideals reminiscent of the covenanters's 1641 programme. Those ideas lived on in the country party which sniped away at crown powers throughout the 1690s. Its most articulate spokesman was Fletcher of Saltoun, who also drew inspiration from 1641 (although denying any covenanting influence), and was attracted to classical republicanism. In 1697, in *A Discourse Concerning Standing Armies*, he attacked the idea of a professional army as a threat to the people, while his 'limitations', published in 1703 as *Speaches by a Member of the Parliament*, were designed to restrict the powers of a British imperial monarchy. Fletcher proposed a constitutional monarchy subject to an annual parliament which would appoint an executive committee and officers of state. He opposed the union of parliaments as it would bind Scotland to a Westminster system in which the crown-in-parliament had absolute powers. Concern at the tyranny of Westminster also was expressed by a jacobite member of parliament, George Lockhart of Carnwath. In 1703 George Ridpath, another anti-unionist, wrote *An Historical Account of the Ancient Right and Power of the Parliament of Scotland*, in which his case for a limited monarchy was founded on the nobility's traditional role as constitutional watch-dogs and on covenanting ideas. The reform programme failed precisely because the nobility was seduced by the court, but the subjection of the prerogative to the legislature was accepted by the whig court party which ignored the rightful royal succession and offered the throne to the house of Hanover.

Church and State

Scots of every persuasion agreed that religious uniformity held the hierarchic order in place and ensured greater homogeneity within society, and all religious dissidents were seen as threatening the stability of the community as well as defying God. Dissenters themselves, whether they be catholic recusants or cameronians, were convinced of their own monopoly of the truth. This commonplace intolerance was demonstrated in 1637-8, 1660-1 and 1688-9 when episcopalians and presbyterians turned the tables on one another. Even those presbyterians suffering persecution opposed toleration since it implied an acceptance of the royal supremacy, and James Renwick's *Testimony against the Toleration* (1688) was an uncompromising statement of this position from a man who was executed that same year. In fact Renwick died for his political views, and most persecution took the form of fines and civil disabilities for offences concerned with outward demonstrations of non-conformity, attending mass or a conventicle, or with the direct political implications of religious views like refusing to take the test oath in the 1680s. There was no inquisitorial concern with people's beliefs. Roman Catholics suffered under a wide range of political and civil disabilities, but catholics were not put to death for their faith. John Ogilvie, hanged at Glasgow in 1615, was exceptional, but he was punished for his treasonable activities not for holding catholic beliefs. Of course, ranting against the catholic menace aroused excitement, and George Gillespie's *Dispute Against the English Popish Ceremonies* struck a popular chord in 1637 with its equation of liturgical reform and creeping catholicism. More savage persecution was visited on those accused of witchcraft, especially in the witch crazes of the 1590s, 1629-30, 1649-50 and 1661-2 when hundreds of women were burned. However, Thomas Aitkenhead, the Edinburgh student who was hanged in

1696 for foolishly expressing atheistic ideas, was the sole martyr to his untimely views.

There was a muted strain of tolerant thought in the early seventeenth century, but Drummond of Hawthornden's irenical thoughts found little favour in the 1630s. The Scots' instinctive intolerance unwillingly bore the limited religious plurality foisted on them by the English republicans in the 1650s. However, native support for a modest level of toleration was expressed in 1653 with the publication of the late William Forbes, bishop of Edinburgh's *Considerationes Modestae et Pacifica*. After the restoration a more secular attitude was in evidence in Mackenzie of Rosehaugh's *Religio Stoici* (1663), while Robert Leighton, archbishop of Glasgow advocated a more lenient approach to the covenanting problem. However, attempts by Charles II's ministers to strengthen the prerogative by introducing indulgences and comprehension failed, and James VII's toleration policy of 1686–8 should not be mistaken as anything other than a camouflage behind which he promoted catholicism. When toleration of episcopalians finally was introduced in 1713 it was for partisan political reasons, and was opposed by the presbyterian majority. The most genuine plea for toleration came in 1676 from Robert Barclay, whose controversial *An Apology for the True Christian Divinity*, published in Amsterdam, attacked the idea of the confessional state and became a quaker manifesto.

Scottish protestants were united in their calvinism. Attempts by Charles I and Archbishop Laud to encourage arminian ideas in Scotland were unsuccessful, and it was not until the second decade of the eighteenth century that the calvinist uniformity began to crack. However, from 1560 there was an on-going debate on authority within the church which had its origins in the nature of the reformation as a popular revolution. The roots of an episcopal church lay in the policies and ideas of Archbishop Patrick Adamson who defended the royal supremacy and bishops in the 1580s, and in the ambitions of James VI. James made his erastian ideas explicit in *Basilikon Doron* in 1599, and his preference was shaped by political rather than theological concerns. Arguing that church government was not a matter of doctrine, but was an external affair subject to the king, James preferred bishops because they were more biddable than the presbyterian clergy who appeared as bad as papists in demanding a church separate from and independent of the state. A form of royal supremacy existed in statute from 1584, making the king head of the church with powers of patronage over appointments, but it was 1610 before James acquired an unequivocal recognition of the supremacy from parliament.

From 1603 James had the additional motive of wanting to move towards conformity between the churches in England and Scotland, and unionists like John Gordon believed religious conformity was the most secure basis on which to build a British empire. In 1608 a deputation of English bishops was sent to persuade the Scots of the merits of episcopal government, saddling the bishops with the popular perception of them as agents of anglicisation, a view which was heightened by Archbishop Laud's policies in the 1630s. The presbyterian attack on episcopacy provoked some Jacobean bishops like James Law of Orkney, Patrick Forbes of Aberdeen and William Cowper of Galloway to mount a defence, but their arguments primarily were pragmatic and were helped greatly by James's image as a godly prince. A more militant claim for *jure divino* episcopacy was made by John Forbes of Corse in his *Irenicum* (1629), but it was the Laudian bishops who took a doctrinal position on episcopacy and the royal supremacy. The latter led to a growing interference in matters within the rightful province of the church, chiefly the liturgy. Consequently, presbyterians like John Murray in his *Dialogue* added the charge of crypto-catholicism to those already levelled at the bishops. The collapse of the episcopal church in 1638, and with it the hurried exile of the bishops and the abjuration of episcopacy by two of them, exposed an intellectual and spiritual vacuum. Even the 1639 *Declinator and Protestation* by the exiled bishops moved little beyond a pragmatic defence of the royal supremacy. Archbishop John Spottiswoode's *A History of the Church of Scotland*, written before his death in 1639 but unpublished until 1655, made a weak historical case for episcopacy, failing to disguise the true nature of the bishops as servants of the state. Not surprisingly, it was an English bishop, Joseph Hall of Exeter, who went on the offensive in 1639 with *Episcopacy by Divine Right, asserted*. The Aberdeen Doctors made a spirited defence of the royal prerogative and of non-resistance, but it was 1644 before the Laudian John Maxwell's *Pro-sancta* demonstrated that Scottish episcopacy had an ideological basis, although even here it was the royal supremacy which inspired Maxwell.

Charles II's restoration of episcopacy in 1661 also was politically motivated. Apologists for an episcopal church again were found, most notably Robert Leighton, but the hallmark of the restoration bishops was obedience to royal authority. Any dissent was crushed, and when Alexander Burnet, archbishop of Glasgow objected to the royal supremacy in 1669 he was sacked. Obedience was so fundamental to the restoration church that its clergy found themselves supporting the catholic James VII, and their inability to escape from this dilemma left the episcopate paralysed in 1689. Even more than the tory Church of England, the Scottish episcopalians were harnessed to the doctrine of non-resistance. Subsequent to the revolution they split into those prepared to give an oath of allegiance to the new government of King William, and those obstinate and jacobite non-jurors. The best episcopalian apologist, John Sage, adopted a more controversialist tone and argued from rational principles, but after 1689 episcopalian thinkers became intransigent in their adherence to non-resistance, passive obedience and the indefeasible hereditary rights of the Stewarts. It was no accident that the most effective exponent of divine right monarchy, Mackenzie of Rosehaugh, continued to defend episcopacy after 1689. While there were episcopalians who supported William II, it is appropriate that a religious party constructed by the crown to make the church into an instrument of state should fall with the dynasty which had promoted it. This is not to say that there was no constituency for bishops in the country. The north-east became a region deeply committed to an episcopal church, and much of the support gathered for the jacobite rebellion of 1715 came from frustrated episcopalians. However, even before the defeat of

1715 many episcopalians were turning away from active politics to a more contemplative religion, having at least won toleration from the act of 1713.

Presbyterian ideology was rooted in the popular history of the Scottish reformation, in Knox and Buchanan's political ideas, and in Andrew Melville's advocacy of a separation of church and state. The two kingdom theory, which excluded the king from church affairs while claiming the right of the church to instruct the king on civil matters pertaining to the godliness of the community, was central to royal objections to presbytery. The crown also disliked the parity of ministers and the system of government by concentric church courts. These ideas were contained in the *First Book of Discipline*, hurriedly produced in 1560, and the more polished 1578 *Second Book of Discipline*, and were disseminated widely in lowland parishes before the crushing of the presbyterian leadership in 1606. The *Second Book of Discipline* was republished in 1621, dissident ministers inculcated popular support, and conventicling spread their ideas beyond the literate public. Some ministers formed a presbyterian diaspora in Ulster, the Netherlands, and even France, from where they continued their attacks on the bishops. John Forbes kept alive the presbyterian interpretation of the 1606 state trials in the unpublished 'Certaine records', David Calderwood reconstructed the continuous presbyterian tradition from the reformation until its interruption in 1597 by the king in *De Regimine Ecclesiae Scoticanae Brevis Relatio* (1618), William Scott outlined the decay and corruption of the church from 1597 in *The Course of Conformitie* (1622), and John Row's manuscript *An Apologetical Narration* circulated among presbyterians from 1635 and was a savage attack on the bishops. The Glasgow assembly of 1638 condemned bishops on political and doctrinal grounds, resurrecting a situation in which church and state co-operated while remaining distinct. There also was a feeling that a presbyterian church was a patriotic church, and the excitable apocalyptic element to calvinist ideas was enhanced by the success of the revolution. The belief that God had entered into a covenant with the Scottish people was fused in the solemn league and covenant with the common view that the English reformation had been incomplete. The presbyterians saw it as their divinely appointed responsibility to conform the church in England and Ireland to their own. The Westminster assembly which sought to arrive at an agreed formula for the British churches ultimately was a failure, but it did provide the Scots with the Westminster Confession of Faith which became the touchstone of presbyterian belief in Scotland.

The arguments which split the presbyterians after 1648 were not over church government, but on the extent of church co-operation with the ungodly in pursuit of its aims. Herein lay a division over whether the church was a national church, or a gathering of the godly claiming to speak before God for the nation. The division into resolutioner and remonstrant factions in 1650 demonstrated the weakness of presbyterian ideas on authority. In refusing to accept the majority decisions of the resolutioners in the general assembly, the remonstrants invited the idea that individual conscience and understanding of the bible was a better guide to the will of God than the collective view of the church. Yet the Scots remained steadfastly opposed to independency, and sects like the baptists made little headway during the 1650s when they were granted toleration by the English occupying regime. In essence, little changed in presbyterian thought for the remainder of the century. The idea of the covenants remained powerful throughout the restoration period, but sensibly was dropped in 1690 when presbyterians again assumed control of the national church. The cameronians refused to accept the 1690 settlement, which they saw as a betrayal of the covenants, but the settlement was an attainment of the greater part of the sixteenth century presbyterian programme. Church and state were divorced from one another, while church government was placed in the hands of the church courts, the key role of the presbyteries being strengthened by the 1696 barrier act. The triumph of popular calvinism was short-lived for in 1713 the tory government restored patronage along with toleration. The accompanying oath of loyalty again split presbyterians many of whom saw this as state interference in a matter which involved their conscience.

The Idea of Britain

The idea of Britain formed a major undercurrent in the political thought of the sixteenth century, and was not simply the creation of royal propaganda in 1603 in support of James VI's imperial British vision. However, the muted unionist ideology of the Scots was understandable since British imperial ideas were associated with English efforts to conquer the country and with ceasaro-papalist notions of kingship. The most ardent unionist was James VI, whose visionary Britain drew on ancient history, and was expressed in the semi-mystical language of marriage. James imagined an imperial British monarchy presiding over a powerful protestant state in which Scotland would be assimilated to England through a union of parliaments, government, laws, churches and peoples. Royal propaganda stressed the certainty of strength, prosperity and peace in a united Britain, drawing parallels with the unity in nature or in divinity. Enthusiasts like John Gordon saw the regal union as the work of God, an event of cosmic proportions heralding an apocalyptic age in which a messianic king would rule an elect British nation. However, Scottish unionists like Gordon, David Hume, James Maxwell, Robert Pont and Sir Thomas Craig, whose *De Unione Regnorum*, written c. 1604, is perhaps the best known unionist work, desired a union of equals which preserved the Scottish identity. Even an esoteric court unionist like Sir William Alexander retained a strong sense of Scottish identity within the imperial world which he inhabited.

Unionist ideas were most prominent at court and in crown artistic patronage. The union was celebrated by the English playwright, Ben Jonson, in his 1606 masque *Hymenai*, and in the iconography accompanying royal occasions such as the 1604 entry to London unionist images were given due prominence. For Jonson and other unionists the imperial idea overlapped with an enthusiasm for classical learning and forms, and much of their inspiration was drawn from Roman Britain. Britain, it was claimed, was united in the distant past, but had been divided and troubled with instability ever since. Under James's imperial peace the golden age had returned and Britain – the Fortunate Isles – once more could enjoy harmony and prosperity. A mythical history was reconstructed in which figures like Brut, the first and last king of a united Britain, the British born and Christian Emperor Constantine, and the legendary British King Arthur were employed by crown propagandists. The most impressive artistic legacy of this spate of British ideology is Rubens' allegorical decoration of the ceiling of the New Banquetting hall in Whitehall. British imagery continued to appear in the Caroline masques of the 1630s, but Charles I never shared James VI's passion for Britain.

Scottish suspicions of union were exacerbated by English arrogance, and only respect for the king kept the lid on the racism expressed by Sir Christopher Piggott in the House of Commons in 1607. A major problem with the unionist argument was that English unionists like Sir Francis Bacon and John Thornborough talked and wrote in terms which implied English superiority, and James himself encouraged this view. More extreme English members of parliament like Sir Edward Sandys advocated a 'perfect' union and spoke of a legal conquest of Scotland in which Scottish institutions and laws would be submerged in or replaced by English alternatives as in Ireland. Such attitudes outraged many Scots, some of whom retorted that England had become a mere accession of the Scottish crown. Sir Thomas Craig attacked the English historian Ralph Holinshed who had argued for the superiority of the English crown, and in the posthumously published *Scotland's Sovereignty Asserted* he indicated the reservations felt even by supporters of union.

One major concern was the future status of Scottish fundamental law, a matter which vexed a stubborn Scottish parliament in 1604 and led a pro-unionist like John Russell to argue that Scots law and the English common law must remain separate. Yet the idea of legal pluralism was difficult for contemporaries to envisage. In his *Jus Feudale* of 1603 Craig demonstrated that English concerns over a union of laws were groundless, and that the two legal systems shared a common European heritage. But on this issue English common lawyers were not persuaded, and genuinely feared the imposition of the civil law code which so influenced Scots law. The decision of the English judges in 1604 that a change in the name of the kingdom implied a conquest and the overthrow of the law highlighted the problem. A simple matter like the alteration by proclamation of the king's style to King of Great Britain and Ireland provoked a storm of protest in England where the new style never was adopted by statute. The English saw no advantage in union, suspecting the Scots would exploit their markets, and there was a belief that union would strengthen the royal prerogative. Forced to question their identity by British ideas, English antiquarians developed Anglo-Saxon origin myths. In 1586 John Camden's *Britannia* had claimed the Scots were English in origin, and in response to the British onslaught Richard Verstegen celebrated the Germanic roots of the English in his *Restitution of Decayed Intelligence* (1605), while John Speed looked to an Anglo-Saxon history for the beginnings of English liberties in his *History of Great Britain* (1614). The effect of such history was to sustain English xenophobia, especially when fused with a belief in the elect nation set apart by God.

More overtly Scottish unionism was expressed by David Hume in his 1605 tract, *De Unione Insualae Britanniae*, in which he advocated a united presbyterian church for the whole of Britain. This presbyterian vision came to fruition in 1643 in the solemn league and covenant, the alliance between the Scots and English parliament in which the Scots agreed to invade England and both sides bound themselves to introduce religious uniformity and a federal political structure. Covenant theology appealed to patriotic instincts, flattering the nation by holding that God had entered into a unique relationship with Scotland. This uniqueness attracted the interest of royalists like Alexander and covenanters like Rutherford, both of whom were obsessed with the idea of Scotland as a second Israel. Since 1603 Scottish unionists had favoured a federal programme – both the Spanish monarchy and the Dutch republic were seen as useful models

– and throughout the 1640s the covenanters repeatedly sought to renegotiate the union on federal line. However, the desire for closer union was not intended to bring about a convergence of England and Scotland. Instead the aim of the covenanters was to preserve a Scottish identity within a regal union perceived to be eroding that separateness. That the solemn league and covenant was a Scottish solution to the British problem was clear to the English. Even the Westminster assembly failed to create sufficient unity in religion to provide the Scots with the security they craved. Instead, the vision of covenanters like Rutherford of a British church purified by the Scots' second reformation degenerated into quarrels over church-state relations.

Without the restraint of a shared monarchy the English readily abandoned British ideas, unleashing the naked nationalism of the English republic. The very concept of Britain became unpatriotic in England, being too closely associated with royalist ideology. As early as 1642 John Hare in his *St Edward's Ghost* called for the subjection of the whole of Great Britain and Ireland to England. By 1658 Richard Hawkins could celebrate that dream in *A Discourse of the Nationall Excellencies of England*. The English nationalist propaganda of the royalists in the late 1630s and early 1640s was happily echoed by republicans, while the arch-royalist earl of Strafford's plans for the imposition of an English hegemony were realised by the republican Oliver Cromwell, two very different men who shared a similar contempt for the Scots and Irish. Of course, the experience of conquest dampened Scottish interest in union, but there were those like the eccentric Sir Thomas Urquhart who expressed support for the idea of a union of laws, a project which aroused little English interest. Insofar as the unionist dream remained alive it did so in the minds of radical covenanters committed to the solemn league and covenant, but the restoration in 1660 ended all hope of a presbyterian Britain. Nor was there a revival of British ideas by royalist image makers. There was interest in Arthurian matters at Charles II's court, and the figure of Britannia made her first appearance during his reign, but Charles was content to govern Scotland independently, attaching the monarchy to the rising tide of English assertiveness which the republic had fuelled. The experiences of the 1640s and 1650s left a legacy of mutual suspicion between the two kingdoms. This wariness was reinforced by residual imperialism in England which found expression in publications like the anonymous *Discourse upon the Union* (1664), advocating the imposition of English law on Scotland, and by the tenacious clinging to the covenants by many Scots. The language in which unionist ideas were expressed earlier in the century now was old-fashioned, and origin myths were ridiculed by the likes of John Milton when he published his *The History of Britain* in 1670.

In the early eighteenth century the idea of Britain became the tool of a particular political programme – the control by Westminster of the Scottish parliament. The fundamental issue was one of sovereignty, but if union was to become popular it would have to find new arguments. The discussions surrounding the union project of 1668–70 revealed some shifting in positions with the paramountcy of legal union losing ground. The codification of Scots law by Stair and Rosehaugh rendered legal union almost impossible, and even pro-unionists like the earl of Cromartie were determined to resist the incorporation of the law and the legal system. A more intractable difficulty, religious union, was obviated as the concept of a confessional state was dropped by the crown and politicians accepted that the Britain of the eighteenth century would be ecclesiastically pluralistic. Essentially the idea of Britain was realised in the creation of an effective instrument of government, the new parliament of Great Britain, and an enlarged and protected market.

It was the latter which held out attractions to the Scots. By the early 1700s, English economic confidence was running high and Scotland was vulnerable to economic persuasion. English mercantilists argued that the formation of a bigger market would provide greater opportunities for English capital, but supporters of union had to demonstrate that both countries would gain. This was the main thrust behind Hugh Chamberlen's work *The Great Advantages to Both Kingdoms of Scotland and England by an Union* (1702). Scots who favoured economic union also had to demonstrate that they had something material to offer the English, and in 1705 John Spreull tried to demonstrate this in his *An Accompt Current betwixt Scotland and England Balanced*. The most effective Scottish unionist pamphleteers were George Mackenzie, earl of Cromartie who contributed *Parainesis Pacifica: or a perswasive to the union* (1702), and William Seton of Pitmedden who wrote a number of essays on the subject including *Scotland's Great Advantages by an Union with England* (1706). Both men were among a minority of genuine unionists, convinced by the economic arguments they presented while also seeing in union the prospects of peace and political security. Seton rejected the idealisation of Scotland before 1603, pointing out the poverty and instability of the country (this would become an eighteenth century orthodoxy), and arguing that the nation would survive without parliament. Yet the underlying feeling that it was the association with England which had caused Scotland's economic ills found expression in the writings of Fletcher of Saltoun, James Hodges and William Black, whose *Essay upon Industry and Trade* (1706) blamed the regal union for destroying Scotland's international trade. Fletcher accepted that the economy was weak, but in his *Two Discourses Concerning the Affairs of Scotland* (1698) he advocated decisive and authoritarian government intervention to regulate economic affairs as a realistic alternative to union.

The Anglo-Scottish tension of these years revealed that in spite of efforts by the crown to play down nationalist feelings, animosity between the two nations and racial stereotyping was as great as ever. In his *An Essay at Removing National Prejudices aganist the Union* (1706) Daniel Defoe, the union's most effective propagandist, avoided the sovereignty issue in order not to offend the Scots. However, both imperialism and racism continued to surface, most notoriously in James Drake's *Historia Anglo-Scotia* which was burned by the hangman in Edinburgh at the command of the privy council. A more persistent advocate of the kingdom of England's legal superiority was William Atwood whose *The Superiority and Direct Dominion of the Imperial Crown of England, over the Crown and Kingdom of Scotland* (1704) could not have stated the case more bluntly or offensively. Atwood's ramblings were thoroughly refuted by James Anderson in his *An Historical Essay, showing that the crown and kingdom of Scotland is imperial and independent* (1705), but clearly the Scots were rattled. Naturally, it was opponents of union who focused on the sovereignty issue. In 1695 George Ridpath finally published Craig's *Scotland's Sovereignty Asserted*, and went on to publish a succession of his own essays asserting Scottish sovereignty. James Hodges even resurrected national origin myths, and presented a case for the most loose of federal unions in *First Treatise on the Rights and Interests of the Two British Monarchies* (1706). Sovereignty was at the heart of the opposition to union expressed by Fletcher of Saltoun in *The State of the Controversy betwixt United and Separate Parliaments* (1706), but two years earlier, in *An Account of a Conversation,* he had indicated a willingness to speculate on some kind of federal arangement for Europe in which the British problem would be subsumed. Concern at preserving Scottish fundamental law and Scottish institutions exercised men of very different political traditions, and were echoed by an old adversary like Mackenzie of Rosehaugh whose *Arguments Against an Incorporating Union Particularly Considered* was posthumously published in 1706. In spite of the impressive case against union, its opponents were hamstrung by a lack of any clear way forward. Instead there were variations on the union theme with even Fletcher and Hodges suggesting a renegotiated relationship with England. The kind of Britain the Scots got in 1707 might not have been to their liking, but it is difficult to avoid the conclusion that already they were finding it impossible to imagine an existence outside of Britain.

4

THE IMPERIAL EXPERIMENT, 1603–37

Union and its Limits, 1603–15

James VI was a relatively successful Scottish king in the twenty years of adult rule before his departure to England in the spring of 1603. He defeated counter reformation catholicism, tamed the presbyterian party in the church, pacified aristocratic factionalism and charted a diplomatic course which brought him to the English throne. By 1596 James had mastered his own kingdom through a combination of political skills and good luck, for as king of Scots there could be no pretence to absolutism. Yet the revival of royal power over which James presided did not mean that in 1603 he left behind a kingdom without problems. King James was not a popular ruler, and indeed made no effort to court popular approval. During the terrible 1590s when raging inflation, famine, dreadful weather, unemployment, rebellions, widespread feuding, witch crazes and religious controversy had been the norm a more image-conscious king would have taken greater care to counter popular perceptions of a connection between harsh times and inadequate government. The aristocracy wanted strong government, but only if it provided stability and did not interfere with their privileges. Within the church there remained unsolved problems which would not disappear simply because

James had bullied the presbyterian opposition. Royal finances were a muddle for reasons which were both structural and a consequence of the king's personal mismanagement. Law and order was only beginning to show signs of improvement in parts of the lowlands, and was precarious in the borders and highlands. Even the acquisition of the crowns of England and Ireland evoked mixed responses from those who were unsure of the implications for Scotland.

James himself had a vision of a new British imperium in which he would preside over united royal courts, parliaments, administrations, legal systems, churches and peoples. However, James greatly under-estimated the difficulties both in adapting to being the king of England and of managing multiple kingship, and within a year his dream of a British kingdom was dashed. James moved too far too fast, and the slick presentation of unionist ideas in the London entry of July 1604, the officially backed flurry of supportive pamphlets, and the careful preparation of crown ministers in both kingdoms collided with deep national prejudice and innate conservatism in both countries. In 1604 commissioners from the two kingdoms discussed a union of parliaments, and agreement was reached on common citizenry and free trade. However, the two parliaments were hostile to the idea, blocking any further progress, and only James's personal interest kept the issue on the political agenda until 1607–8. Opposition was widespread in both kingdoms, and in 1607 Scottish noblemen and councillors, suspicious of English talk of a 'perfect union', petitioned the king against any further union. The Scottish nobility feared a loss of political influence in a British parliament, while the English nobility believed the former would exploit their intimacy with the king to acquire political dominance. Lawyers on both sides claimed that legal union was impractical, and the exclusive claims of the English common lawyers made compromise impossible. Scottish bishops feared subjection to Canterbury, while popular opinion wanted nothing to do with what was perceived as an unreformed English church. For their part, English bishops were concerned that the Scots would strengthen the puritans. Commercial interests in Scotland thought free trade would destroy domestic manufacturing, while the English had visions of being swamped with cheap and favoured goods, and were suspicious of Scottish links with France. Both sides feared political eclipe, although the English obsession with the threat of legal conquest if the common law was united with Scots law was more contrived than the Scots common sense comparison of the relative size and wealth of the two kingdoms. Concern that union would strengthen the royal prerogative was an issue, but the dissent which wrecked the king's project was rooted in more primitive political instincts which negated any advantages of a common language, religion, monarchy and island mentality. National antagonism and outright racism surfaced occasionally in the House of Commons among populist Scotophobics like Sir Christopher Piggot, and on the streets of London, where Scots were in danger of being attacked; while in Edinburgh in 1610 the privy council had to outlaw widespread oral and written polemics against Englishmen.

The king's personal authority and the royal prerogative achieved minor progress on some cosmetic aspects of imperial kingship. James proclaimed himself King of Great Britain in 1604, although the English parliament continued to use the alternative style of King of England, Scotland, France and Ireland. A new union flag was adopted in 1606, and the royal arms were redesigned. However, the basis of the decision of the English courts in Calvin's case in 1608 to recognise the right of naturalisation of all subjects of the crown born after 1603, raised fears that property rights were threatened by a Scottish invasion, while at the same time appearing to strengthen the prerogative. Yet regal union did create conditions in which a degree of Anglo-Scottish governmental co-operation was possible. Communication between Edinburgh and London was improved by the creation of a regular postal service. The coinage was unified, a ratio of twelve to one in favour of sterling was adopted, and customs rates were abolished until 1610 when they were reintroduced. The borders were pacified after being brought under unified administration, especially with the creation of the Anglo-Scottish border commission in 1605. The western isles and Ireland were policed more effectively, the old mercenary route between the two regions being severed, and from 1610 the Scots joined the imperial policy of colonisation in Ulster. Anglo-Scottish relations now rested on an apparently secure base and, with the signing of an Anglo-Spanish treaty in 1604 and the flight of the catholic earls from Ireland in 1607, the omens were good for the new golden age of peace.

At the court the king's visionary empire became visible in the masques, iconography and art which royal patronage sustained. Here James deliberately sought to create a melting pot, encouraging marriages between aristocratic families of the two kingdoms, and ensuring that the Scots had a high profile. The king's loyalty to old friends, his notorious generosity, and his long established habit of listening to household advisors ensured for the Scots a powerful and envied position. This unwelcome Scottish influence contributed greatly to the breakdown in relations between James and a large constituency within the English body politic. A meddlesome and influential bedchamber was not new to Scottish politicians, but what was unsettling was the advantage the court now enjoyed over the privy council in counselling the king and in securing patronage. It was unsurprising, therefore, that the crucial political figure in the post union years was Sir George Hume of Spott, a trusted household servant as well as treasurer since 1601. His financial acumen and clear understanding of the political value of patronage brought him control of all the revenue departments in the Scottish administration and in addition he became keeper of the privy purse in the bedchamber and chancellor of the exchequer in the English government. Hume, who was created earl of Dunbar, was James's closest advisor, courted by politicians in both kingdoms, and his combination of servility to the king and ruthlessness in dealing with others made him an effective and feared political operator. Between 1603 and 1605 James and Dunbar largely were concerned with English affairs and with the union programme. The administration in Scotland was left in the safe hands of Alexander Seton, first earl of Dunfermline, the younger son of a catholic peer and the most brilliant lawyer of his generation. His legal and administrative skills made Dunfermline an ideal man to manage the king's business in Edinburgh, and in 1604 he was appointed chancellor. However, Dunfermline's catholicism left him vulnerable on religious issues, and it was his lack of confidence in dealing with presbyterian dissent in 1605, and the mischevious meddling of John Spottiswoode, archibishop of Glasgow, that persuaded James to send Dunbar home to take charge.

Between 1606 and his early death in 1611 Dunbar dominated Scottish politics, travelling regularly between Edinburgh and the court, thus retaining his close working relationship with the king. His impact in Scotland was instant and the five year partnership with Dunfermline saw a substantive extension of royal power. In the church the last remnants of presbyterian resistance to James's ecclesiastical programme was broken. The disappointment of the English puritans at the Hampton Court conference in 1604 was a clear signal that James had no intention of altering the Elizabethan church, and instead it was to become his model. One man who attended the conference was Spottiswoode, who had rejected entirely his Melvillian education and was already proving an effective royal servant in ecclesiastical affairs. However, it was Dunbar who initiated the prosecution in January 1606 of John Forbes and the five other dissident ministers of the unauthorised Aberdeen general assembly, securing convictions for treason and sentences of exile after the jury was bullied into returning a guilty verdict. Andrew Melville and the remaining presbyterian leaders were summoned to London, held without trial, and subjected to a sustained period of political education by the English clergy. Melville remained a prisoner in the Tower of London until 1611 when he was allowed to go into exile. Meanwhile in 1606 parliament recognised James as supreme governor of the church, and the king manipulated his right to decide the time and place of meetings of the general assembly to complete by stealth his programme of creating an erastian episcopacy. In 1607 the bishops were appointed as constant moderators of presbyteries; two years later their consistorial authority was restored; in 1610 the courts of high commission were restored and a royal supremacy was erected, and in 1612 the general assembly recognised the episcopal authority of the bishops. James had begun moving towards an erastian episcopacy in 1584, and it was 1596 before he acquired sufficient leverage over the presbyterians to make progress on restoring the bishops. However, it was the regal union which gave James immunity from presbyterian pressure and a new momentum, in that an episcopal church met his requirements for a British monarchy. The king's own Constantinian ambitions were bolstered by the Guy Fawkes conspiracy in 1605 (a plot which was almost as anti-Scottish as anti-protestant), assuring him of divine protection and correcting any latent sympathy towards catholics. James was careful not to offer his critics the opportunity to complain that his bishops were the agents of Anglicisation, and when three of them were consecrated in England in 1610 it was made plain that their action did not imply subordination to Canterbury. In other respects too the church retained its Scottish character, with the lower church courts holding onto their presbyterian structure because interference at this level was too difficult. There also was common agreement on a calvinist theology in Scotland and England where the appointment in 1611 of the calvinist George Abbot as archbishop of Canterbury, a man generally approved of in Scotland, eased progress towards religious convergence.

Elsewhere Dunbar's energy and Dunfermline's management advanced a range of royal policies concerned with law and order. As a borderer himself, Dunbar took a particular interest in overseeing the work of the joint border commission. Between 1606 and 1610 a brutal campaign of state terror imposed an unprecedented level of peace on a region long known for cattle raiding and violent feuding, although the 'middle shires', as James dubbed the borders, never entirely shook off their lawless reputation. In the highlands the rationale for intervention was as much fiscal as judicial, James's officials having persuaded him that clan chiefs were withholding revenue. There was another aspect to highland policy, and a bloody raid by the Magregors on Glenfruin early in 1603 resulted in a revival of an attempt to exterminate this troublesome clan. The king's prejudice against highlanders was heightened by the embarrassment such incidents caused for the new emperor of Great Britain, and he sanctioned a number of violent schemes to **pacify** the western isles before the idea of a general extermination was abandoned as impractical in 1607. A policy of colonisation, first tried in Lewis in 1599, was initiated again in 1605, but the Gentlemen Adventurors of Fife were killed or driven out within five years. Instead Ireland became a more attractive land of opportunity for the colonial entrepreneurs and economic migrants of lowland Scotland. In the highlands the crown turned to the old fashioned methods of control exercised by favoured noblemen like Lord Kintail in Lewis and the earl of Argyll in Kintyre and Islay. In 1608 Lord Ochiltree took an Anglo-Scottish naval expedition to the isles and treacherously captured a large batch of chiefs. They were taken to Edinburgh, forced to submit to the king, and a year later they agreed to abide by the statutes of Iona which were negotiated by Andrew Knox, bishop of the Isles. The statutes tried to turn clan chiefs into responsible landlords answerable to the privy council in Edinburgh, and sought to dismantle clan society by promoting churches, outlawing temporary marriages, masterless men and itinerant bards, limiting the import of alcohol, restricting the size of households, and demanding the education of the eldest sons of landowners. However, the law and order issue was not confined to these two problem regions. The campaign against feuding which began in 1598 continued to gather momentum with a number of major bloodfeuds being settled over the next ten years, and a reduction in the incidence of duels and gun-fights, while the sensational execution of Lord Maxwell for murder in 1613 clearly indicated that aristocratic violence would no longer be tolerated.

Dunbar's other interest was fiscal policy. In 1606 he persuaded parliament to vote the large sum of 400,000 merks over four years, and in 1610 he combined his office of treasurer with that of comptroller as a preamble to reorganising the management of crown revenue. Like the king, Dunbar viewed money as a political tool, being less concerned with balancing the accounts, and it was in these years that crown income was diverted into one huge patronage lake. The tax revenue in

1606 was funnelled into pensions, but its collection was the first sign that the crown in Scotland could not pay its way, even with the costs of the court being met by the English. As a number of aristocratic families could tap into English revenue at court the increase in patronage available to the nobility was substantial, accounting for their subdued political activity. In 1606 the creation of the lordships of erection, new lordships created from former monastic lands, was another form of pay-off to lesser noblemen who had acquired former church lands, often in crown service. For the aristocracy the union offered the prospects of a beneficent state pouring out pensions, lands and titles in their direction. Such optimism was reinforced by the upturn in the prevailing economic conditions, and courtiers and councillors alike continued to exploit the get rich quick schemes which passed for economic policy.

Amidst the scramble for spoils there was little interest in substantive political issues once the union issue was settled. The disgrace in 1608 of the secretary of state, Lord Balmerino, for supposedly carrying on a correspondence with the pope in the king's name some years earlier, aroused only minor interest. Dunbar's death in 1611 might have been expected to have a siesmic effect on political life, but outside the court little changed. At court Dunbar recently had strengthened his position by allying with the Howard family and getting his candidate, George Abbot, elected as archbishop of Canterbury. Leadership of this faction fell to his protegé, Sir Robert Ker, who was ensconsed already in the bedchamber and emerged as the king's new favourite, monopolising his affections and acquiring a dominant position in the dispensing of patronage. By 1613 he was created earl of Somerset, was acting secretary in England, and had Dunbar's old office of treasurer in the Scottish administration. However, unlike Dunbar the new favourite was a political light-weight and was uninterested in Scotland except in matters affecting patronage. The treasurer's job was done by his cousin and depute, Lord Elibank, and an influential voice in the administration was found in his new brother-in-law, Thomas Hamilton, Lord Binning, the secretary. However, government was left essentially to Dunfermline whose conservative and aristocratic instincts ensured a slowing of the pace after the hectic years between 1606–10. Orkney was annexed to the crown in 1612, and a half-hearted rebellion by the Macdonalds on Islay was crushed without much enthusiasm by the earl of Argyll, but there were no new initiatives. Behind this slowing down lay a switch in the king's interests away from Scotland, removing pressure on the privy council in Edinburgh to do anything beyond maintaining the status quo. Meanwhile, Prince Henry's death in 1612 was a blow to James's diplomatic efforts to negotiate a general European peace, but Princess Elizabeth was married to the Elector Palatine in 1613. In the following year tentative negotiations began with an unenthusiastic Philip III of Spain for a marriage between Prince Charles and the Infanta. It was a policy bound to raise hackles in England where James's political difficulties were mounting. After the collapse of the union negotiations, relations with the English parliament never recovered, and the parliaments in 1610 and 1614 ended in serious rifts with the king, primarily over money. Somerset's disgrace in 1615 appeared to complete James's disappointment, and it was against this background that he turned again to Scotland.

Absentee Government Exposed, 1615–25

The relative success James enjoyed in Scotland until 1617 was founded on his own knowledge of Scottish affairs, Dunbar's shuttling between London and Edinburgh, adequate patronage, general prosperity, the absence of controversial policies, and the fact that Dunbar was succeeded by another Scottish favourite. All these conditions now deteriorated. James's experience was a declining asset, Dunbar was dead, patronage was drying up, economic conditions throughout Europe changed for the worse, the king embarked on new and more sensitive religious policies while simultaneously making higher tax demands, and the court became dominated by the new English favourite, George Villiers, first duke of Buckingham. The only positive factor to remain unchanged was Dunfermline and his senior colleagues on the privy council. The chancellor's position was strengthened by an alliance with John Erskine, second earl of Mar who returned to Edinburgh as treasurer in 1616, leaving his cousin, Thomas Erskine, first earl of Kellie, to manage their affairs at court where he was groom of the stool and head of the bedchamber. Lord Binning ceased to be a threat after the fall of Somerset, and while Archbishop Spottiswoode's translation to St Andrews increased his eminence he could not mount a challenge against Dunfermline. Besides, in spite of their petty quarrels the privy councillors had no real differences over policy. Scottish politics were nursed into a dull, mundane routine of familiar business, punctuated by minor disputes over patronage and the occasional outbreak of highland gangsterism. The elderly men who ran the Scottish government – Dunfermline was sixty in 1615 – already had done their most creative work in crown service and were content to manage the system.

It was the king who promoted change and with it instability. James's determination to accelerate the pace of religious change, moving the Scottish church closer to that in England, placed strains on absentee kingship. Yet there was nothing new in his preference for a congruous development in the English and Scottish churches and, besides, the idea of religious conformity within the realms of a ruler was commonplace in Europe. James now was convinced of the correct form of the English church's ceremonial and ritual, and he wanted to reduce the grounds for Scottish criticism of the English church by moving the Scots towards the anglican model. With the death in 1615 of the unco-operative Archbishop Gledstanes and his replacement at St Andrews by the more competent Archbishop Spottiswoode movement on ecclesiastical reform was more likely. Yet concern among the Scottish bishops when the catholic marquis of Huntly was released from excommunication by Archbishop Abbot in 1616 underlined the need for sensitivity. The rigorously calvinist confession of faith of that year served to reassure a large section of opinion that the church's doctrinal purity was not threatened, but the switch from issues affecting church government to liturgical reform was dangerous. It was more difficult for the crown to argue that this was an indifferent issue over which the secular power had authority. The first hints of substantial change appeared at the general asembly of 1616, and James's visit to Scotland in the summer of 1617 (he had promised to return every three years) served to publicise the king's departure from the simple ceremonial of the Church of Scotland. James wanted reform, but his privy councillors and bishops dragged their feet, achieving nothing at the general assembly in November. Undeterred, the king bullied his servants and undermined the clerical opposition with a mixture of threats and bribes. The general assembly at Perth in 1618 passed the five articles, providing for kneeling at communion, observence of holy days, private baptism, private communion and confirmation by bishops. It proved to be the last general assembly for twenty years.

Many Scots, even among those who had supported the king against the presbyterians, thought the articles had the appearance of popery. Objections to conformity with England were strengthened by innovations there like the introduction in 1618 of a *Book of Sports*, undermining strict sabbitarianism and providing further evidence of the drift of an already flawed Church of England away from reformed practices. James did give his support to the synod of Dort's denunciation of arminian ideas in 1619, but arminians were making an impact at court, and by 1621 the king conceded to Buckingham's pressure to grant William Laud, the leading arminian exponent, a bishopric. James now lost patience with opposition in Scotland to the implementation of his liturgical reforms, and in 1621 an unprecedended level of management was required in parliament to give the five articles of Perth statutory authority. However, both the privy council and even the episcopate made it clear they were unwilling to risk pushing the issue any further. Already the presbyterians had been gifted a platform on which to mount an attack against creeping popery and erastian corruption. Open air conventicling by congregations committed to carrying on their own style of worship gained support in the lowlands, especially the south west. Religious revivalism and a sense of apocalyptic foreboding and war fever was fed by the defeat of protestantism in Bohemia and the Palatinate between 1618–23, and by the slow decline in the economy leading to the terrible famine of 1623. At this stage the presbyterians remained a popular party led by dissident ministers, a steady trickle of whom appeared before the two courts of high commission to be sentenced to domestic exile in an unsympathetic locality or outwith the country. However, the 1621 parliament provided an opportunity for aristocratic support to be expressed more publicly. By accepting that he could go no further James avoided a crisis, but the destabilisation of the church could not easily be put to rights.

The five articles almost cost James the huge and controversial taxation voted by parliament in 1621. The convergence of fiscal demands and religious change was an explosive mix, and one that would return to destroy Charles I. The underlying problem for the crown was that its ordinary revenue, drawn from rents on crown lands, customs and the profits of justice, was inadequate. However, the increase in trade in the early seventeenth century – exports in linen, coal and salt all were up – produced a growth in customs revenue, and the buoyant state of the rural economy made financial issues less pressing for everyone. In reality the revenue after 1603 paid for the Edinburgh administration and for pensions, contributing little if anything to the court or diplomacy, and the entire income of the Scottish crown amounted to less than three per cent of the king's total revenue. However, the growing financial constraints which James faced in England, especially after the failure of the great contract in 1610, required that some effort be made to tighten up financial management in Scotland. In 1616 Mar was appointed treasurer in the hope he could reduce the deficit, and in the last few years of the reign the books were balanced. However, there was a cost. Cutting expenditure was an unpopular solution, and while savings were made Mar was aware of the poltical problems associated with disappointed pensioners. After 1619, the treasury was unable to make use of the preferred monetarist option of regulating the money supply and currency values, as the spreading European war induced a trade recession which reduced the value of customs revenues. Further heavy borrowing was too expensive, and there was no alternative but further taxation. Tax had been collected throughout 1607–10 and again 1613–18 when landed and mercantile incomes were rising. But taxation remained irregular, with opposition being aroused to the demands made for money to pay for the king's visit in 1617, and there was no further supply collected in 1619 and 1620. The king's request for a very large tax in 1621 arose in part from a general need to supplement the royal income and from the specific request to provide aid for James's son-in-law in the Palatinate. The £1,200,000 over four years dwarfed previous taxations, and in addition parliament agreed to a new tax on annual rents, or interest, for a limited period. The latter especially did not please the merchants, and the granting of trade monopolies to favoured courtiers was another grievance which soured attitudes towards the king. Due to his personal reputation, the skills of his officials, and the relative prosperity of the kingdom even in the midst of a recession, James got the tax. It was not until 1623 that conditions were really such that taxation hurt, and taxation became a serious issue. Fortunately, perhaps, James took little interest in economic affairs, allowing the privy council to manage the economy as best it could. The advantage of this was demonstrated in 1622 when courtiers backed a scheme advocating that Scottish wool exports be restricted to England. Councillors acted with a combination of self-interest and national pride to quash the idea, keeping at bay the development of anything suggestive of an imperial economic policy.

Nevertheless, the wool scheme, like the five articles of Perth, was indicative of the growing distance between Scotland and the court. The latter now was dominated by Buckingham who created a monopolistic patronage structure based on his willingness to indulge James's homosexual tastes, a keen political intelligence, and the king's desire to be shielded from the press of suitors who daily harassed him. Yet the price was high, as Buckingham's rapacity, support for arminians, and espousal of a pro-Spanish foreign policy all aroused resentment in England, contributing to the stormy 1621–2 parliament. He took little direct interest in Scotland, but Buckingham's patronage did extend to Scots. Among his clients were men like the earls of Nithsdale and Morton who supported controversial royal policies after 1625. Others who rose to prominence in the next reign were Sir William Alexander and Sir Robert Ker, household servants of Prince Charles, who became Buckingham's close ally in the last years of James's reign. Court careers based on subservience to Buckingham and Charles produced men of a very different stamp from James's councillors. As early as 1623 Charles unsuccessfully attacked the latter by using his own men to manipulate a committee of grievance. Of the older councillors, Dunfermline died in 1622, Mar, Archbishop Spottiswoode and the earl of Melrose (formerly Lord Binning) were all over sixty, and the new chancellor, Sir George Hay was only a few years younger. At court the great aristocratic grandees, the duke of Lennox and the marquis of Hamilton, died in 1624–5, and James himself died on 27 March 1625. A younger and less patient generation who had grown up with the idea of an imperial British monarchy waited in the wings.

The Making of a National Revolution, 1625–37

Charles I was a Scot and he retained an awareness of Scotland's distinct political identity. However, he was committed to the idea of imperial monarchy which in practice meant a rational and authoritarian direction of affairs throughout Britain from the centre, and a more aggressive foreign policy. The latter brought war with Spain in 1625, followed by war with France in 1627, only two years after marrying Henrietta Maria, daughter of Louis XIII. Fighting was sporadic but disastrous, and peace was made in 1629 after a great waste of men and resources which served only to demonstrate the inability of the British kingdoms to mount a war in Europe. War also exposed the limited nature of the state apparatus. In Scotland this was no great surprise, and the privy council struggled to supply a few under-strength regiments, to press-gang sailors, and to forward a small contribution to the war chest. The biggest impact the war had was on Scotland's remaining trade links with France, which were disrupted permanently. However, there was little public criticism of the war in Scotland, in comparison to the storm it aroused in England where parliament cut off supply, and where the campaign against Buckingham's influence reached fever pitch prior to his assassination in 1628. Angered by the petition of right in 1628, and still unable to get supply, Charles dissolved his English parliament in 1629, knowing he was denying himself any opportunity to conduct an active foreign policy, but comforted by the knowledge that he preferred a pro-Spanish policy which was served by neutrality in Europe. James, third marquis of Hamilton's Anglo-Scottish army in Germany in 1631 was really a mercenary force of which the king was one of the backers. In the absence of war the British kingdoms would continue to muddle along, and Charles could concentrate his energies on their independent domestic affairs.

In Edinburgh the cosy, incestuous cabal which had administered the kingdom for over a quarter of a century was shattered immediately by a king unprepared to accommodate himself to the obstructive conservatism of his father's councillors. In effect Charles engineered a coup against his own government. He broke the overlap in personnel between the privy council and court of session which served principally to ease the racketeering of councillors and judges, and reduced the king's power over each body. Charles also cleared unqualified noblemen from the bench, which now would be staffed only by men formally trained in law. In 1626 he concentrated Robert Maxwell, first earl of Nithsdale and other loyal servants in an influential committee of war which was used to by-pass the full council. Older councillors complained about the king's arbitrary manner and his unwillingness to listen to their point of view, but Charles was uninterested in objections to his policies. Melrose was demoted, Mar was ignored and Chancellor Hay was bullied into compliance. While the latter remained nominally head of the administration, Charles chose to operate through William Graham, seventh earl of Menteith who was appointed president of the council and justice general in 1628. The latter proved reasonably effective in getting business done, and in maintaining contact between the court and the privy council, but Charles acquiesced in his disgrace in 1633 as a consequence of political faction and Menteith's own stupidity. Chancellor Hay died in the following year, and the king turned to Archbishop Spottiswoode, a man of sixty-eight, to replace him. The latter's high profile was founded more on his office than person, and the appointment was only the king's most blatant example of his preference for biddable councillors drawn from the episcopate. By the middle of the 1630s ten of the fourteen bishops were members of the council and they formed the most active group within it. However, the leading councillor now was John Stewart, first earl of Traquair, a nobleman who progressed through the administration to become treasurer in 1636. Charles had the privy council he wanted, a body of men utterly dependent on himself and afraid to contradict him. As for the counsel the king received at court from the likes of Hamilton, the earl of Morton, or the secretary of state, Sir William Alexander, that too was self-serving.

Yet for all the ignominy heaped on it, Caroline government was far from ineffective. Like its Irish counterpart after the appointment of Sir Thomas Wentworth in 1632, it was if anything too energetic. It was the announcement on 14 July 1625 of the king's intended revocation which signalled that government in Scotland was moving up a gear. A royal revocation was a mechanism designed to allow kings to recover land alienated during their minority, but Charles had no minority and reached his twenty-fifth birthday on 25 November 1625. Hurriedly conceived and drafted at court, arbitrarily announced, and poorly explained, the revocation threatened landed rights by claiming for the crown lands secularised by the church since 1540. It is unknown who devised the project, but as early as 1617 the genesis of such thinking appeared in the plan for a register of sasines, or land titles, and a commission to augment ministers' salaries. The proclaimed intention of the revocation was to provide income for the church, liberate heritors from feudal dependency on the nobility, abolish heritable offices, and alter feudal tenures from blench-ferme back to ward and relief which was more lucrative for the crown. The immediate impact was to create panic and fury throughout the landed community, uniting landlords and heritors against a seeming threat to property rights from arbitrary confiscation.

After the first damaging impact of the scheme in the summer of 1625 attempts to explain the king's policy early in 1626 served only to highlight its lack of foundation in law, and to broaden the opposition by revealing the wide-ranging nature of the revocation. There was excitable talk of rebellion in 1626–7, but there was no need for such extreme action as the entire project collapsed in on itself. Even leading members of the privy council opposed the scheme, accelerating the purge of the Jacobean old guard. Those more established nobility who were the principal target of the plan soon found themselves leading a united campaign against it. The lords of erection, who stood to lose most since their lands were granted from former church estates, lobbied Charles in London in November, but were fobbed off to a committee chaired by Buckingham. A convention of heritors in the spring of 1627 was unimpressed by claims that teind (tithe) reform was in their interests, seeing only the increased annual duties they would have to pay the crown. Consequently the convention refused to back the revocation. The clergy remained suspicious of the suggestion that some of the income clawed back for the church would be spent on education, poor relief and augmented stipends. They were later to pay for a lobby to obstruct the teind commission. Only the burghs stood aloof, negotiating a bilateral deal with the king which freed them from the implications of the revocation.

Although Charles refused to back down or to listen to advice, the establishment in February 1627 of a commission for surrenders and teinds was in effect a retreat. The teind commission was empowered to compensate landlords for the surrender of kirklands and to valuate teinds, a crucial shift away from the more drastic idea of confiscation. What the teind commission was being asked to do was rationalise the muddle created by secularisation and to sweep away some of the more anachronistic aspects of feudal landholding. Its remit was to buy out heritable offices, compensate owners of kirklands for the loss of superiorities over their feuars, and redistribute teinds. The latter would ensure the crown acquired an annuity, the church received a proportion of the income, and heritors could buy out superiors at sums set by the commission. Implementation would require an unprecedented level of governmental interference in local affairs as detailed investigations had to be made of every parish in the country, and in June 1629 local sub-commissions were established to carry out these inquiries. However, the lack of local crown officials left the king no choice but to rely on the existing local community to assess itself, and heritors and ministers were forced to serve on the parish committees. The result was widespread collusion to frustrate and stifle the scheme at every level. By 1630 only four noblemen had made voluntary surrenders of their superiorities, on condition the crown met their price, while in the parishes the entire process ground to a halt. The revocation was ratified formally by parliament in 1633, but it was an empty gesture, and while some administrative reforms did follow, the price of the revocation was the disaffection of the whole landowning community. Not only had landowners adopted a hostile attitude towards the crown, but they had won, exposing the nakedness of royal government in the localities in much the same way as would happen from 1639 in England with the failure to collect ship money.

In contrast to his success in reducing the role of the higher nobility in central government, Charles failed in his attempt to dislodge their local power. In *Basilikon Doron* King James identified the power of the nobility in their localities as a great obstacle to his own authority and a burden to their feudal inferiors, but concluded that there was little he could do about it. In 1609 James tried to introduce commissioners of the peace, but it proved impossible to make any inroads into the immense hereditary power of the nobility, and there was a reluctance to serve on the commissions which were left with little power and only the more mundane aspects of local government. From 1617, James also made desultory efforts to reduce the number of hereditary jurisdictions when an opportunity arose to confiscate or purchase a franchise court, but by 1625 only eight sheriffs could be appointed by the king. Charles pursued this policy of bringing justice and local government under crown control more vigorously. Yet instead of eroding aristocratic power the revocation strengthened it by making the nobility the leaders of local communities in their opposition to teind reform. Attempts to persuade noblemen to surrender their jurisdictions failed due to aristocratic opposition and the prohibitive cost. There were some successes, such as in 1629 when the marquis of Huntly was bullied into resigning into the king's hands the sheriffdoms of Aberdeen and Inverness. By 1632 the number of sheriffs appointed by the king had doubled to sixteen, but this remained a small share of local jurisdictions and many of the resigned sheriffdoms were compromised by regality courts. A revival of justice ayres in 1629 was inspired by efforts to prosecute tax evasion, but these were undermined by local resistance to outside interference. The attempt to relaunch the peace commissions in 1634 was no more successful, and collapsed by 1637 for similar reasons as before – chiefly their sabotage by the nobility and an unwillingness to staff them. Besides, there is no evidence to suggest that this interference in local government was an improvement, and the meddling with traditional patterns of power undermined order. The erosion of Huntly's once vast power in the north-east led to renewed feuding and increased recusancy in the 1630s. Elsewhere, the lack of any sure direction was equally damaging. The control James VI had exercised over the chiefs of the west highlands and islands slackened, and in 1631 they failed to appear before the privy council to account for their activities. The decline of Campbell power since the exile of the earl of Argyll in 1617 created conditions in which there was no-one to police the region effectively, and throughout the 1630s there was a build up of tension and outbreaks of feuding between the Campbells and their neighbours. On the borders the premature disbandonment of the border commission and guard in 1621 was followed by an increase in disorder. The large number of border aristocrats who were absentees – Nithsdale, Roxburgh, Annandale and Buccleuch – left something of a vacuum, and the revival of the joint border commission in 1634 was an admission that the middle shires had not yet attained normalcy. Added to all this muddle was the undermining of the work of the teind commission, widespread tax evasion and growing conventicling adding up to a picture of disintegrating government in the localities.

By Charles I's reign the growth in the economy which accompanied the first fifteen years of the regal union had ended. The union itself had been one factor in the upturn in the economy, but the principal influences had been climatic factors and international peace. Poor, marginal economies such as that of Scotland balanced precariously on the outcome of the harvest, itself a product of the weather, and swung violently from good years in which grain was exported to dearth. The ten per cent of the population who emigrated every year in the early seventeenth century were largely trying to escape from an economy with an unfavourable population pressure on land. The reasonably good run of harvests which prevailed throughout most of the first two decades of the seventeenth century came to an end in the 1620s. There were food shortages throughout 1622–4 and the worst famine of the century in 1623. A further serious bout of bad harvests struck from the middle of the 1630s causing heavy emigration to Ulster. Furthermore, Scotland was vulnerable to international trade patterns, and the decline in the Franco-Scottish trade made the country more dependent on less reliable and increasingly mercantilist English and Dutch partners. The outbreak of war in Bohemia in 1618 and its subsequent spread throughout Germany seriously disrupted Scottish markets in north Germany and the Baltic, while the growth in privateering threatened shipping. Charles I's own wars with Spain and France between 1626–9 were even more damaging to the balance of trade, and a growing bullion shortage destroyed exchange rates already operating at a market rather than official level.

This background of growing economic difficulties made people sensitive to fiscal policies which appeared to exacerbate the situation. The surpluses in the crown's current account which were a feature of the last years of James's reign disappeared, largely because of falling customs revenue brought about by slack trade. With an ordinary income of around £250,000 per annum and an inherited pensions bill of £159,000 per annum, Charles had little choice but to rely more on borrowing and taxation. The ordinary income in fact fell by twenty-five per cent between 1625–30 during the war, and while it did rise again there was a debt of £138,000 by 1630. In 1633 the ordinary income recovered to £238,000, but routine expenditure stood at £260,000 and the crown was heavily dependent on the £100,000 land tax and the tax on annual rents voted in 1630. However, the ongoing increase in pensions and the huge level of borrowing from William Dick of Braid and other merchant creditors meant that most of the tax revenue was going to service an unmanageable debt which by 1633 had risen to £853,000. The taxes granted in 1625 and 1630 were relatively generous, but had not been acquired without opposition, and the discontent with royal fiscal policies which had surfaced in 1616 and 1621 intensified. Taxation now was regular and higher than ever, the new tax on annual rents was viewed as intrusive, and increased customs taxes on coal and salt were damaging to business. Yet at the 1633 parliament Charles gave his critics further cause for complaint by tightly managing a vote for an extension of the 1630 tax for another six years, a rise in the tax on annual rents from five per cent to six and a quarter per cent, and a highly irregular benevolence which allowed the two per cent reduction in interest rates (from ten per cent to eight per cent) to be paid to the crown for three years. All sections of the political community were hit hard by taxation, but none more so than the merchants, especially in Edinburgh, which was burdened with additional bills to pay for the new Parliament House and the redesign of St Giles cathedral. Similarly in Glasgow there was anger at the increase in the customs rate by two per cent, and at Archbishop Lindsay's manipulation of fiar prices. Crown retrenchment meant that no money was spent on royal buildings after 1633. From 1634, when he became treasurer, Traquair also tackled the issue of pensions but in a highly selective way, with the result that there was a substantial political cost in aggrieved and indebted noblemen.

In other respects, too, the crown's economic policies were hurtful, driven as they were by a combination of imperial mercantilism which perceived Scotland in provincial terms, and by the narrow needs of royal financial managers to profit the king and themselves. The former was demonstrated in the common fishing policy, initiated in 1630, which sacrificed Scottish trade to English interests, and in Charles's pursuit of tariff reform in 1636 which resulted in the two and a half per cent increase on Scottish goods which made the important coal and salt exports less competitive. Although malevolent court influences were at work behind both these schemes, they were more obvious in the encouragement of monopolies, such as Lord Erskine's tanning monopoly which was singled out for attack by the convention of royal burghs in 1630. Sir William Alexander believed that Scotland's underlying economic problem was over-population and recommended emigration to Nova Scotia, but the enterprising secretary would have been the principal beneficiary of such a scheme, just as he expected to receive a windfall from the damaging 1632 debasement of the coinage which caused widespread hardship for ordinary people. A sharp devaluation in February 1636 aroused further discontent with currency management, since it caused the export of good coinage, increased the cost of imports, created a credit squeeze and reduced the value of landed incomes.

The problem which faced the political community after 1603 was how to express dissent. Prior to the union it was easy enough to confront James personally, and the court, the privy council, parliament and general assembly were all forums for frank and vigorous debate. The nobility also had recourse to physical force when it was felt necessary. After 1603 the English spoiled James with flattery and deference, and the tightening up of royal control over parliament and the general assembly, which last met in 1618, began under him. Charles completed the process, forbidding the privy council to contradict his orders, stifling debate in parliament in 1633, and authorising no general assembly until 1638. Yet from 1621 opposition to royal policies became more vocal whenever a platform was provided for expressing it. Resistance to the five articles of Perth and the new tax demands in parliament in 1621 was followed by a repeat of dissent in the conventions of 1625 and 1630 and in the parliament of 1633. In 1630 there was discussion of petitioning against grievances, and three years later the opposition went public in Charles's presence in parliament. At the same time these critics held private discussions among themselves and circulated clandestine documents expressing their discontent. Among these was a supplication drawn up by William Haig which amounted to a damning indictment of Charles's entire government, and which was said to have received wide, if subdued, support from noblemen. An identifiable group of nobles led the dissent throughout this period, most notably John Leslie, sixth earl of Rothes, John Campbell, second Lord Loudon and John Elphinstone, second Lord Balmerino. These men also had been at the fore in opposing the revocation, Rothes and Loudon both being on the deputation which lobbied Charles in London in 1626. It was Balmerino whom Charles chose to make into an example, ordering his trial for treason in the summer of 1634 after a copy of Haig's supplication was passed on to him. Significantly it was the bishops who pressed hardest for the trial. Balmerino was charged with leasing making, in effect with not revealing his knowledge of a treasonable document, and was found guilty by Traquair's casting vote. The sentence of execution never was carried out, but the political cost of the trial was to make Balmerino a martyr and convince the king's critics that constitutional opposition was impossible. In spite of the trial the impression is that clandestine ideas circulated more freely in Scotland than in England, where in 1630 a Scottish minister, Alexander Leighton, suffered the loss of an ear and was sentenced to life imprisonment for attacking the English church.

In common with Charles's other two kingdoms, however, it was his religious policy which caused most controversy and which provided the popular support for aristocratic action against the king. James's legacy in the church was unsatisfactory both within Scotland and in terms of the Church of Scotland's relationship with a multiple monarchy. At the late king's funeral Archbishop Spottiswoode uncharacteristically highlighted this latter point by refusing to give precedence to the archbishop of Canterbury or to wear English vestments. Charles's determination to pursue a more vigorous policy of conformity was dangerous, but logical enough, and his later enforcement of the thirty-nine articles of the Church of England on Ireland in 1634–5 demonstrated the British dimension to his plans. The size of the presbyterian population in Scotland is difficult to estimate, but presbyterians were probably in a majority south of the Tay, and certainly the church hierarchy received a fright at a convention of the clergy in 1627 when presbyterian strength was revealed. Charles made his task even more impossible by supporting a shift within the Church of England away from calvinism towards the arminian theology and the authoritarian politics of William Laud, his principal religious advisor. The latter did not become archbishop of Canterbury until 1633, but even before that he was exercising an influence on Scottish ecclesiastical affairs. By the later 1630s only four of the fourteen bishops were Laudians, but the latter were in the ascendancy, with the likes of John Maxwell, bishop of Ross vigorously supporting royal policies. As in England and Ireland Charles's ambitions for the church were to establish for it a more secure financial base, give the bishops a more prominent role in government, and bring the liturgy into line with Laud's high view of ritual. The former was tied up with the revocation, but although the king tried to maintain the rise in ministers' minimum stipends these fell throughout the 1630s because of the drop in victual prices. However, a new bishopric of Edinburgh was funded, including the upgrading of St Giles to a cathedral, and in 1635 there even was talk of the restoration of abbeys and priories to the clergy. There was much less interest in the business of providing schools, hospitals and poor relief which were longstanding aims of the presbyterians. The use of bishops in crown business as privy councillors, lords of the articles and local magistrates was revived by James, but Charles was less sensitive and packed his council with tame bishops. However, the reconstitution of the court of high commission in 1634 with civil powers based on the royal prerogative proved to be less controversial than in England.

It was the reform of the liturgy which aroused the deepest anger. In 1626 Charles insisted only that all new ministers observe the five articles of Perth, but the campaign for conformity gathered momentum from 1629. The royal visit to Scotland in 1633 both convinced the king that worship in Scotland needed reforming, and shocked many Scots by making so public Charles's approval of a ritual which in outward form was popish. It was this above all else which made the belated coronation such a failure as a public relations exercise. Anti-catholicism always was rife in Scotland, but was especially virulent because of events in Europe and the crown's own campaign against catholics in 1629–30. Charles was not in the least sympathetic to catholicism, but his queen was a French catholic and there was a catholic circle at court including Scottish courtiers like Nithsdale. Furthermore, leading arminians in the Church of England, like Richard Montagu, deliberately set out to minimise the differences between Canterbury and Rome. The king's introduction of a new book of canons in 1636, and a new prayer book in 1637, therefore not only aroused resentment on account of its Anglicising influences, but because of its apparent and imagined connection with a popish plot at court. The new liturgy certainly was directly borrowed from England, Laud himself having been involved at every stage of its preparation since 1629 (he had lobbied for the Anglicising of the Scottish church since his visit to Scotland in 1617), and there were only minor modifications by the Scottish bishops. Besides, regardless of whether Laud, Spottiswoode or the canterburian John Maxwell had the greatest influence, the public perception was that Archbishop Laud was behind a scheme to restore popery to Scotland. The liturgy was intended to shift the emphasis in worship away from a preaching ministry towards rigidly defined ceremonial, and was alien to the reformed tradition in Scotland. This was a very dangerous development in a country already deeply concerned about the erosion of political self-determination since 1603, and which had invested a great deal of national self-consciousness in the church. In addition, Charles interpreted the royal supremacy as meaning he had absolute personal authority over the church, a more extreme position than James, who at least went through the form of consulting the general assembly and parliament. The canons and prayer book, therefore, were introduced by royal prerogative, forced on Scotland by a despotic absentee surrounded by popish advisors, or so it seemed. All this took place against a background of religious revivalism and expectation seen in the outburst of fasting and communions which characterised the 'awakening' throughout the south-west from the 1620s, and in the very large increase in the number of religious publications in circulation. Presbyterian dissent was growing stronger in spite of the tough treatment of ministers like Samuel Rutherford, who was banished to Aberdeen in 1636. The arrival back in Scotland of presbyterian ministers driven from Ireland by Wentworth further radicalised opinion, at least in the south-west. At a parish level the networks and mechanisms utilised to wreck the revocation were mobilised against the prayer book in a popular but co-ordinated campaign which gathered momentum throughout 1637 as the time for the launching of the new prayer book approached.

5

REVOLUTION, WAR AND CONQUEST, 1637–60

The Scottish Revolution, 1637–41

The public announcement of the introduction of the prayer book at St Giles cathedral on 23 July 1637 provided the occasion for an organised protest by the king's political and religious critics which turned into a popular riot. An outpouring of religious dissent followed throughout August, fuelled by economic grievances, especially in and around Edinburgh, Fife and the west. The aristocratic leadership was surprised at the level of popular support, but retained control of events. However, the privy council pretended the incident was a spontaneous, popular riot, exploited by dissident presbyterian ministers, and was reluctant either to inquire further or to inform the king of the growing momentum of the protest. The attack on the crown's religious policies focussed on the single issue of the prayer book, which was condemned as popish, against the reformed tradition and unconstitutional. A copy-cat riot took place at Glasgow on 30 August, and by 20 September a petition against the prayer book was signed by around a third of the peerage, as well as many lesser noblemen and about one hundred clergy. The riot in Edinburgh on 18 October demonstrated to the dithering privy council that it had lost control of the capital. A supplication was distributed to the localities for signing, widening the attack to include the bishops and liturgical reform. The disintegration of royal and episcopal authority proceeded apace as dissident noblemen and lairds co-operated with presbyterian ministers in taking over local government. On 15 November the opposition established a committee based provisional government in Edinburgh, subsequently known as the tables, to represent the interests of each estate – peers, barons, burghs and clergy with an executive committee being added later – and to direct their affairs.

Responsibility for the collapse of royal control lay with Charles, who dismissed the supplicants as a rebellious rabble, stirred up by a conspiracy of trouble-makers. From an early stage in the crisis he listened to royalist extremists like Nithsdale and the catholic clique around the queen, who urged the employment of the catholic nobility to crush the rebels. However, the majority of Scottish courtiers, bishops and especially lay councillors like Traquair advocated an accommodation, but when he returned from court to Edinburgh in February 1638 Traquair brought only an uncompromising proclamation to the supplicants to disperse. Charles thus identified his personal authority and reputation with the prayer book. Faced with a more dangerous riot, a panicky privy council abandoned Edinburgh for Stirling. The opposition's response was the national covenant, the culmination of the petitioning campaign, first signed by noblemen in Greyfriars kirk in Edinburgh on 28 February. The national covenant was composed principally by Archibald Johnston of Warriston, the clerk of the tables, and Alexander Henderson, minister of Leuchars, both presbyterians and political radicals. However, the aristocratic leadership of Rothes, Balmerino and Loudon understood the need for a broad appeal. This was evident in the format of a traditional bond, the avoidance of overt presbyterian rhetoric, the expression of loyalty to the king, and the clearing of the document with legal counsel to avoid treason charges. Yet there was an implicit radical agenda aimed at the destruction of Charles's authoritarian, imperial monarchy and the episcopalian church. The national covenant appealed to the commonplace and vitriolic anti-catholicism of the Scots by repeating the 1581 negative confession, thus implying a connection between the king, his bishops and popery. There was no overt attack on the bishops or the royal supremacy, but episcopacy and the five articles of Perth were shown to be alien by highlighting earlier presbyterian legislation which had been ignored or circumvented, while the liturgy and canons were attacked as arbitrary innovations. Parliament, the general assembly and the law were upheld against the prerogative of an absentee king, although the critique of royal policy went back to the later 1590s. Bishops, Anglicisation and prerogative rule were rejected. Finally, the covenant bound the signatories to a common defence of one another, the church and the king, the last being conditional on godly government.

The avoidance of an overt presbyterian programme, and the national covenant's apparent conservatism attracted widespread support. It appealed to landowners infuriated by teind reform and tax demands, mercantile interests adversely affected by Charles's wars and fiscal policies, and farmers, craftsmen and ministers hurt by a range of unpopular government actions. It also provided a rallying point for discontent with a regal union which exposed the kingdom to absentee monarchy, provincialisation and British imperialism. The national covenant even appealed to moderate episcopalians who disliked recent liturgical reforms. Later, in 1638–9, the covenant was popularised and given a more evangelical dimension by a powerful, excitedly apocalyptic preaching campaign, and copies were distributed to the localities. In the parishes of the south, where presbyterians had nursed their hopes in conventicles and privy churches, and where the rabid anti-popish element was outraged by rumours of a crypto-catholic court, the covenant was perceived as a crusade against popish innovations by the bishops and their corrupt friends in London. It was at this level that the national covenant was most dangerous, politicising the masses and appealing to individual consciences.

The covenanters hoped their impressive support would persuade Charles to compromise, and Traquair led the lay councillors in advising concessions on the liturgy. A resident king would have had no option, but Charles refused to compromise and decided on war. He had secure military bases in England and Ireland, a fleet capable of blockading Scotland, the English exchequer at his disposal, and considerable residual support in Scotland, especially in the north-east and on the borders. But the king had no army, and while he had financed his court and government since 1629 without subsidies from the English parliament, there were no reserves and the crown had no credit in the city of London. With widespread discontent and tax strikes in the English counties the king was aware of the risk in summoning an English parliament which was unlikely to sympathise with demands for supply to finance a war in Scotland. Furthermore, there was a danger in allowing the revolt to spread across the border, and in his determination to contain the problem Charles did not brief the English privy council on the seriousness of the revolt. Those English councillors who were consulted, Archbishop Laud and Sir Thomas Wentworth, were determined to impose an imperial peace on Scotland, subjecting it to the English church, law and administration. Wentworth and the marquis of Antrim were ordered to mobilise troops in Ireland, and while Charles tried to scrape together an army in England, the marquis of Hamilton was sent to Scotland in June to buy time.

Charles believed the covenanters represented a minority of radical activists who could be disengaged from a moderate following, and it was left to the conciliatory Hamilton to implement this strategy. On Hamilton's advice Charles revoked the canons and prayer book, dismantled the court of high commission and suspended the five articles. Hamilton also issued the king's covenant on 22 September, attempting to generate popular support for the king's cause. It attracted only 28,000 signatures and there was little enthusiasm outside the north-east, where a handful of academics at Aberdeen's two universities provided ideological resistance to the national covenant. Many royalists were offended by the document, especially the catholics since it too contained the negative confession, while a number of nervous privy councillors signed only because the ambivalence of the text allowed it to be construed as anti-episcopal. Charles also agreed to a meeting of the general assembly in November, the first since 1618, but no effort was made to prepare a royalist party. By contrast, the covenanters managed the autumn elections and had a majority in the assembly when it met in Glasgow on 21 November. Glasgow was chosen because of its proximity to Hamilton's Lanarkshire estates, but the king's commissioner was deserted by his followers, the bishops and most of the lay councillors. Instead, Glasgow was packed with armed covenanters, fearful of a royalist coup. Inside the cathedral, Hamilton faced a well organised and numerically dominant presbyterian caucus which met in privy conference to agree their tactics in advance. Leadership was provided by the new ruling elders, elected by the presbyteries. This astute innovation, based on earlier precedents, gave the aristocracy, who constituted ninety per cent of the ruling elders, a powerful voice in the church's affairs. In the absence of royal nominees in the assembly, Hamilton could not prevent the election of Henderson as moderator and Johnston of Warriston as clerk of the assembly. The latter expertly assumed control of the procedural mechanisms, and forced Hamilton into an impossible position. The commissioner's humiliating walk-out on 28 November when the assembly asserted its right to try the bishops completed the rout. With a haemorrhage of defectors from the privy council signing the national covenant, the last remnants of royal authority collapsed. Among the defecting councillors was the powerful Archibald Campbell, eighth earl of Argyll, a staunch calvinist with strong ideas on limited monarchy. Asserting its right to meet without royal sanction, the assembly overthrew the royal supremacy, abolished and abjured bishops, swept away the five articles, canons and liturgy, and dismantled the court of high commission. When it dispersed on 20 December the assembly had completed a religious revolution, but the political situation was precarious, and war now was inevitable.

The covenanters appreciated the value of propaganda, and their presses and lobbyists worked hard to persuade the English that no threat to their interests was intended, exploiting the popish plot, blaming the bishops for creating the crisis, and emphasising their commitment to the regal union. English puritans and members of puritan bodies like the Providence Island Company were receptive to the covenanters' propaganda, and contacts were made with those politicians who saw in the Scottish troubles an opportunity to force Charles to summon an English parliament. Charles, however, neglected the propaganda war, and his belated efforts to stir up English national sentiment against the Scots failed. In Ireland, where Wentworth had been harrying presbyterians since 1634, the lord deputy feared an uprising of Ulster Scots, but was unable to take pre-emptive military action because it would compromise the king's Scottish policy. Instead he enforced an unpopular anti-covenant oath which further alienated the Scots who showed more enthusiasm for the national covenant. Scots in Ireland and at home responded to the patriotic appeal of the national covenant and the 'true' Scottish church, especially in the face of English aggression.

Throughout 1638–9 the covenanters consolidated their grip, exploiting the widespread confusion, uninterest and neutralism, to establish control of the localities. By the summer of 1639 the covenant was signed in most lowland parishes, presbyteries were purged of hostile moderators, or rival presbyteries established – a process eased by the flight of the bishops – individual noblemen were pressurised into conformity, and shire and burgh government was usurped. The covenanters recruited mercenary officers from Scots serving on the continent, purchased arms in Europe, established a national military apparatus with shire committees of war answerable to Edinburgh, prepared muster lists in the parishes where there was little resistance to conscription, siezed control of strong points, set up an early warning system on the borders, and overawed Aberdeen and its hinterland in a quasi military expedition. Revenue was raised by voluntary contributions and loans from noblemen and merchants. Nevertheless, the covenanters were unsure of their army, commanded by the veteran mercenary, General Alexander Leslie. Its committee based command structure was unwieldy, there remained a shortage of arms, supplies and trained troops, and men were reluctant to fight the king. However, the royalists, a potentially powerful grouping of magnates and bishops, either abandoned their localities and fled to court, or retreated into the intense localism which hampered the royalist war effort throughout the next decade. Charles himself began recruiting troops in January 1639, ostensibly to resist a Scottish invasion of England, but the arrival at Berwick in late May of a badly equipped and ill-disciplined royal army exposed the English state's antiquated military organisation. With the king's over-complicated strategy foundering, Charles was fortunate that the army did not have to fight. The planned invasion from Ireland by Wentworth and Antrim did not materialise, although the threat pinned Argyll down on the west. In the north-east, where royalist support was greatest, George Gordon, second marquis of Huntly was imprisoned and James Graham, fifth earl of Montrose deprived Hamilton of a secure base for his fleet to land. Fighting was avoided because on both sides the aristocracy wanted to find a compromise. An uneasy truce, the pacification of Berwick, was agreed on 18 June, obliging neither side to make concessions, but the 1639 campaign was a political and military victory for the covenanters, who strengthened their hold over the country and brazened out the threat from the imperial monarchy which had exhausted its financial and military resources for nothing.

Charles's defeat was underlined when the general assembly met on 12 August 1639 and declared episcopacy to be against God's will, a decision with implications for the churches of England and Ireland. The assembly demanded compulsory adherence to the covenant, a necessary but ultimately unpopular step for a covenanted people. The focus of political activity passed on 26 August to parliament, which ratified the decisions of the recent general assemblies. The two institutions worked in partnership, but final authority lay with parliament. There the great majority of peers and shire commissioners and all the burgh commissioners – in keeping with their belief in the separation of church and state the ministers did not press for representation – were covenanters. A beleaguered Traquair failed to control the procedure for electing the lords of the articles which subsequently was disregarded, and after refusing to be prorogued on 14 November, parliament elected a standing committee of the estates to replace the tables as the effective government.

At Whitehall Charles established a committee of Scottish affairs composed predominantly of English councillors. The key figures were Wentworth, who returned from Ireland in September 1639, dismissing all talk of compromise, Hamilton and Laud. Traquair remained in Scotland at the head of an emasculated privy council, riddled with covenanting sympathisers. A military solution required an adequately financed English army. Therefore on 13 April 1640 Charles summoned the English parliament, hoping it would follow the example of the Irish parliament which Wentworth had bullied into voting £150,000 sterling to support the king. However, the strains of puting together an army in 1639, combined with obstructive localism, had broken what remained of county administration and heightened feeling against the court. The elections were a disaster for the king, and members of parliament were unimpressed by government scaremongering about the covenanters' links with France. Instead those activists who had established ties with the Scots, and who knew their own fate was linked to the success or failure of the covenanters, attacked the crown in England. Worried by the threat posed by an Anglo-Scottish alliance against him, Charles dissolved the Short Parliament on 5 May. The king chose to go to war without the backing of the English political community and without any money. Persistent local obstructionism and the unavailability of credit meant that his army had to be cobbled together from his own resources and those of his courtiers.

In Scotland the presbyterian clergy completed their ecclesiastical revolution, appointing the commission of the assembly which acted as a powerful executive manager while the general assembly was not sitting. Lay participation in church affairs remained high, but the clergy were regaining control in the kirk sessions and presbyteries. Even in the general assembly and on the commission the ruling elders were less prominent once parliament assumed its political leadership of the nation. Parliament met on 2 June 1640 without royal permission, and

119

a constitutional revolution was hammered out in ten days: triennial parliaments, free debate, the sidelining of the lords of the articles, the doubling of the shire vote in response to the demands of the lesser nobility, the abolition of proxy votes, the formal abolition of the clerical estate, and the continuation of the committee of estates when parliament was not sitting. A national tax to support the war also was voted. The covenanters refashioned government entirely, replacing the old model with one based on committees in parliament and the general assembly, and locally in the shire committees of war and the presbyteries.

On the military side the covenanting government interred prominent royalists, and conducted military operations in the north-east and in the central highlands in the spring. The royalist naval blockade was effective, but the threat from Ireland evaporated because of Wentworth's dependence on English supplies, arms and naval transport. Fearing an attack from the south, and encouraged to invade by English sympathisers, the 18,000 strong Scottish army crossed the border on 22 August, swept aside the English forces at Newburn and occupied Newcastle by 30 August. Charles wanted to fight, but his under-equipped army, undermined by Scottish propaganda, was mutinous. The emphatic defeat of the imperial monarchy in the second 'Bishops' War' destroyed any hope of restoring royal power in Scotland, and precipitated revolution in England. Charles tried to salvage something from the wreckage at a conference of peers at York on 24 September, but had run out of both options and money. The covenanters resisted the temptation to advance further into England, and concentrated on working with their English allies. In turning the king's position in British politics against him, the covenanters recognised that their own security was dependent on dismantling Charles's power in England, and they therefore refused to negotiate until the English parliament was sitting. The army occupied the north of England, cutting off London's coal supply, and demanded £850 sterling a day for its maintenance. By making the English pay and quarter the army the covenanters maintained the political pressure on the king, and protected their English allies. Peace was agreed at Ripon in October, and the English parliament met in November after an election which the court lost. Remarkably, Charles believed the English would fight against the rebels in Scotland. Instead his troubles were multiplied as English members of parliament sought to repeat the Scottish revolution. Ireland too showed signs of growing discontent with Wentworth's administration, and on 7 November the Irish remonstrance was signed, appealing to the English parliament against his oppressive policies.

At Westminster the pro-Scottish faction exploited the menace of the Scottish army and their close contact with the covenanting leadership to break the king's power throughout the winter and spring of 1640–1. It was a brittle alliance, and in the long term the radicalism of the Scots revealed differences between themselves and the English, and within the English parliament. The covenanters successfully pressed support for the root and branch petition in November, and initiated the attack on Archbishop Laud and Wentworth. The latter, now earl of Strafford, was hated on account of his treatment of presbyterians in Ulster, his willingness to use Irish military strength against the covenanters, his desire to continue the war after Newburn, and his contempt for Scottish independence. The Scots pressed hard for his execution which came on 12 May 1641, but Laud survived as a prisoner in the Tower of London. Charles remained unyielding, plotting with the remnants of the royal army, defending Strafford as long as possible, and convinced his enemies would destroy one another. Certainly the growing demands of John Pym and other leaders of the English opposition, and their association with the Scots, were damaging, especially as the covenanters were pressing for the reform of the English church. Consequently there was reluctance in England to address the union issue. Charles conceded that the making of war and the stopping of trade required the consent of both parliaments, while the appointment by the parliaments of conservators of the peace was designed to improve the mutual security apparatus in Britain. Some effort was made to draw the Irish parliament into the system, but the covenanters had a secret agenda for 'a perfect amity' between Scotland and England. This programme was based on the continuation of the regal union, but with guaranteed autonomy over internal affairs, separate and co-operative parliaments, regular consultation between privy councils with dual membership for leading councillors, joint foreign and trade policies, free trade between England and Scotland, greater Scottish representation at court, and uniformity of religion. Scottish suspicions that the Church of England was unreformed and was a threat to their own church could not be concealed, but their English allies knew unity in parliament would not survive an open attack on the anglican church. In itself this made a resolution of the union issue difficult, and in the treaty of London which Charles ratified in August 1641, the English parliament was left to settle the Church of England.

The reduction of the king to a figure-head and the destruction of the royal prerogative in both kingdoms created a royalist backlash among moderates. In Scotland, doubt among the covenanters surfaced first in August 1640 with the signing of the Cumbernauld bond by Montrose and seventeen other noblemen. Montrose wanted to preserve royal authority, distrusted the oligarchic power of the committee of estates, and was jealous of Argyll's growing influence, but his clique had no alternative programme. Charles meanwhile failed to raise support in Ireland where he disbanded the army for lack of funds. He therefore visited Scotland in the late summer of 1641, hoping to take the Scots out of English politics. A less realistic objective was to create a royalist party to intervene on his side in England. It was inconceivable that the king could build a party around the 'malignants', ultra-royalists like Huntly, while among moderate covenanters Montrose had been arrested in June for plotting and Rothes died in August. Instead Charles faced demands for parliament's control over the appointment of officers of state and judges on the court of session, and for a greater Scottish say in the policies and personnel of the imperial monarchy through a strengthened union. He acceeded to these demands, reconstituting the privy council with covenanters (thus superseding the committee of estates), and heaping honours on the covenanting leadership. A reduced standing army was retained to protect the regime. Charles also agreed to the institution of treasonable proceedings against Traquair and four other 'incendiaries' accused of counter revolutionary activities. The king bowed to the revolution, but in doing so he freed himself to concentrate on his English enemies. However, the visit ended with the discovery on 11 October of the Incident, a royalist plot to assassinate Argyll, Hamilton – who had adjusted to the new political order – and his brother, the earl of Lanark. Following two army plots in England that year, the Incident confirmed the covenanters' opinion of the king's integrity. It also frightened his opponents in England.

The War of the Three Kingdoms, 1641–51

Charles's strategy of conciliating the covenanters as a premise to recovering power in England was shattered by the surprising outbreak in October of a well-planned rebellion in Ireland. Inspired by the actions of the Scots, alarmed at the increasingly militant anti-catholicism in Scotland and England, and angered by the two parliaments' collusion in asserting English imperial claims and rights of jurisdiction over the Irish kingdom, the Old English and Irish catholic populations united in an insurrection against the British colonists. Irish intentions were not to achieve independence from the crown, but to free themselves from the English parliament and negotiate a new relationship within Britain similar to that of the Scots, thus preserving catholic and Irish national interests within a restructured regal union. For Charles the Irish rebellion meant he could not dissolve the English parliament, and fears of a popish plot were fanned by the refugees' tales of Irish atrocities, exaggerated deliberately by Pym and his colleagues, worried by their declining popularity. With a less secure political base than the covenanters, the English opposition embarked on a collision with Charles for control of the government and army. Repeating the covenanter agenda, they argued that the king could not be trusted to employ an army in Ireland without being tempted to turn it, and even the catholic Irish, against his English subjects. One solution to the dilemma was offered by the Scots, and as early as 28 October Charles asked for Scottish assistance. With some 50,000 Scots having emigrated to Ireland since 1603, many as recently as the mid-1630s, the covenanters also were concerned for their kindred and were equally unwilling to trust the king. Military intervention allowed the covenanters the opportunity to advance presbyterianism in Ireland, and to sustain an army at someone else's expense. This option offered Charles and his English enemies an escape from the stalemate in the south, but English pride and suspicion of Scottish territorial ambitions in Ireland prevented an agreement until January. The first of 10,000 Scottish troops arrived in Ireland in April 1642 where they cleared much of eastern Ulster of rebels.

The Irish rebellion polarised English opinion around rival myths of a catholic plot and a puritan conspiracy. The grand remonstrance, attacking the English bishops and calling for discussion of religious uniformity with the Scots, narrowly passed through parliament amidst an atmosphere of mob violence in London. Yet concern at the growing disorder and for the welfare of the anglican church was generating a royalist reaction. Charles's failure to carry out a counter-coup by arresting five leading members of the Commons on 5 January 1642 ended any hope of a surgical resolution to the conflict. It also irritated the covenanters, especially as one of the king's justifications for his action was the incitement of the Scots to invade England in 1640 by the dissident members of parliament. Charles deserted London just as his councillors had deserted Edinburgh in 1638. However, in contrast to Scotland where the localities were mobilised quickly against the king, and the Cumbernauld bond came too late to rally support, the royalist cause was well organised. The collapse of order in the localities, the threat to the anglican church, the radical demands of parliament, and the role of the Scots in English affairs ensured that the king had greater success in winning the middle ground. Therefore, in spite of the local desire for consensus and the lack of military preparation which delayed the onset of fighting, the appearance of two determined parties in England ensured that civil war broke out there three years earlier than in Scotland. The last opportunity for compromise was dashed in June by Charles's rejection of the English parliament's nineteen propositions, which he viewed as a statement of war aims, and he raised his standard at Nottingham in August.

With his access to greater available capital and professional experience Charles raised a powerful army, and gained control of much of England and Wales. Outright victory escaped Charles and his Scottish commander, the earl of Forth, at the battle of Edgehill on 23 October, preventing a march on London, but as the 1643 campaign unfolded royalist successes made an outright victory likely. However, from the spring of 1642 both the king and the English parliament wooed the Scots. Hoping to exploit their position in order to negotiate a favourable union, the covenanters aspired to a mediating role, but the king rejected this in April 1643, and was content to neutralise the Scots from the war in England. The covenanting leadership, headed by Argyll, interpreted this refusal to negotiate with the English parliament from a position of strength as an indication of the king's intransigence and determination on total victory. In Scotland, as in England, there was a growing feeling that the revolution had gone far enough. Hamilton, now a duke, campaigned in the privy council, parliament and general assembly for non-intervention. He argued that Charles could be trusted, drawing attention to the English parliament's neglect of its fiscal obligations to the Scots army in Ireland, warning about the dangers of being sucked into a war in England, and raising aristocratic fears of social anarchy. By keeping his distance from Huntly and Montrose, both implicated in the recent Antrim plot to land Irish troops in Scotland, and by posing as a moderate covenanter, Hamilton succeeded in winning over a majority of the peerage. The Cross Petition of January 1643 revealed forty-one noblemen, including eight peers or their heirs, who wanted to re-establish royal authority. Hamilton's efforts delayed intervention, but faced with covenanting majorities in all the government committees, the solid opposition of the shire and burgh commissioners in the convention of the estates, and the well drilled presbyterian phalanxes in the general assembly, Hamilton found himself outvoted in late June by Argyll. This defeat cost Hamilton the trust of the king, who ordered his arrest on his return to court in December. Argyll's argument for intervention was sound as only the king's defeat would guarentee the constitutional settlement of 1641, and a royalist victory would be a disaster for the covenanters. There now was a real threat from the north of England where the earl of Newcastle's army with its catholic officer corps was stationed. Even more frightening was the danger facing the army in Ulster from the Irish confederacy which had negotiated a treaty with the king in September, reawakening the nightmare of an Irish catholic invasion of the west coast.

Between August and November 1643 the solemn league and covenant was agreed between the two parliaments. The Scots promised to provide paid military assistance in return for a closer relationship between the two kingdoms, cemented by religious conformity. The latter reflected the crusading zeal and national pride of the radical wing of the covenanters. However, the political leaders who negotiated the treaty were concerned to provide a framework for a future Britain in which Scottish political and religious freedoms would be protected. A presbyterian church throughout the three kingdoms was only part of a federal package which the covenanters had pursued since 1640. Unfortunately for the covenanters, this unionist agenda aroused little interest in the English parliament where divisions had appeared over war aims and over Scottish involvement. The treaty pushed the king to the political periphery, popularised Scottish resistance ideology in England, and brought an intensified religious bitterness to the war. However, the English negotiators succeeded in diluting Scottish demands, and religious uniformity was to be pursued according to the adaptable 'Word of God', a phrase which allowed both sides to have their own models for reform in mind. The Scots accepted the qualification to secure the treaty, confident that their military strength would guarantee a dominant role in the final peace process. In the meantime

Scottish representatives were invited to attend the Westminster assembly to debate the future of the English church.

The covenanters' escalation of the military conflict in Britain in 1644 strengthened the English parliament and ensured the king's defeat. The army of the covenant, 20,000 strong and commanded by General Leslie, now earl of Leven, crossed into England on 19 January. In a war conducted largely by sieges it destroyed or captured most of the important royalist strongholds in the north of England, including Newcastle which fell on 19 October 1644. The Scots relieved pressure on their allies in the south, cut off the supply of royalist recruits from the north, and secured control of the London coal supply, while their army in Ulster ensured the king was not reinforced from Ireland. Leven also commanded the allied army which defeated the king at Martston Moor outside York on 2 July 1644, but his strategic triumph was negated by his premature flight from the field, and the English parliament credited Oliver Cromwell with the victory.

The establishment of the committee of both kingdoms in January of 1644 was an attempt to ensure that military and political co-operation between the allies was co-ordinated. However, the committee lacked power over either army and the Scots were unable to influence English policy. Crucially, the Scottish army failed to win the war outright in 1644, and in spite of occupying Newcastle, Carlisle, Durham and York, the English parliament carped about the Scots' shortcomings and the burden the army of the covenant placed on their resources. Parliament was all the more sensitive because Charles still appeared to be winning the war. However, the formation of the new model army in April 1645 and the subsequent growth in parliament's military power altered the relationship with the covenanters. The Scottish contribution to the war was talked down in contrast to the publicity given to the successes of parliament's own armies, and pay was diverted from the Scots to English soldiers. This calculated disregard for the Scots was facilitated by the Scottish army's unpopularity in the occupied counties, where its predatory practices and evangelising efforts were resented. Leven's refusal to campaign south of the Trent in 1645 while Montrose was at large in the north, also served to make the covenanters appear unenthusiastic about prosecuting the war.

England was the principal war theatre in Britain, and the covenanters rightly committed the major part of their forces to the conflict in the south. However, in the long term the scale of military involvement in England and Ireland destabilised the covenanter government, while the concentration of force in the south allowed the royalists to apply pressure on the peripheries. In Ireland, where the first presbytery had been established in June 1642, the solemn league and covenant was received with suspicion by British colonists more concerned about the catholic threat and distrustful of Scottish ambitions. The Scots were less concerned with the British predicament in Ireland than with preventing Charles getting Irish reinforcements to England. Enthusiasm for the covenant only surfaced in the spring of 1644 when it was confirmed that Edinburgh would maintain its army in Ireland. However, in the summer of 1644 Antrim sent Irish mercenaries under Alastair MacColla to Scotland to recover Macdonald lands from the Campbells, an action approved by the Irish confederacy government at Kilkenny. This invasion cut off reinforcements for the Scottish army in Ulster, encouraging Montrose's strategy of a war on three fronts. As in 1639 this complex strategy collapsed. Antrim was unable to reinforce MacColla in the west, Huntly was reluctant to stir in the north-east where a rising was crushed in the spring of 1644, and Marston Moor destroyed any threat to the covenanters from across the border. Montrose therefore returned to Scotland to link up with MacColla, and between September 1644 and August 1645 their small army of Irish and highland irregulars won a succession of tactical victories over covenanting reservists.

This string of defeats undermined the covenanters' standing in England and humiliated Argyll who was routed at Inverlochy in February. However, without the support of royalists like Huntly who stood aloof, or the Hamilton faction, Montrose was unable to create a sufficiently large army or political alliance to control Scotland. There was even less likelihood that he could alter the strategic balance in Britain. The covenanters resisted the temptation to withdraw from England, sustaining the pressure in the north, while the new model army smashed the king's last hopes of victory at Naseby on 14 June 1645. Another stunning victory at Kilsyth on 15 August 1645 allowed Montrose to press on and invade the central lowlands in the later part of the summer, but it was a superficial victory, and the localism of the royalists undid his achievement. Huntly and other royalists still refused to join, while MacColla and many of the highland troops returned north. Montrose's quixotic march to join the king in England came to a predictable end when David Leslie's veteran army surprised him at Philiphaugh in the borders on 13 September. Montrose's brilliant but brutal campaign delayed the emergence of support for the king from among moderate covenanters who distrusted him and feared his catholic-Irish troops. He did push the covenanting regime to its limits in fighting a domestic war, supplying armies in England and Ireland, and coping with the effects of poor harvests and plague in 1644–5. However, his victories came too late to save the king who surrendered to the Scots at Newark in May 1646.

In surrendering to the covenanters, Charles hoped to exploit the deteriorating relations between them and the English parliament. English coolness towards the Westminster assembly's recommendations, which the Scots adopted late in 1644, exposed differences between Scottish presbyterians and both the anglicans who opposed the overthrow of their own church, and the independents who objected to the powerful role of the presbyterian clergy. More generally, the English parliament disliked the idea of a church which was not subordinate to the state. The execution of Archbishop Laud in January 1645 was something on which the covenanters and the independents agreed, but the tension between the two was dangerous. Already in December 1644 the covenanters had attacked Cromwell as an 'incendiary', triggering off the self denying ordinance which cleared the way for the formation of the new model army. The Scots now were worried by the growing influence in England of the independents, sectarians in presbyterian eyes, and of those who wanted an unconditional victory for parliament. They persuaded the English parliament to negotiate with the king at Uxbridge in January 1645, hoping to draw Charles and the English presbyterians into an agreement with themselves. But the king remained intransigent, and the talks collapsed. Further negotiations after Charles's surrender took place at Newcastle in July–December 1646. Charles objected to the English parliament exerting control over the government and militia, and continued to oppose Scottish demands for a presbyterian church throughout Britain. Incompatible religious aims also placed a strain on Anglo-Scottish relations. Those English anxious to retain a national church to which all must belong agreed by the spring of 1646 to impose a settlement very different from the Scottish model, transferring significant powers from the clergy to the laity and diluting the powers of parish officers. Furthermore, the independents in the English army objected to the very idea of a confessional state. Irritation at the Scots' religious demands, and impatience at the continued presence of the Scottish army in England threatened to create an open rift between the allies. There was no doubt now that the Scots were the weaker partner, and the English were showing less and less interest in a British solution. A further blow to the Scots' declining military reputation was dealt in June with the rout of their Ulster army at Benburb by the Irish confederates. The covenanters were unable to enforce a settlement, and as they had nothing to gain from detaining the king, he was handed over to the English parliament in January 1647. The Scottish army withdrew from England in February, after making an agreement for the payment of its arrears of £400,000 sterling. Hopes that relations with England would improve were dashed when the new model army, which also was owed arrears and was furious at parliament's efforts to disband it, siezed control of the king on 4 June and marched on London. The moderate heads of proposals which formed the basis of negotiations between Charles and the army over the summer wholly disregarded the solemn league and covenant.

Fighting in Scotland fizzled out over the winter of 1646–7 after the king ordered his supporters to lay down their arms.

Montrose went into exile, Huntly was captured, and MacColla was killed in Ireland in November 1647. The covenanting government achieved remarkable feats in keeping the country on a war footing from 1638, especially with recurrent plague striking throughout 1644–7, but the regime was under strain and peace was welcome. The defeats of 1644–5, the human and material devastation of regions like the south-west highlands, high taxation in the form of an excise from 1643 and a monthly cess on rental from 1645, the disruption of international trade, poor weather, and bad harvests eroded the government's popularity. That unpopularity was heightened by the regime's growing centralism, based on many of Charles's innovations of the 1620s and 1630s, and its increasing willingness from 1643 to crush dissent, principally through the use of crippling fines. Furthermore, the radical trend of events was worrying to the nobility who lost control of the revolution in 1643, and were being challenged in their localities by committees of war and presbyteries they were unable to dominate. The leveller contribution to the debates in the English army at Putney in the autumn of 1647 was a worrying indication of the dangers in upsetting the social order.

Intervention in England failed to create the federal security structure for which the covenanters had worked. Instead a Scottish king was a prisoner of English sectarians intent on weakening the union and discarding the solemn league and covenant. Leadership of the disparate groups of royalists, neutrals and moderate covenanters was provided by Hamilton who saw the opportunity to restore the king's authority in England provided Charles conceded to the covenanters' religious programme for Britain. The king's rejection of the heads of proposals, and his temporary escape to the Isle of Wight was followed by another round of talks with the Scots. On 26 December 1647 an 'engagement' was agreed between Charles and the moderate covenanters, Chancellor Loudon, the earl of Lauderdale, and Hamilton's brother, Lanark. The king promised to observe the 1641 settlement, including the covenanters' federal programme, and to allow a three year trial of presbyterianism in England in return for military assistance in regaining his freedom and suppressing the independents. The engagement never represented a return to the pre-1637 situation, but it was an abandonment of the solemn league and covenant. This betrayal of the covenants, and the high military risks involved, led Argyll and the general assembly to oppose Hamilton's scheme. The church's reaction was all the more virulent because of the laity's failure to control the commission of the general assembly, while the decline of moderate influence after Henderson's death in 1646 lead to the greater prominence of radical ministers like George Gillespie. However, Hamilton persuaded parliament to back the engagement, gaining the support of most of the peerage, more than half the shire commissioners, and almost half the burgesses. This aristocratic reaction breached the alliance between parliament and the general assembly, and the church used its pervasive influence throughout lowland localities, especially south of the Tay, to obstruct the engagement. In addition, the reduced army remained aloof, its officer corps committed to the covenants but torn by loyalty to parliament and gratitude to Argyll who prevented its disbandment. The engagement was hampered by war weariness, a shortage of seasoned soldiers and equipment. Furthermore, in the west where radical ideas and economic discontent were prevalent, a church campaign of conventicling – in spite of general assembly disapproval, privy kirks endured in some parishes – encouraged opposition to the raising of levies and physical resistance. The struggle, which spawned the abusive terms whig and tory, culminated in the engagers winning a skirmish at Mauchline Moor on 12 June. With difficulty Hamilton raised an army of 20,000 men, but the long delays, and the guerrilla activities of the western covenanters, prevented him from marching until Sir Thomas Fairfax and Cromwell had wiped out royalist risings in Wales, Yorkshire, Kent and Essex. Badly led, hampered by appalling weather, and deprived of English support, the engagers were portrayed as a foreign invasion. Cromwell's new model army destroyed the outnumbered Scots at Preston on 17–19 August. The captured Hamilton was treacherously, but understandably, executed a few months later.

Preston underlined the shift in the balance of military power in Britain back towards England. Within Scotland it shattered the engagers who were ousted from power by the whiggamore raid, a coup carried out in September 1638 by those radical covenanters of the west who had formed the western association in November to protect the regime. More immediate insurance against the engagers, who brought over reinforcements from Ireland, was provided by Cromwell's arrival in Edinburgh on 4 October. The covenanters whom Cromwell installed in power under Argyll's nominal leadership were wary of the English and detested the independents, but they hated the engagers more. Therefore they were willing accomplices in agreeing to Cromwell's demand for a thorough purge of their enemies from all civil and military offices, a measure confirmed in the act of classes on 23 January 1649. This act gave the church a veto over office holders, but it undermined the military effectiveness of the shire committees. Convinced that the radical covenanters would remain grateful and conciliatory, Cromwell returned to England, where parliament was pursuing a settlement with the king. Colonel Pride's purge of parliament on 6 December mirrored events in Scotland, providing the army and the independents with the majority they needed to put the king on trial at the end of January. Not before time, Charles I was executed at Whitehall on 30 January.

The government which ruled Scotland throughout the two years after Preston was composed and sustained by the godly. Although the more radical wing of the presbyterians had grown in influence over the 1640s, gaining a dominant voice in the assembly commission, mainstream covenanters remained in the majority, and even in 1648 the radicals could not get their candidate elected as moderator of the general assembly. These covenanting noblemen, lairds, merchants and clergy believed fervently in the covenants and in the idea of a second reformation. It was an astonishing period when the greater aristocracy were largely incapacitated from holding office – only sixteen peers attended the first session of parliament in 1649 – and Scotland teetered on the edge of political and social revolution. Only now did the aristocracy's negligence in exploiting their influence as ruling elders in the general assembly and presbyteries become apparent. Control of the church did not lie in the assembly, which met only for a few weeks a year, but in the commission of the general assembly and in the sixty presbyteries and almost nine hundred kirk sessions. There the clergy's leadership was accepted by the lay elders, predominantly tenant farmers in the countryside and merchant burgesses in the towns. While Argyll and a number of radical peers provided figure-heads for the regime, it was these social groupings which now dominated parliament. Lay patronage in the church was swept away, ministers' stipends were increased, the lairds were permitted to buy up feu duties from feudal superiors, tenants were granted greater protection from exploitive landlords, justices of the peace were encouraged, and poor relief was improved. This activity was accompanied by a narrowing of religious vision, more intense moral policing, and the persecution of witches, which took place against a background of military exhaustion and a severe famine in 1648–9. There also was a heightened degree of political intolerance, although the beheading of the dithering marquis of Huntly, following a minor royalist rebellion in the spring of 1649, was necessary in the light of the north-east's repeated revolts.

The engagers' defeat wrecked lingering hopes of federal union as there was no possibility of the English independents pursuing a common British agenda with the covenanters. The king's execution ought to have ended the regal union, but the Scots proclaimed Charles II King of Scotland, England, France and Ireland on 5 February 1649, salvaging the monarchy even before the Rump Parliament abolished it in England in March. The covenanters' desire for a covenanted monarchy was at odds with the sectarian republicans of England, or the royalists. The latter was seen as the more desirable ally, and the crown was offered to Charles on condition that he agreed to the covenants and enforced religious uniformity throughout Britain. His unwillingness to negotiate with the covenanters led to Montrose's futile campaign in the far north in the spring of 1650 in an effort to pressurise the government into concessions. Instead the rout at Carbisdale on 27 April, followed by Montrose's capture and justifiable execution, strengthened the government. The English commonwealth appeared less secure as it faced royalist regimes in Ireland and Scotland, and deep domestic divisions. However, Cromwell's savage campaign in Ireland between August 1649 and May 1650 closed off Charles's preferred option. In June, Charles II reluctantly arrived in Scotland to sign the covenants, demonstrating his dependence on God and the people for his authority. Faced by a Scottish government committed to imposing both the king and presbyterianism on Britain, and having experienced three Scottish invasions in the last decade, the nervous English republicans had to attack Scotland. In spite of unhelpful clerical interference, David Leslie came close to achieving a strategic victory over Cromwell's overstretched army in the summer of 1650. But in the last stages of the campaign he was manouevred into tactical mistakes, allowing Cromwell to win his greatest military triumph at Dunbar on 3 September.

Dunbar gave Cromwell control of south-east Scotland, but it did not end the war. It did end the dominance of the radicals, who lost control of the commission of the general assembly. Nevertheless, the western remonstrance of 17 October showed a hardening of their ideological resolve and a willingness to defy the government and split the church. It was the defeat of the western association army by English troops in December, and the occupation of the south-west which broke the remonstranters' power. A failed royalist coup – the Start – in October forced Charles to work with the majority party of mainstream covenanters whose resolution of 14 December, expressing a more conciliatory attitude towards engagers, allowed the formation of a coalition committed to defending Scotland, the covenants and the king from foreign invasion. Charles was crowned by Argyll at Scone on 1 January 1651, the act of classes was repealed, and the king took limited command of the war. However, Scotland was militarily broken, the southern half of the kingdom was occupied, and political divisions paralysed resistance. Economic ruin had also taken a high toll; huge sums had been expended on military equipment, and the country had suffered plague and famine, war damage and the killing of ten per cent of the male population. The committee of estates was captured on 28 August 1651, while Dundee was stormed on 1 September, opening up the royalist recruiting grounds in the north-east. The remnants of the Scottish army, which followed Charles in a desperate invasion of England, was cut to pieces at Worcester two days later. Most of the country was occupied by the end of the year. The covenants were not rejected by the Scots. Instead it proved impossible to contain them in a Great Britain in which the nationalism of the English elect proved stronger than that of their covenanted neighbours.

The English Hegemony, 1651–60

The English republicans did not set out to conquer Scotland, and even after Dunbar Cromwell wanted a negotiated settlement. It was Scottish intransigence over the united monarchy which forced the English to seek security for their own unstable regime by subjugating the Scots. That conquest was based on English military superiority, and Scottish economic collapse and political sterility, but it was not an easy war to win. Fighting died out towards the end of 1651, but it was the following summer before Argyll submitted, and the highlands remained unconquered. Throughout 1652 an English administration was installed, a punitive tax was imposed, and so secure did the regime feel that a twenty per cent cut in the size of the army was made.

However, the superficiality of English control was exposed in 1653 when a poorly co-ordinated royalist rising under the earl of Glencairn and John Middleton succeeded in panicking the occupying force. Guerrilla activities spread throughout the highlands and western shires as far south as the border. Divided leadership, lack of support from the exiled court, a shortage of military supplies and horses, and the collaberation of Argyll and other Scots opposed to the royalists allowed the English to ride out the rebellion at a time when the London government was enmeshed in constitutional crisis, fighting the Dutch, and policing royalists. Cromwell's coup against the Rump Parliament, the surrender of authority to him by the Barebones Parliament and the creation of the protectorate in December 1653, and the end of the first Dutch war (1652–4), provided a favourable background to the smashing of Scottish resistance by General George Monck in 1654. The highlands were invaded and subjected to systematic terror, but many chiefs like Sir Ewen Cameron of Lochiel were able to retain their arms by striking bilateral deals with the hard-pressed English military. After the flight or surrender of royalist leaders the war ended in the winter of 1654–5. Control was established by a powerful army of 10,000 troops, the construction of an effective fortress complex based on Ayr, Leith, Perth, Inverlochy and Inverness, the widespread use of spies, informers, surveillance and the arrest of political suspects, the suppression of all dissent, restrictions on the possession of arms, horses and castles, strict control of movement around the country, the threat and enforcement of punitive financial punishments, heavy taxation, and the employment of English personnel in government. The English created an alien, oppressive police state, detested by all but a tiny minority of republicans and sectarians. It was not contentment which left the Scots unmoved by Penruddock's rising in England in the spring of 1655, but fear.

The English empire of the 1650s was a repudiation of the federal union of the covenanters. Cromwell rejected pressure to annex Scotland, and wanted a union in which Scotland would become a dependent province within the English imperial world. In October 1651 'A declaration of the commonwealth of England, concerning the settlement in Scotland' intimated the English government's intention to unite the former kingdoms by incorporation. The political instability of the commonwealth era pushed the issue off the agenda, and while in the summer of 1654 a union was created by an ordinance of the English government, it was 1657 before the protectorate parliament passed an act of union. Consultation with suitably vetted Scots was conducted in 1652, but little account was taken of Scottish views, and the final settlement did not conceal the reality of conquest. There was no equivalent to the 12,000 former soldiers who were settled in confiscated land in Ireland in lieu of pay, but those deemed enemies of the protectorate had their land confiscated, and there was little difference in the status of the two subjugated kingdoms. The involvement of a small number of Scots in government was an attempt by an over-stretched occupying regime to facilitate its job. Provision was made for Scotland to have thirty seats in the protectorate parliament (a few nominated Scots sat in parliament in 1653), but most of these were filled by English officers, and at the 1656 election sixteen seats went to Englishmen. In 1659 there were only eleven Scots, all but Argyll being English nominees. Those who collaborated with the occupying power included some enthusiasts for the ideals of the English revolution, and self-interested quislings who exploited the demise of the traditional status quo. The disqualification of so many noblemen from office ensured that initially those Scots prepared to collaborate were drawn from a relatively low social status. However, by 1656 the status of members of parliament had risen, reflecting the government's need to involve noblemen whose co-operation was essential in keeping down the cost of military government. This was also true in the administration and local government. By 1653 a majority of the commission for the administration of justice was Scottish, two Scots sat on the nine strong Scottish council formed in 1655, Scots predominated in the lower levels of the administration, and the proportion of Scottish sheriffs steadily increased. Many of those who filled these posts hated the regime, but feared more oppressive policies if they refused to co-operate. Noblemen were browbeaten into conforming by the threat of the full rigours of the act of grace and pardon which imposed fines on enemies of the occupying regime, although these were reduced as the English found it needed the co-operation of the local aristocracy. Even at the level of burgh government, burgesses and freemen had to swear an oath of loyalty.

The attempt to involve the Scots in government reflected the ideas of Roger Boyle, Lord Broghill, the Anglo-Irish president of the council of state in 1655–6. At the very time Cromwell was unleashing the major-generals on England, Broghill reduced the military profile in Scotland by recruiting civilians into government. The attraction of this conciliatory policy for General Monck and the council of state in London was one of cost and effectiveness. Although Scotland was less heavily taxed than Ulster, the £10,000 a month cess which the government tried to levy from 1652 proved impossible to raise. The sum was reduced by twenty five per cent within the year, and fell as low as £6,000 in some poorer districts. The economy was in a deep depression with foreign trade having collapsed, shipping destroyed, and much of the country devastated, with areas like Argyll or burghs like Dundee taking years to recover. The imposition of Anglocentric economic legislation was unhelpful, and the previously longed for free trade meant the freedom of English merchants to exploit Scottish markets, turning the country into a source for cheap raw materials. Nevertheless there was some indication of recovery in Glasgow by the mid-1650s, and the absence of very bad harvests prevented a total collapse. Monck drew a lesson from 1653–4, realising that to press an impoverished people for high taxes would maintain the cycle of social instability which would only benefit the royalists. Yet in spite of managing its finances better than either of the administrations in England or Ireland, the occupying government was unable to fulfil its ambition to be self-supporting. More than half its income came in subsidies from England where high taxation was contributing to the protectorate's unpopularity. The most expensive item was the army which, in 1659, was devouring ninety per cent of the total budget of £307,000, and it was essential to keep down military costs. Involving politically acceptable Scots in policing their localities, dispensing justice and in administration was in part cosmetic, but by reinforcing traditional elites the role and cost of the military was reduced.

Broghill's attempt to cloak military government in civilian clothes was partially successful. The council of Scotland tried to fulfil its remit to preserve the union, promote the preaching of the gospel, maintain the peace, reform education, remove undesirable office-holders and encourage trade. The employment of soldiers to collect the excise was reduced, and civilians played a greater role in government from 1655. However, the menacing presence of an army which was resented even in England could not be ignored, and General Monck was the final arbitrer of power. The army provided a measure of stability and effective policing after the violence of civil and foreign warfare, as well as the anarchic pillaging of freebooting mosstroopers, high-landers and vagrants which followed the collapse of gov-ernment in 1651. The dependence on the army to pro-vide justice and fight crime was heightened by the aboli-tion in 1654 of the hereditary regalian and baronial courts. However, in the highlands the army was unable to cope without the assistance of trusted clans who operated their own private policing. The occupying regime's wider pro-gramme of social and economic legislation was designed to destroy the power of the nobility and create a grate-ful tenancy. Sheriffs and justices of the peace appointed by the government were to co-operate with English officers in replacing these hereditary courts. Yet in spite of a rec-ord of impartiality and fairness, the new order was unable to match the broad range of social control and cohesion of the former courts. Those lairds who acted as justices needed constant encouragement from the military, and Eng-lish officers acting as sheriffs-conjunct supplied the backbone to the sheriff courts. It was the church courts which provided the bulk of justice for ordinary people, and the regime lacked the resources to fulfil its intention of depriving the church of its social control. There was more success in the central courts, and in the newly formed commissions for justice, where English judges, having abandoned early hopes of introducing the common law, struggled with the technicalities of Scots law to produce speedier and generally just decisions.

The presbyterian split was exploited successfully by the Eng-lish. The majority resolutioners were committed to Charles II and were prepared to allow a separate religious settlement in England. The minority remonstrants or protestors, were hard-line solemn league and covenant supporters, uncommitted to Charles II. At first Cromwell preferred a united church, and tried to work with both parties. After 1653, when the resolutioners backed the rebellion, he favoured the protestors, who predominated only in a sixth of all parishes, and who were concentrated in the south and west. The introduction of religious toleration for all but catholics and episcopalians led to the establishment of a handful of independent sects during the 1650s, but the Scots were unimpressed by these alternative church structures. Opposition to religious toleration was particularly vehement among the protestors whose inability to negotiate with Broghill in 1656–7 led to their eclipse by the resolutioners, especially when the latter ceased praying for the king. Yet neither was persecuted, and while the general assembly was abolished in 1654 and clerical influence in national affairs disappeared, there was no interference in the internal business of the church, where ministers retained the dominance they had acquired on the collapse of the engagement in 1648. The universities, however, were purged of resolutioner professors.

Cromwell's death on 3 September 1658 initiated a bitter struggle between factions in the army and parliament that brought chaos to England. The collapse of the protectorate was followed by the paralysis of the revived commonwealth. Civil war in England appeared likely by the winter of 1659–60, and Scotland was not unaffected. As supporters of the Cromwellian usurpation, the Scottish members were ejected from the restored Rump Parliament in the spring of 1659, and the nature of the union was left unresolved. However, in contrast to the disintegration of military discipline in much of Britain, Monck's army remained a powerful force, sustained by Scottish taxes. He cautiously backed the English parliament, but in order to intervene in England a greater measure of trust had to be invested in the Scottish aristocracy. It was the royalist earl of Glencairn who emerged as the politician most able to ensure peace and a continuation of stable government when the bulk of the army, purged of any dissidents, marched south. Monck crossed the border on 1 January 1660 with no clear programme other than to end the uncertainty and restore some form of parliamentary government. The Scots watched events unfold in England, while the nobility gradually resumed control of the localities. Once Monck's coup ensured the recall of the Long Parliament in February the momentum for the return of the monarchy gathered pace, and even before the declaration of Breda on 4 April, sketching out Charles's conciliatory intentions, the issue to be decided was the nature of the restored monarchy, not its desirability. Monck and Charles consulted Scots in this process, but the making of the restoration was an English event. Charles returned to England on 25 May, never again to set foot outside that kingdom. Nevertheless, Scottish politicians now could seek a new role in a Great Britain united once more by the slender threads of the Stewart monarchy.

6

RESTORING THE KINGDOM, 1660–88

The Restoration, 1660–6

Disillusioned by the experience of co-operation with the Scots in the 1640s, and desiring to dismantle anything associated with the republican adventure, the English wanted to minimize their political ties with Scotland in 1660. Furthermore, the 1650s underlined English superiority, and there was no economic advantage for England in strengthening the relationship. Fuelled by aggressive mercantilist ideas and agricultural depression, the English put up a wall of protectionism in the navigation acts. For their part the Scots associated union with conquest and wanted their liberty. Only the protestors were ambivalent about the implications of a royal restoration and how to respond to the end of the protectorate. Some urban commercial interests saw advantages in free trade with England, but public opinion overwhelmingly was against union. Charles II and later James VII's preference for keeping English and Scottish affairs separate contributed to the retreat from union. Charles resisted the suggestion from Edward Hyde, first earl of Clarendon that Scottish affairs be subordinated to English ministers through the Whitehall council. Yet Charles was protective of Scottish independence since it gave him more freedom, and he operated chiefly through the secretary of state, John Maitland, second earl of Lauderdale, who was determined to keep Clarendon at a distance. As for the administration in Edinburgh, except in the case of foreign policy, it had considerable freedom.

The English cavalier parliament which met in May 1661 was dominated by an aristocracy determined to use the crown to restore their own authority over the clergy and army. The revolution was not overthrown entirely, but most of the English crown's prerogative powers were restored. Charles therefore had greater freedom to shape the nature of the restoration in Scotland than would have been the case if the English crown's powers had been more limited. However, the Scottish nobility proved to be even more reactionary, believing the recovery and preservation of their power, privileges and wealth lay in an alliance with the crown. Therefore they favoured a complete restoration of monarchical authority as a guarantor of stability and order. In the spring of 1661 parliament passed the act recissory, sweeping away all legislation enacted since 1633. For moderates there was some attraction in a device which appeared not only to abolish covenanting legislation, but also the more controversial of Charles I's reforms. Careful management by the king's ministers, and the combination of royalists seeking help in recovering their estates and former covenanters hoping for indemnities from prosecution, produced this stunning crown victory. The extent of the crown's triumph surprised a king who hated to be crossed, never admitted to being wrong, and was capable of calculated cruelty. Yet his pragmatic approach to problems and his underlying caution meant that Charles II knew when to compromise. He wished to restore in full the power of the monarchy, and he fought to preserve the royal prerogative. However, unlike his father and brother, Charles II never gambled what he had already on future prospects or high ideals.

The restoration settlement returned to the king authority to make war and peace, complete control over central government patronage – officers of state, privy councillors, judges and the army – and the prerogatives and mechanisms used to manage parliament. The latter experienced greater freedom of debate than before the revolution, but Charles enjoyed the right to summon, prorogue and dissolve it, to interfere in elections, and the lords of the articles again dominated proceedings. The problem for the restored monarchy lay in translating political dominance in central government and the legislature into action in the localities, where the aristocracy regained their private jurisdictions and hereditary influence and where the crown relied on their co-operation. A small army was retained, but the scaling down of the military establishment in 1667, and its replacement with a militia commanded by the nobility, left the king's coercive power at the mercy of the local aristocracy. The price of co-operation was non-interference, especially in the highlands, where the private fiefdoms of magnates like the earls of Argyll, Atholl, and Seaforth operated like autonomous regions, while a region like Lochaber witnessed a revival of cattle raiding and feuding. It was hoped the king's own finances would be placed on a sound footing when parliament granted a generous tax of £480,000 per annum raised from the customs and an excise on ale and beer. As in England the government was over-optimistic in estimating its income and underestimated the level of spending. Parliament's intention (as in England) was to remove the burden from the landed community and place it on consumers. Charles promised never to raise taxation by the efficient but intrusive cess, but a land tax of £666,667 over five years was voted in 1665 to support the Dutch war, and the cess was reintroduced in 1667 to provide £864,000 to pay for military requirements. This growth in unpopular taxes meant that the most common for of employment for soldiers was as tax collectors.

Charles sought to create security by conciliating former royalists and their opponents. In England this proved more successful in the household and administration than in the localities, while in Ireland much of the existing government was retained. Both Monck and Broghill went on to serve Charles in England and Ireland after 1660. In Scotland the Cromwellian regime over which they once had presided was swept away, although it was 1662 before the last English troops left the country. For Charles the problem of compensating loyal friends and balancing political interests was complicated by the inadequacy of patronage. However, the restoration of aristocratic power was reflected in the high number of peers holding crown offices. It was Monck who began this recovery in the late 1650s, and throughout 1660 the nobility tightened their grip on government and the localities, helped by the absence of any representative body until January 1661, and by the divisions in the church. The competing political factions were predominantly covenanters, and the one group marginalised by the power-sharing in 1660 was the old pre-engagement royalists. Most of the men recruited to Charles II's government had a record of opposition to his father, having supported the covenants, but now they backed a strong monarchy as the route to stability and the recovery of their own fortunes. As in England and Ireland where the pre-eminent figures in the government, Clarendon and the duke of Ormonde, were members of the exiled court, the man entrusted with running Scotland was a former exile. The king's commissioner to parliament was John Middleton, first earl of Middleton, a professional soldier who switched to the royalist side at the time of the engagement. Middleton shared the leadership of the 1653–4 rising with Glencairn who had made his peace with Monck and assumed the pivotal position in Scottish politics in 1659–60. He was appointed chancellor. The other leading members of the administration, the earls of Rothes, Lauderdale, Crawford and Cassillis, all had covenanting credentials.

The reputation of the restoration administration has suffered from an exaggerated picture of incompetence, corruption, drunkenness and vicious factionalism. The last certainly was true and there was an intense struggle for ascendancy within the regime, and with it control of royal policy and patronage. The ideological split in the government between presbyterians and their sympathisers like Lauderdale, and episcopalians around Middleton was resolved in favour of the latter, who had the backing of Clarendon. By 1662 presbyterians like Cassillis and Crawford were forced out of office, and in 1663 Middleton surreptitiously attacked Lauderdale, attempting to add his name to those exempted from the act of indemnity. However,

Lauderdale was a skillful courtier and was liked by the king. He turned the 'billeting affair' against Middleton by appealing directly to Charles who was outraged at this attempt to veto his choice of servants. Consequently, Middleton and his court allies were disgraced. The death of Glencairn in 1664 removed the last of Clarendon's clients. Lauderdale remained vulnerable to criticism in England of being soft on presbyterians, but he had now no Scottish rival at court, and Clarendon, whose own influence in England waned from 1663, no longer had access to Scottish affairs through the abandoned Whitehall council. In Edinburgh the dominant figure after 1663 was John Leslie, seventh earl of Rothes who picked up the offices of treasurer and king's commissioner while also acting as chancellor. Also influential was James Sharp, archbishop of St Andrews, who desired to preserve the church's independence from overt state interference, and who launched a bid for the chancellorship in 1664.

Returning royalists expected to settle old scores in 1660, but there was less bitterness among the Scottish aristocracy than their counterparts in England or Ireland where the transfer of land had been greater and had led to post-restoration squabbles over land claims. The low number of royalist forfeitures in Scotland before 1651 when Charles granted an act of indemnity, and the fact that the English government on the whole employed punitive fines rather than confiscations eased the return of the royalists. Widespread aristocratic debt provided a very useful weapon which the crown used regardless of previous political affiliations, and many families never were compensated for their losses. However, there were victims of the restoration. Charles complied in the vindictiveness of the earls of Middleton and Glencairn to take revenge on old enemies, especially the protestor ministers. James Guthrie went to his execution defending the right to resist, Samuel Rutherford was fortunate to die in 1661 while awaiting trial on treason charges, his writings proscribed, and while Patrick Gillespie was acquitted of treason, he was imprisoned until his death in 1675. This crack-down on the protestors took place with the connivance of the resolutioners and with aristocratic approval. The politicians were treated less harshly, but Argyll was judicially murdered in May 1661, a deranged Warriston was dragged back from exile to face the block in 1663, and Sir John Chiesley, prominent in the protectorate government, was allowed to rot in prison for years. Some seven hundred people were excluded from the act of indemnity in September 1662 and were subject to heavy fines, although most of these were mitigated following good behaviour.

What ensured the continuation of repression beyond 1660–1 was the restoration of an erastian and episcopal church. There were no signs throughout the 1640s and 1650s of support for the return of bishops. In fact the prevailing mood in 1660 was a virulent anti-clericalism which encouraged the crown and nobility to seek a church settlement characterised by lay domination of the clergy. Episcopacy was chosen simply because bishops were the most effective tools for creating order in the church. Ironically, subsequent efforts by the bishops to exercise a degree of independence were criticised by crown ministers as 'presbyterian'. Yet in 1660 encouraging reports from James Sharp, who was sent to persuade Charles to adopt the resolutioner programme, and the presbyterian preferences of noblemen like Lauderdale and Crawford, lulled the majority resolutioner party into expecting the king to agree to a presbyterian church. Even in England a primitive episcopacy staffed by presbyterians and retaining elements of presbyterian government and puritan worship was expected to survive. Certainly Charles's own lack of committed opinion – he worshipped according to anglican rites in exile – encouraged those who hoped for a moderate settlement in both king-doms. But the king's experience in Scotland in 1650–1 left him with an enduring prejudice against the Scottish clergy, and the reaction against presbytery was strong in all three kingdoms, stronger even than the king wished. In Ireland episcopacy was restored before Charles reached England. The refusal of English presbyterians to accept bishoprics, the overwhelmingly anglican composition of the cavalier par-liament, and Clarendon's determination to impose bishops ensured that the Church of England was returned to staunch episcopalians under the leadership of Gilbert Sheldon, who became archbishop of Canterbury in 1663. Any residual hopes for the presbyterian Britain envisaged by the solemn league and covenant were dashed long before the Scottish church was settled.

Episcopacy in England added conformity to the case being advanced for bishops in Scotland. The anglican Middleton, with Clarendon behind him, persuaded parliament in early 1661 to impose on office holders an oath of allegiance, recognising the royal supremacy and condemning the covenants. Cassillis was the most notable victim of this purge. The act rescissory abolished the changes made in the church since 1633, both the Laudian innovations and the presbyterian reforms, while the act anent religion left the church settlement to the king. Lauderdale distanced himself from the presbyterians, while the opposition in parliament, led by the young William Hamilton, third duke of Hamilton, was weak and disorganised. Middleton, Rothes and Glencairn siezed the initiative, pressing for an immediate restoration of episcopacy and lay patronage. As in England, the king expected no more than a primitive episcopacy, and he appreciated the flexibility of toleration. Charles therefore was surprised when in the autumn of 1661 Middleton secured the full restoration of diocesan episcopacy. The crown's refusal to recall the general assembly had worked to the king's advantage, depriving the divided presbyterians of a formal negotiating medium. The resolutioners were also more concerned with defeating their protestor rivals, and were so confident of victory that they approved the outlawing of conventicling. Faced with the *fait accompli* of a restored episcopacy, resolutioner leaders like Robert Douglas refused the offer of bishoprics. Only James Sharp sold out, providing the king with an archbishop capable of leading a second choice and second rate episcopate. As none of Charles I's bishops had survived, the first four bishops were consecrated at Westminster in December 1661 without implying any English jurisdiction over them, and by the autumn of 1662 an episcopal church was in place. The presbyterians were left isolated and exposed in the church courts, where their protests were overawed by the bishops. However, doctrine, liturgy and the moral discipline of the parish was untouched, and with anglicanism heading off down a divergent path there was no repeat of the attempt in the 1630s to create a British church. Nevertheless, the return of prelatical bishops, lay patronage, and the royal supremacy – formally enacted in 1669 – proved to be the fundamental blunder of the restored monarchy.

The insecurity of the restoration monarchy is often overlooked. The biggest worry was the army which in England was whittled down to a rump of loyal regiments. In Scotland the English garrison was replaced by a small and loyal standing army under Middleton's command. The threat from republican sympathisers never existed in Scotland, but in spite of Charles's efforts to isolate genuine enemies from the mass of non-conformists, his ministers behaved as though there was a British republican underground. Thus in 1660 the Scottish government banished all protestors from Edinburgh following Venner's rising in England, and outlawed unlicenced public meetings. Similar half-baked conspiracies in England, like the 'Tong Plot' of 1662, or the attempt by protestant radicals to sieze Dublin castle in 1663, reinforced royalist fears of revolt. Support for increased repression in England came from Clarendon, Archbishop Sheldon and the powerful anglican lobby, and from eager-to-please magistrates. Particular attention was paid to any hint of covenanting ideology. The cavalier parliament ordered the solemn league and covenant to be burned publicly, the corporation act of 1661 required all English town councillors to sign a declaration against it, and anglican militants like Dr Herbert Croft publicly blamed the king's earlier misfortunes on his alliance with the Scottish presbyterians. In spite of their staunch monarchical principles, the covenanters represented the most intransigent and, because of their subversive political ideology, the most dangerous opponents of the British monarchy.

In Scotland the presbyterians formed a majority of the highly politicised lowland population south of the Tay, and a direct assault on their beliefs was very risky. However, Middleton and

Glencairn followed Clarendon's lead, provoking a purge of the church which they hoped would smoke out leading protestor ministers. The campaign began in 1661 and was a disaster for the church as the net was cast too wide, allowing deprivations for a range of offences, such as refusing to commemorate the anniversary of the king's birthday and restoration. However, it was the 1662 act requiring all ministers appointed since 1649 to seek presentation from their patrons and collation from the bishops which created most difficulties. By 1663 the government had deprived of their livings 268 ministers, around twenty-five per cent of the total (compared to ten per cent in England). A disproportionate concentration was in the south, especially in the west where Galloway lost thirty-four of its thirty-seven ministers. Many ministers acquiesced in the change, but their conformity cannot necessarily be interpreted as support for episcopacy. Archbishop Sharp was left to fill the empty charges, often with unsatisfactory candidates, and to ensure that congregations conformed in the face of non co-operation from the local nobility and widespread non-attendance at church. He was compelled therefore to turn to the state for enforcement, completing the breach with his old colleagues. In order to isolate the ousted ministers from their congregations punitive legislation, principally fines for non-attendance at church, was introduced in 1663. Behind Sharp's growing hawkishness lay the influence of Sheldon, who initiated severe repression in England in 1664–6 and to whom Sharp turned for advice. Sharp also sought greater episcopal control over the coercive process through the church commission established in 1663. His own arrival on the privy council that same year launched a campaign to succeed Glencairn as chancellor, a prospect which the anti-clerical nobility viewed with misgiving. Meanwhile the appointment of Alexander Burnet as archbishop of Glasgow in 1664 brought new energy to the church in the west. Against this background Crawford resigned as treasurer rather than renounce the covenants, but Lauderdale gave public support to the campaign while criticising it on pragmatic grounds in private. His analysis was to prove perceptive and the reluctance of landed presbyterians to enforce the law created a *de facto* toleration by 1664–5, exposing the limits of the regime's authority in the localities.

Meanwhile, Scottish recovery from the economic devastation of the 1640s and 1650s was slow, especially as the economic provincialism of the years of military occupation was replaced by a trade war with England. The English navigation acts of 1660 excluded Scotland from English colonial or continental trade while Scottish foreign policy remained subordinated to aggressive English commercial interests. New customs rates on Scottish linen, cattle, salt and coal were imposed by 1663, forcing the Scots to retaliate with duties on English woollens. In fact there was a strong protectionist lobby among Scottish coal owners and salt masters to preserve the domestic market from imports. Government efforts to stimulate trade and industry in 1661 made little headway, but Lauderdale succeeded in persuading the English government to lower the customs rates in 1664, alleviating some of the popular discontent aroused by high indirect taxes.

War with the Dutch, England's principal trade rival and Scotland's major trade partner, arose in 1665 as a result of court interests in tropical trade ventures and English ambitions to continue the foreign successes of the protectorate government. Scotland had nothing to gain from war, but contributed funds and men, and suffered a loss of trade which reduced crown customs receipts, hurting the pockets of officials and pensioners, and leading to new tax demands in 1665. A jittery privy council introduced greater security measures following alleged presbyterian links with the Dutch, and talk of a rising by militant covenanters like John Brown of Wamphray whose An Apologetical Relation justified resistance to the crown. Control over the south-west was minimal, and Rothes, the effective head of the Edinburgh administration, sent the army into the region to harass illegal conventicles. However, the gradual build-up of troops in the south was achieved only by withdrawing them from the highlands where they were employed in tax gathering. It was in this latter capacity that Rothes' men made a nuisance of themselves in the south-west when they set about collecting old fines imposed at the restoration and which now were pocketed by the corrupt military. The steadily rising level of repressive activity which Rothes and Archbishop Burnet initiated was insufficient to crush dissent but provocative enough to incite rebellion in the region in November 1666. The Pentland rising was both spontaneous and desperate, and only military incompetence allowed it to gain any momentum. Some 1,000 ill-equipped men made a winter march across country in the hope of pressurising the government to make concessions. The failure to attract support outside the south-west, or to persuade any noblemen to join, forced a retreat and they were dispersed by regular troops in a bloody skirmish at Rullion Green on 28 November. Nevertheless, the government was shaken, and it reacted with characteristic brutality, sending more troops into the region to fine and disarm suspects, employing torture, executing some thirty-six prisoners, and consigning many others to the slave plantations on Barbados.

Provincial Devolution, 1667–78

The war limped to an inglorious end after the successful Dutch raid up the Thames in June 1667 forced Charles to sue for peace. Defeat at the hands of the Dutch, in conjunction with domestic problems throughout Britain, precipitated a major change in the political landscape. Ministers fell in all three kingdoms, but the principal casualty was Clarendon who was forced into exile in 1667. Charles now took more interest in business, entrusting power to a team of ministers who attracted the acronym Cabal after the names or titles of its principal members, one of whom was Lauderdale. Clarendon's fall was popular in Scotland, and Lauderdale now enjoyed an unimpeded monopoly of Scottish business at court. No English ministers intruded on Scottish affairs, and Lauderdale's personal ambition was matched by his patriotism in keeping them at a distance. By contrast his own influence on British policies and at court grew. Lauderdale succeeded in blaming the Pentland rising on Rothes and Sharp's mishandling of the presbyterian problem. Rothes was demoted to the largely honorary chancellorship in exchange for the treasury which was placed in commission. He too was stripped of his military commands when an investigation into corruption and incompetence persuaded the king to disband the army. Sharp was bullied into compliant acceptance of the indulgence and the royal supremacy of 1669. Freed of rivals, Lauderdale became commissioner in 1669, and employed a succession of dispensable lieutenants. Thus in 1671 John Hay, the second earl of Tweedale, a presbyterian sympathiser, was dropped in order to enforce harsher measures against conventicles, and as a result of a disagreement with Lauderdale over the management of the customs farm.

Lauderdale brought a powerful Scottish voice to the conduct of foreign policy, and after the fall of Clarendon he became a member of the committee of foreign affairs which formed a cabinet within the English privy council. He also had a voice on the committees for trade and colonial policy, but found it difficult to influence his English colleagues. Trade languished into the 1670s, hamstrung by the navigation acts, interrupted by the Dutch war, and hurt by the new French tariffs of 1667. However, Lauderdale secured a victory for the cattle trade, lobbying for the Irish cattle bill which passed through the English parliament in January 1667 and reduced competition from Ireland. He also persuaded Charles to use his prerogative to lift the duty on Scottish cattle imports in England in 1669. The trade flourished, bringing much needed profits to Scotish landowners, and attracting foreign investment from the likes of the earl of Shaftesbury. A depression in 1667 persuaded Tweedale to secure court backing for discussions on an Anglo-Scottish commercial treaty in 1668, but there was open opposition to the idea in the 1669 session of the Scottish parliament. In England protectionist interests, especially in the north-east, were heightened by demands from the Scots for a reduction on import tariffs on their goods and exclusion from the navigation acts. Government ministers in both kingdoms supported commercial union, seeing an expansion of trade as a means to increase crown revenue through rising customs receipts. However, the talks collapsed due to lack of interest in

England and suspicion in Scotland. Lauderdale and the king switched the emphasis of the negotiations to political union, believing the Scots could be persuaded that the benefits of free trade would offset any loss of sovereignty, and that the crown would gain a solid phalanx of Scottish votes in a British parliament. In fact neither side was interested in union. Charles and Lauderdale kept the process going until 1670, using it as a smokescreen to secret dealings with Louis XIV who was seeking to end French isolation.

War with either France or the United Provinces was undesireable for Scotland. Lauderdale was privy to the secret treaty by which Charles agreed to join in a French assault on the Dutch in return for a subsidy (although he knew nothing of the secret clause in which Charles bound himself to declare his conversion to catholicism), and he was the most vociferous advocate of the surprise attack on the Dutch in 1672. The Scottish contribution to the war again was meagre, and economic hardship was less severe than in the previous conflict. Yet criticism in parliament of war profiteering by monopolist courtiers forced Lauderdale to offer concessions. In England, where the government was bankrupt even at the outset of the war, the outcry against its conduct was louder. With the French army bogged down in Flanders, a quick, decisive victory proved impossible, and Charles made a separate peace in 1675. Under pressure from the English parliament he agreed a treaty with the Dutch in 1677, the new relationship being sealed by the marriage of William of Orange to James's eldest daughter, Princess Mary. The marriage was popular in Scotland, but Charles continued to have underhand dealings with the French, and only the earl of Danby, the king's chief English minister from 1673, and Lauderdale knew of yet another secret agreement with Louis in February 1676.

Royal religious policy was equally erratic. Charles' hopes of turning non-conformists into loyal subjects dependent on the prerogative power of the crown to grant toleration was advanced throughout Britain by a stop-go policy of repression and conciliation. In the summer of 1667 the government began reducing the size of the army, replacing it with the militia. An offer of an amnesty to the great majority of those involved in the Pentland rising indicated that the government felt in no way threatened by the covenanting remnant, and by 1669 Lauderdale and Tweedale were confident enough to initiate a policy of indulgence. Their strategy was to isolate the radical covenanters and regulate the majority of dissenters within the church by allowing deprived ministers to return to their pulpits after making a limited submission. The campaign had a disappointing impact, persuading only forty-two ministers to conform, and it met with a storm of protest both from covenanters and from the hawkish Archbishop Burnet. Burnet and Sharp were furious at the 1669 act of supremacy which made explicit the king's absolute control of the church, but while Sharp kept his head down, Burnet was sacked for protesting. The church's vulnerability to crown pressure was in contrast to England where Sheldon and the anglican vote in parliament formed an obstacle to Charles's religious policy, particularly as toleration was perceived as an attack on statute law. Charles gave limited protection to English dissenters after the lapse of the first conventicling act in 1668, but passed more severe legislation in 1670 to ensure the English parliament's co-operation over finance. In Scotland, Burnet's *de facto* replacement was Robert Leighton (he did not accept office until 1672) who was equally opposed to toleration, but tried to promote the comprehension of the presbyterians within a moderate episcopal structure. However, the overt erastianism to which the bishops were subjected in 1669 fatally damaged whatever credibility they had acquired, and the effect of the first indulgence was to create a presbyterian fifth column within the church. Leighton's efforts at accommodation failed by 1671, although he struggled on for another three years before resigning. The tough measures Lauderdale reluctantly introduced in 1670, including the clanking act which made preaching at conventicles a capital offence, also failed in their intention of encouraging the accommodation process, or in driving a wedge between the ministers and their landed supporters who bore the brunt of the fines.

Once again it was war which exacerbated domestic tensions. As a perparation to war Charles tried to win over non-conformist support, and a second declaration of indulgence was issued in England in March 1672. In Scotland a second indulgence was issued six months later, and as a result the number of conforming ministers increased to 136. Unfortunately for the king a hardened minority of clergy remained outside the law, and these now were being reinforced by a new generation of presbyterian leaders. These dissident clergy attracted substantial followings, particularly in the south-west. In England the indulgence achieved the opposite of what was intended, and was interpreted as an extension of the prerogative both by critics and by supporters like Lauderdale. Fears that toleration would not only allow the king to suspend the law, but was part of a popish plot, intensified the clash with parliament and threatened to bring the war to a standstill. The British dimension of the growing rift was highlighted when the row between the crown and the English parliament was exploited by the Irish protestant lobby to whip up anti-catholic feeling. Lauderdale pressed Charles to make peace, arguing that control over religion and the preservation of the suspending power in England was too high a price to pay for a successful foreign policy. Instead in March 1673 the king withdrew the indulgence in a humiliating climb-down. The anglican backlash which followed resulted in the imposition of a test act in England which restricted the king's choice of ministers, and exposed James, duke of York as a practising catholic.

In Scotland opposition to Lauderdale (now a duke) in parliament was not new, and surfaced ineffectively in 1669, 1670 and 1672. However, in November 1673 Hamilton and Tweedale, now an opponent of Lauderdale, held up business in order to compel the king to listen to Scottish grievances, most importantly complaints about the duties on malt, brandy and tobacco. Hamilton and his 'party' were acting as a focus for opposition which embraced moderate religious dissent, economic discontent, and political rivalry which centred on Lauderdale's monopoly of patronage. Ostensibly they favoured more toleration and pressed for a national synod to discuss the church. Lauderdale also found himself under attack in England at the beginning of 1674 from his recent colleague, Anthony Ashley Cooper, first earl of Shaftesbury, who joined forces with Hamilton. However, while English ministers either were toppled or eclipsed by the new treasurer, Thomas Osborne, first earl of Danby, Charles and Archbishop Sheldon gave their backing to Lauderdale. The latter not only survived, but was granted an English earldom and thereafter was able to sit in the House of Lords and enjoy immunity. More significantly, the Scottish privy council was purged of opponents, and parliament was dissolved. However, since 1667 when provisions for raising Scottish militia for service anywhere in Britain had first been made, English members of parliament had feared Lauderdale was using Scotland as an absolutist testing ground. In 1675, the House of Commons returned to the attack while Hamilton maintained the pressure in Scotland. Charles continued to show complete confidence in Lauderdale, but the secretary now was on the defensive.

The arrival of Danby at the head of a government dependent on anglican support was parallelled in Scotland by Lauderdale's growing reliance on the bishops. Just as the policy of indulgence caused an anglican reaction in England, Rothes, Burnet and even Sharp blamed the indulgence in Scotland for the widespread conventicling, the attacks on orthodox ministers, and the non-observance of the king's birthday. Lauderdale, like Danby, therefore set out to silence critics by applying repressive measures, thus feeding his enemies with evidence of absolutist policies. In 1674 troops were deployed in the south-west, and the replacement of Leighton as archbishop of Glasgow with Burnet ensured a tougher approach to dissent by the church. Yet in spite of the harsh treatment, there was every sign that conventicles were growing larger and spreading beyond the south-west – Fife had particularly large conventicles – and were more willing to take up arms. Also, the underground church was better organised, partly as a consequence of the government's encouragement of unofficial meetings of dissenting clergy to discuss its accomodation proposals. The limits of the state's authority were exposed by the shortage of troops to police the trouble spots, and the militia's lack of enthusiasm for the job. Many local landowners were sympathetic to the covenanters, especially in Ayrshire and Clydesdale where, in October 1677, the nobility refused to implement the law. Equally dangerous was the growing discontent with the crown's arbitrary policies among those noblemen gathered around Hamilton. Ironically, the purge of Hamilton and his allies from the council made it easier for them to oppose the secretary. Lauderdale now found himself the hostage of the English bishops whose support he needed to hold off impeachment in Westminster, and of Sharp and Burnet who were setting the pace of repression in Scotland. With no room to manouevre on toleration, tentative moves towards another indulgence collapsed.

By 1678 the crown faced the disintegration of its local control. In the highlands government influence was minimal due to the predatory private wars of noblemen like Archibald Campbell, the ninth earl of Argyll and John Campbell of Glenorchy who exploited their control of independent highland companies. While the highlands could be ignored (both Argyll and Glenorchy were Lauderdale's clients), the collapse of control in the south-west was dangerous. The government deployed Irish troops on the Ulster coast, strengthened defences in the north of England, and ordered the quartering of the militia on the region in January 1678. Troop levels had risen steadily since 1673, but the quartering of the 'highland host', a militia force of 8,000 men drawn primarily from the southern and central highlands (a third were lowlanders) was a provocative means of crushing dissent, and of exposing Hamilton's inability to protect his clients. However, the brutal behaviour of the militia was easy propaganda for Hamilton and his friends, who now included James Scott, the duke of Monmouth, the king's illegitimate son and something of a champion among English non-conformists. Another attack was launched on Lauderdale in London as part of a wider onslaught on the ministry's handling of foreign policy. While Lauderdale survived accusations that he was preparing an army for use in England – Danby does appear to have been preparing a contingency military force in England – Hamilton had at last dented the king's confidence in his secretary. Far more importantly, the volatile situation in Scotland was beyond the control of London or Edinburgh, and events in the localities were developing their own momentum.

The Limits of Absolutism, 1678–88

The growing identity of interests between the crown's critics in Scotland and England threatened a British crisis in 1679. The emergence in England of an increasingly plausible popish plot over the summer of 1678, and the damaging revelations by Ralph Montagu in December of the king's secret dealings with France led parliament to pass a test act and begin impeachment proceedings against Danby before Charles dissolved the cavalier parliament. The subsequent election of a whig House of Commons in February 1679, and its passing of a bill to exclude James, duke of York from the throne provided the background to the outbreak of rebellion in Scotland at the beginning of the summer. It seems unlikely that the militant activity of the covenanters was unaffected by events in England, especially the popish plot. Sporadic guerrilla activity in covenanting regions was followed on 3 May 1679 by the assassination of Archbishop Sharp outside St Andrews, and the *Rutherglen Declaration* denouncing the successive betrayal of the covenants since 1648. Mutual recriminations between Lauderdale and Hamilton over the merits of toleration, and further attacks on the former by Shaftesbury in the English parliament increased the sense of a government under siege and out of touch. The spark which ignited the rebellion was the defeat of John Graham of Claverhouse's dragoons in a botched attack on a very large, armed conventicle at Drumclog on 1 June. As in 1666, however, the lack of aristocratic leadership, and the usual division between radicals and more moderate covenanters who hoped their demonstration of strength would convince the king of the need to compromise, lost the rebels their initiative. English troops were mustered, and it was an Anglo-Scottish army commanded by Monmouth, ally of Hamilton and Shaftesbury, which routed the rebels at Bothwell Brig on 22 June, killing between 200–400 of them. A small number of executions and transportations followed, but Monmouth had no desire to be seen as a persecutor of non-conformists in Scotland, and the subsequent repression was mild. Lauderdale hung on to preside over a third indulgence which legalised privy kirks and pardoned most of the rebels, but the programme was that of Hamilton and Monmouth.

The relative ease with which Charles II defeated the coven-anters in 1679 was possible because, in contrast to the events of 1637, popular anger was not fused with aristocratic dissent. Furthermore, the privy council in Edinburgh acted swiftly and had force available at its command. Yet the rebellion exposed the crown's inability to command consent throughout a large region of the country. In British terms the crushing of revolt in Scotland was fatal to the English whigs – a derisory term for Scottish rebels – on whom Charles now concentrated without fear of a war in the north. Ireland was under control, in England the king had the support of the tories, he was well served by competent ministers, and he had a small, reliable army. Nevertheless, fear that the popular Monmouth might return in triumph to London where Shaftesbury and the whigs controlled both the city and the House of Commons, and were pressing hard for exclusion, persuaded Charles to dissolve the English parliament. The second 'exclusion parliament' proved as difficult as the previous parliament when it met in October 1680, but the king's control of the House of Lords, and the whigs' unwillingness to compromise, allowed Charles to dissolve parliament again, claiming that Shaftesbury and his friends threatened the constitution.

Certainly the actions of the whigs threatened the regal union, as they had given no thought to the implications of exclusion for the united monarchy. Had the exclusion bill passed both houses of parliament, James still would have inherited the Scottish crown. There were echoes here of 1649, with the prospect of a war to place a Scottish king on the English throne. In contrast to England, there was no support for exclusion in Scotland, but the *Sanquhar Declaration* of June 1680 by a remnant of radical covenanters led by Richard

Cameron, a thirty-two year old former school-master who had been ordained in Holland, was a declaration of war on the state. Unlike the English whigs, the cameronians took up arms against the crown, but their apocalyptic ideology was viewed as extremist, and their ruthless repression raised no objections among the political elite. The cameronians were defeated in a skirmish at Aird's Moss on 22 July 1680 when Cameron himself was killed, the remaining leaders being rounded up and executed in the following year. Only now did the crown begin to detach the radicals from the bulk of the presbyterian population. Defeat for the king's enemies in England took the form of a royalist coup in the spring of 1681. The whigs were purged from the privy council, household and local government, before the third 'exclusion parliament' was dissolved in March at Oxford. Deprived of their parliamentary platform, Shaftesbury and his allies knew the king was too powerful to risk appealing to the country.

The tory reaction in England left Charles to govern for the remainder of his reign without a parliament and with little freedom to conduct an active foreign policy – the price of Louis XIV's pension. However, peace suited him, and adequate funds were forthcoming due to the earl of Rochester's financial management and the increase in trade. The rout of the whigs was followed in 1683 by the Rye House plot which was manipulated by the crown to give Charles an excuse to execute whig leaders who now were branded as revolutionaries. In Scotland too repression was stepped up. In August 1681 the Scottish parliament gave its backing to a brutal campaign to crush the last remnants of dissent, declared James heir to the throne, and passed a test act demanding recognition of the king as head of the church. The test act allowed the government to root out covenanting sympathisers in public office, but its effect was to drive another fifty ministers from the church, predominantly in Lothian, and to recreate a broader dissident opposition rallying behind the defence of protestantism. The 'Killing Times' of the next few years saw the army unleashed on the covenanters, and by 1683 summary executions were carried out on anyone denying the royal supremacy. In addition to the hundred or so victims who were killed, violent bullying, imprisonment, maiming, torture, transportation, billetting, heavy fines, and restrictions on movement were ruthlessly employed against those who rejected the royal supremacy and its prelatical agents. In 1684 the surviving cameronians renounced their allegiance to the king in the *Apologetical Declaration* of James Renwick, another young radical (he was twenty-two) recently returned from Holland, but this dwindling remnant of diehards was separated from the mainstream presbyterian population. However, the crown's victims were not confined to tenant farmers in the west of Scotland. The test act resulted in the flight to Holland in 1681 of Lord President Stair, and of Argyll who had been condemned to death for opposing the oath and was later implicated in the Rye House plotting.

James's enforced residence in Scotland throughout much of 1679–82 not only marked the beginning of more sustained persecution, but heralded a new self confidence in the country. The duke of Albany (James's Scottish title) was enormously popular with the aristocracy who flocked to Edinburgh where a Stewart once again held court amidst a minor artistic renaissance. The rebuilding of much of Holyrood, the commissioning of the Stewart portraits, and the revival of the Order of the Thistle indicated a renewal of crown interest in Scotland and a desire to impose an image of authority rooted firmly in the past. The royalist mood was caught by Sir George Mackenzie of Roeshaugh, who published *Jus Regium* in 1684, advocating absolute monarchy, and two years later went into print in defence of Scotland's mythical kings. Peace in Europe and a run of good harvests heralded an upturn in the economy, benefitting the crown through increased customs and providing the cash to pay pensions and salaries. When he became king in 1685 James was provided with an adequate income by the English parliament, and he proved a good manager of his finances, but the Scottish parliament also granted him the excise for the duration of his reign. It was not only the crown that gained from rising prosperity. By the 1670s the nobility had recovered their confidence, mortgages were being cleared, estate consolidation and improvement was more common, and they indulged in a new level of consumer purchasing and building, epitomised in Sir William Bruce's elegant country house at Kinross. The court in Edinburgh acted as the focus for the patriotic aspirations of a self-assured and wealthy aristocracy. The urban oligarchies too were growing in confidence, and Walter Gibson, the wealthy provost of Glasgow also had Bruce build him a house on his country estate.

Economic recovery owed little to crown policies, but the early 1680s saw government addressing the strategic problems of the economy for the first time since 1668–9. On the whole protectionist policies worked, allowing Scottish salt producers to dominate the home market, but a commercial crisis in 1681 sparked off a new round of protectionist legislation, inviting retaliatory measures from English competitors which damaged the textile industry. The establishment of a committee of trade marked a more imaginative course, and it is perhaps no accident that plans for a Scottish colonial policy were first mooted in 1681 when James, who was an active promoter and investor in colonial schemes, was influential in Scotland. However, the progressive economic ideas of which James approved had another use, and a successful trade policy was linked to the idea of religious toleration. The model here was the Netherlands, and the English declarations of indulgence in 1672, 1687 and 1688 all were justified partly on these grounds. James exploited this idea in Scotland in 1686 by offering parliament free trade with England in return for catholic toleration. Parliament spurned the offer, reminded the king of his duty to secure the protestant religion, and was dissolved for its independent stance. Religion remained more important than trade, and the protestants had their own apologist in Gilbert Burnet whose *Secret Letters*, published in Amsterdam in 1687, argued that it was protestantism, not toleration, which created prosperity. However, once freed of dependence on the English tory landed vote in 1687, the underlying economic policy of James's reign was imperial. An absolutist crown funded by expanding trade required the English commercial sector to become more efficient and ruthlessly competitive, subordinating the interests of Ireland and Scotland to its own markets.

James's experience in Scotland allowed him to create a reversionary interest, a process aided by Lauderdale's failing health and retreat into honourable retirement and death in 1682, and by the more unexpected death in 1681 of the secretary's old rival, Rothes. Hamilton's satisfaction with court patronage and honours alleviated another potential problem. James opened up the privy council to a new generation of politicians with episcopalian and royalist credentials: men like William Douglas, third earl of Queensberry, who became treasurer in 1681; Sir George Gordon of Haddo who was created earl of Aberdeen and appointed chancellor in 1682; James Drummond, fourth earl of Perth, who replaced Aberdeen as chancellor in 1684, and his brother, John Drummond, who acquired the secretaryship in the same year. James also changed government policy in the highlands, encouraging a more conciliatory approach which led in 1682 to the establishment of the commission for securing the peace of the highlands. His cultivation of good will among a wider circle of chiefs, and the forfeiture of Argyll in 1681 acquired for James a large highland clientage. He returned to London in 1682, leaving the government in Edinburgh to determine policy by controlling the flow of information to Charles, especially from 1683 when a secret committee of seven leading councillors was formed. Once he became king this streamlining ensured that the vital decision-making was done at court, and even the secret committee was reduced to carrying out orders. Increasingly power was concentrated in the hands of Perth, who travelled between Edinburgh and London, and his brother who was the king's principal advisor on Scottish affairs at court. The two broad factions which emerged straddled all three British ministries; Queensberry, Lawrence Hyde, earl of Rochester, and his brother Henry Hyde, second earl of Clarendon, the lord lieutenant of Ireland, formed an episcopal-anglican grouping, and were opposed by the Drummonds, Robert Spencer, second earl of Sunderland, and Richard Talbot, first earl of Tyrconnel, Clarendon's rival in Ireland. What determined the success of the latter faction was their willingness to comply with James's religious policy.

Over the winter of 1686–7 James closetted tory politicians and clergymen in England, hoping to persuade them to support his policy of catholic toleration. Purges of the English administration, including Rochester and Clarendon, and of the localities encouraged cynical opportunism. The earl of Sunderland's conversion was intended to give him leadership of the court catholics, but he found himself dealing with a king ever more inclined to follow the rash advice of the jesuit Fr. Edward Petre, Tyrconnel and John Drummond, now earl of Melfort. The number of conversions in Scotland was disappointing. Melfort, his brother, Chancellor Perth, and the other secretary, the earl of Moray, all succumbed to the king's persuasions, but the earl of Seaforth was the only magnate to become a catholic. Possibly James could have had more success with the nobility had he not become so dependent on the Drummonds, and in 1689 James was to pay dearly for neglecting the territorial magnates, none of whom rallied to his support. Even the leading catholic in the kingdom, George Gordon, first duke of Gordon, was ignored. However, there was a steady supply of pragmatists who served James irrespective of religion, including the earl of Breadalbane (formerly Glenorchy), Sir George Mackenzie, Viscount Tarbat, and Sir John Dalrymple, son of the exiled lord president. Opposition came from Queensberry, who was blamed for parliament's refusal to grant toleration, from Alexander Cairncross, archbishop of Glasgow, and from the royalist Sir George Mackenzie of Rosehaugh who all were dismissed. Hamilton cautiously reasserted his earlier leadership of political dissidents, refusing to sign the dutiful reply from the privy council in 1686. However, in spite of accusations that Queensberry encouraged the riot against the mass in Edinburgh in January 1686 there was little if any contact between the restrained opposition of the politicians and popular discontent.

When James VII succeeded his brother in February 1685, the crown's apparent dominance rested on an alliance in England with the anglican church and its tory supporters, and in

Scotland with a broad spectrum of conservative, protestant noblemen who saw the monarchy as the bulwark against chaos and revolution. But in both kingdoms, especially in Scotland, there remained a powerful body of dissent against the crown's religious policies and its authoritarian rule. In 1685 opposition in all three kingdoms was dispirited, the royal prerogative was riding high, the army though small was reliable, and the localities were quiescent. When the accession of this catholic monarch was tested in the early summer by simultaneous risings under Argyll in his own territory and Monmouth in the English south-west, the result was an overwhelming defeat for the rebels. Argyll's power had never recovered fully from his father's execution; his flight in 1681 allowed the crown to break Campbell dominance of the region, and his own leadership was inept. The presbyterians of the south-west had been cowed by the military, the political elite had no appetite for civil war, and the government reacted efficiently, rounding up suspects, crushing the rebels, and capturing and speedily executing Argyll on the basis of his previous conviction. However, the campaign of 1686 initiated a renewed round of violence in highland politics which grew into a regional war lasting intermittantly until 1692. Monmouth's rebellion also ended with his execution and the bloody repression of his followers. The king now retained an enlarged army, almost double its former peace-time size, while allowing the politically unreliable militia to decay. He confidently pursued religious toleration as a smokescreen to leading Britain back towards catholicism, and in November 1685, a month after Louis XIV initiated persecution of protestant huguenots in France, James used the English crown's controversial dispensing powers to promote catholics in public office, especially in the army where there were a hundred catholic officers. Immediately, this led to a crucial breach with the tories and the anglican church. Meanwhile, in Ireland, the militantly catholic Tyrconnel pressed ahead with the catholic remodelling of the army. In the spring of 1686, after an intense campaign of management and propaganda which served only to heighten protestant suspicions, James asked the Scottish parliament to remove the civil disabilities imposed on the kingdom's 2,000 catholics. New doubts about the king's religious intentions were raised publicly, leading to the dissolution of parliament, and rioting in Edinburgh. Toleration by statute having been blocked, James decided to proceed with the appointment of catholics to office, and placed the army in Scotland under the command of the catholic earl of Dumbarton.

James's frustration at the speed of his catholicising programme and the growing opposition from the English tories led to a dramatic *volte face*. Following the dissolution of the English parliament in the summer of 1687, the king turned to the whigs and the dissenters to support toleration. Such an alliance had the added benefit of fulfilling Charles's old ambition of freeing the crown from dependence on the anglican church, but James over-estimated the numerical strength of dissent, and failed to appreciate the degree of protestant unity against catholicism. In Scotland parliament equally was opposed to toleration, and even the lords of the articles resisted the idea of limited freedom of worship in people's homes. A muted form of toleration, excluding presbyterians, was granted by prerogative authority in 1686, and after pressure from Hamilton and other privy councillors, universally in the summer of 1687. At a stroke James cut the ground from under the feet of the Scottish bishops who had no tory party to support them. Unlike in England where seven bishops refused to read out the king's declaration defending his toleration policy and won a victory in the courts in June 1688, the Scottish bishops were paralysed into docile inactivity. Their enemies came out of hiding or returned from exile, many conforming ministers and parishioners declared a preference for the presbyterianism they had nursed covertly for years, and in the west the established church fell apart. Not unexpectedly, James was given little credit for this new freedom as the presbyterians were implacably hostile to the king's catholicism. Nor did the execution of covenanting renegades like James Renwick early in 1688 help the king's reputation. The government's slender control in many localities survived only because of a military presence, or the kind of intrusive bullying which imposed Claverhouse as provost of Dundee.

In many localities control collapsed altogether, with even the episcopalian nobility alienated. The birth of a catholic heir on 10 June produced less of a reaction than in England, but the country was stumbling towards revolution even before William of Orange intervened in England.

7

SCOTLAND AND THE BRITISH REVOLUTION, 1688–1715

The Revolution Settlement, 1688–97

Revolution in Britain was not a peaceful event tidily packed away before the spring of 1689. It was a violent affair which began with a military invasion of England in 1688 and ended with the jacobite rebellion of 1715. Only then was the rejection of the Stewart dynasty irrevocable. The man who made revolution possible, William of Orange, was the son of Charles I's daughter Mary, and was married to James VII's eldest daughter, another Mary. With these dynastic credentials, and with his calvinist faith and hostility to Louis XIV, William was a natural focus for a reversionary interest in Britain. The prickly relationship William had with James before 1685 was exacerbated by the Monmouth and Argyll rebellions, launched unofficially from Holland, and by the protection William granted to British exiles, including a number of Scots. By 1686 William was an active participant in British politics, motivated by James's pro-French foreign policy at a time when the Dutch were rearming in preparation for an expected clash with Louis XIV, suspicions over the direction of the king's catholicising policies, and by a desire to ensure that James did not ignite revolution and lose Mary's inheritance. William decided to invade for reasons which were diplomatic, dynastic and religious, probably in that order, and he had the backing of the Dutch public who believed James would join France in an attack similar to that of 1672. A successful invasion would bring Britain into the war against France, or at least prevent the Franco-British alliance against the Dutch, secure the succession for Mary (both William and Mary accepted the story of the warming pan baby fabricated to discredit James's new heir), and halt James's catholicising programme. Scotland played little part in William's strategic thinking, although Scottish exiles at his court like Gilbert Burnet and William Carstairs had a disproportianate influence, and much of the plotting was done through the less effectively policed Scottish ports. The assumption was that if England fell, Scotland and Ireland would follow.

England fell remarkably easily considering the strategic difficulties involved in making a seasonally late seaborne invasion of a country with a powerful fleet and army. William siezed his opportunity before the Dutch politicians changed their minds, and while the French were entangled on the Rhine where Louis launched a September offensive, believing it was too late in the year for the Dutch to invade England. Also, the longer William waited the more likely it was that James's heir would be accepted and his political retreat would placate the tories. In the end William was lucky. Favourable winds carried his fleet to Torbay in Devon where the 14,000 invasion force was landed on 5 November, and the same winds prevented the English fleet from leaving port to intercept. James, who never had believed in the Dutch threat, panicked and oscillated between paralysis and frantic activity. The desertion of significant supporters, including his daughter Princess Anne, adverse and effective propaganda, the orchestrated disintegration of the royal officer corps, and the siezure of regional centres by William's supporters, combined to allow the Dutch army to achieve an easy conquest of England. James himself fled to France on 23 December. As in 1658–60 Scottish politicians found themselves reacting to events in England, and there is no doubt that the crucial struggle for control of Britain was won there by William in November–December 1688. However, the failure to secure both Scotland and Ireland with the same ease involved William in an unwelcome and protracted civil war in Britain until 1692.

Chancellor Perth fled Edinburgh on 10 December, anti-catholic rioting broke out in the city that evening, and the government fell apart as officers of state and privy councillors did nothing, or scurried off to London to court their new master. The moderate John Murray, first marquis of Atholl made a half-hearted effort at shoring up James's collapsing cause by endeavouring to persuade the king to abandon his catholic programme. But it was too late, and radical presbyterians like the earls of Glencairn and Crawford and Sir James Montgomery of Skelmorlie assumed control. In London, Scottish noblemen asked William to accept responsibility for the government until the estates could meet, while Hamilton saw his opportunity to act as the self-appointed leader of the revolution. In the Scottish localities the king's cause already was lost. Royal control had collapsed in the highlands, governmenttroopshavingbeendefeatedinLochaberinAugust1688. The granting of toleration to presbyterians and the withdrawel south of all 3,000 troops weakened the crown's hold over much of the lowlands. Action by companies of aristocratically led volunteers, the organisation and rhetoric of the presbyterian clergy, and the threat of the mob ensured that before the end of a harsh winter most of southern Scotland, and all the towns, was in the hands of William's supporters.

The English convention parliament which sat in the winter of 1688–9 decided that James had deserted the English crown, which fell jointly to William and Mary (William insisted on nothing less than joint sovereignty with his wife). Here, the revolution was fudged to ensure tory support and to placate William, whose powers as king were left largely intact, although it was the crown-in-parliament in which authority was vested. The convention of the estates which met at Edinburgh on 14 March 1689 faced neither the menacing presence of William's troops nor the organised power of the anglican church. However, the evasion of inconvenient laws, like the 1681 test act, and the limited but effective violence and intimidation which afflicted the elections indicated how opposition to William's cause would be treated. Ultimately, the politicking within the convention was secondary to events in England and the struggle in the localities. Whig magnates like Hamilton and their militant presbyterian supporters would have had no qualms about inviting Dutch troops to quell any counter revolutionary movement. Yet there was a strong desire to avoid civil war and a repetition of the 1640s and 1650s. The hesitancy and self preservation of jacobites like Atholl, the caution of the episcopalians who believed they could preserve their church under William, and James's own political ineptitude in sending the convention a letter demanding unconditional obedience, removed any possibility of a jacobite resurgence. William's supporters carried the day and the most stubborn jacobite leader, James Graham of Claverhouse, now Viscount Dundee, rode north to plan a futile military resistance and stir up a war no-one wanted. By 27 March the Williamites had elected a committee of estates, a provisional executive, composed of their own party, and on 4 April the convention declared the crown forfeit by a massive majority, only five obdurate peers voting against. William and Mary were proclaimed joint sovereigns a week later.

Sympathy for James lingered on, not only among convinced jacobites, but also among episcopalians who disapproved of the resistance ideas which underpinned the revolution. However, James's reputation, and his zealous catholicism made it difficult to support him. Positive support was forthcoming in Ireland, where the native catholic population and Tyrconnel's government remained loyal. But the most immediate challenge to the new regime came from the central highlands of Scotland, where Dundee assembled a makeshift rebel army of clansmen motivated by genuine sympathy for James, fear of the restored house of Argyll, the desire for plunder, and desperation driven by poverty and hunger. Dundee's rising was never more than an irritant to the government in Edinburgh, far less to William in London, and the most he could hope to achieve was to delay the arrival of Schomberg's army in Ireland. Even if Dundee had not been killed at the jacobites' surprising victory over General Hugh Mackay at Killiecrankie on 27 July 1689, James was not going to be restored to his British thrones by an army of 2,000 highland irregulars and bandits. On 21 August the highland threat was broken in the defence of Dunkeld by the presbyterian Cameronian regiment. The last remnants of defiance were mopped up at Cromdale on 1 May 1690.

Elsewhere William's cause faltered and Britain faced defeat at the hands of the French. Ireland appeared lost when in March 1689 James reluctantly landed there with a small French expeditionary force. In spite of the propaganda disadvantages of relying on Irish catholics for support, Ireland was a better base to rally James's cause than Scotland, and Melfort was right to resist Dundee's extravagant claims for mounting an offensive from the Scottish highlands. James took command of the huge, under-equipped and disorganised army which rallied behind him and the cause of Irish catholicism, but his failure to take Londonderry proved costly. Without more time and greater French help, James was unable to avoid the crushing defeat William inflicted on him at the Battle of the Boyne on 1 July 1690. Coming in the midst of defeats at sea and on the continent, the victories in Ireland and Scotland were little compensation to William whose priorities lay in Europe. However, the French army was reluctant to risk a Channel crossing in spite of the control their fleet exercised until its defeat by the English at La Hogue in May 1692. Thereafter Britain was secure from French invasion, but victory in Britain proved easier for William than success in Europe where he lost every battle until the retaking of Namur in 1695. English and Scottish reluctance to participate in their king's ambition to curb Louis XIV's power was expressed annually in the squabble over supply for the war, and by 1696 William faced bankruptcy. The assassination plot of 1696 also emphasised just how precarious the regime remained. But France too was exhausted, and the peace negotiated in the treaty of Rijswijk in 1697 recognised a European balance of power which temporarily contained France. In addition, Louis recognised William as king of Great Britain, promising not to aid James who was now gripped by his own fatalism and dominated by catholic extremists who urged him not to compromise.

The high level of British military commitment in Europe, and the determination of even whig magnates to preserve their private authority prevented William from subjecting the highlands to the same military conquest as Ireland. Instead the government constructed Fort William, but lacked the troops to police the region, and the highlands remained unstable and militarily threatening. Factionalism within the government led Sir John Dalrymple, the secretary, to set himself the task of crushing jacobite dissent in the highlands. A deal agreed at Achallader in the summer of 1691 by Breadalbane and the chiefs gave the clans ample opportunity to recognise William as king by the end of the year. The failure of Alastair McIan to meet the deadline allowed Dalrymple, with William's approval, to order a punitive operation against the MacDonalds of Glencoe. The massacre of Glencoe on 13 February 1692 brought an interlude to the British dynastic war, and was by contemporary standards a minor example of state terrorism – thirty-eight people were killed – but it was blown out of all proportion by ambitious politicians. The orchestrated outcry resulted in the government avoiding further intervention in the region, benefitted jacobite recruiting agents, and in the longer term Glencoe postponed a resolution of the dynastic struggle until 1715.

There was speculation in 1689 that a closer union with England would stabilise the revolutions in both England and Scotland. The onslaught of a trade recession also encouraged the Scots to name commissioners to discuss the issue, but the English were uninterested, and the embarrassed Scots dropped the matter. The constitutional and ecclesiastical settlements in both kingdoms therefore were distinct. In the interests of unity Scottish politicians played down political ideas, but the decision of the convention of estates to forfeit James was an unqualified rejection of divine right monarchy, and a revolutionary whig-presbyterian ideology, embracing contractual and limited monarchy, pervaded the settlement. In future, catholics would be excluded from the throne or from public office, statute law would prevail over the royal prerogative, taxation could only be granted by parliament which was to meet more regularly and conduct its business in freedom, prelacy was condemned, and the use of torture restricted. Here the succession was subordinated to parliament, and government to the rule of law. The attack on the bishops reflected presbyterian influence both inside and outside the convention, but the use of the episcopate by successive arbitrary regimes made the removal of bishops a constitutional and not only an ecclesiastical issue. The Claim of Right was accepted on 11 April 1689 and two days later the Articles of Grievance were passed by the convention, regulating in more detail the rights of parliament in relation to the crown. On 11 May William and Mary took the coronation oath on the implicit understanding that the crown was offered conditionally.

Political insecurity and the European war ensured that William agreed to an unsatisfactory constitutional and religious settlement in the summer of 1690. Failure to create an adequate court party during the 1689 and 1690 parliamentary sessions made ministers vulnerable to the determined opposition of the reformist club. This predominantly presbyterian group of seventy members of parliament, led by Sir James Montgomery of Skelmorlie forced the government to assent to their legislative programme in return for supply. The most important reform was the abolition of the committee of the articles, which freed parliament from overt crown management, leaving William's ministers to construct a court majority with inadequate patronage and from constantly shifting factions. The loss of the bishops also reduced the size of the crown vote. William's ministers struggled not only to manage parliament, but to ensure that the Scottish parliament, freed of ministerial dominance, would co-operate with that in England. The result was at best a patchy level of management which endured until 1702.

As a Dutch calvinist, dependent on presbyterian advisors, William was sympathetic towards the presbyterians and was predisposed to a level of religious toleration. However, he appreciated the value of bishops to the executive arm of government, he wanted to preserve a degree of uniformity in the British churches, and the majority of the Scottish nobility were episcopalian inclined. Yet while William moved reluctantly from attempting to bolster the faltering episcopalian cause to support for moderate presbyterianism, the politicians and clergy ignored his views. Episcopalian hopes of toleration were dashed when at the convention in the spring of 1689 the bishops and the royal supremacy were attacked and episcopacy was declared a grievance by 106 votes to 32. The bishops' close dependence on King James, and their adherence to non-resistance left them to be ground between James's indefensible catholicism and the presbyterians. South of the Tay, the presbyterians had siezed control of a majority of parishes, physically driving out ministers associated with the repressive activities of the episcopal church. In Edinburgh presbytery, twenty-five of the twenty-six ministers were expelled, and by the end of 1689 one hundred and fifty-two ministers were deprived by the commission of the general assembly (sixteen were reinstated by the privy council). In spite of the king's opposition to persecution, aristocracratic preference for episcopacy, and a rearguard action by episcopalian politicians and their English allies, the establishment of some form of presbyterian church appeared increasingly likely. It was the dependence on presbyterian votes in parliament which resulted in a more radical settlement than expected. Episcopacy was abolished in parliament in July 1689, and in the following spring the act of supremacy was swept away and the surviving covenanting ministers who had been ousted in 1662 were restored to their parishes. Finally, in response to difficulties in getting supply from parliament, Commissioner Melville conceded on 7 June 1690 a presbyterian church in return for twenty-eight months cess. William was displeased but had a war to fight. The Westminster Confession of Faith was recognised as the church's doctrinal authority, and the 1592 settlement was established as the model for its government. Clashes with the crown over the assembly's right to meet were resolved in 1694 when the king climbed down, leaving the general assembly to regulate its own affairs. The barrier act of 1697 vested ultimate decision making in the presbyteries rather than the assembly which was susceptible to crown manipulation. Against the will of the king and the nobility, patrons' righ eroded by the act concerning patronages which vested the right to present ministers to vacant charges in the heritors and elders in co-operation with the presbytery.

In Scotland religious toleration was rejected more completely than in England where the tory party was forced to accept a degree of legitimate dissent. Like the king, most clergy and congregations in Scotland probably would have settled for a moderate form of presbytery in which episcopalians were comprehended. However, the equation between presbytery and loyalty to the revolution was drawn, and the privy council colluded in the gerrymandering and bullying which ensured that, when the general assembly met in November 1690, it was dominated by the least compromising of the presbyterian ministers. These sixty elderly men who had been ejected from their parishes in 1662, and the fifty-six ministers they had ordained, formed a solid block of intransigent opinion. Not surprisingly, the two commissions of the general assembly for north and south of the Tay initiated a witch-hunt against ministers who had sympathised with episcopacy in the past, and both the church and the universities were purged in open defiance of the king. This attack on episcopalianism ensured that the partisan bitterness of the pre-1689 years continued after the revolution, giving Scottish jacobites a recruiting ground among the episcopalian nobility and access to the sympathy of the English tories. Crown efforts between 1692–5 to unify the church by test acts designed to allow comprehension within the church had only limited success. Altogether one hundred and sixteen ministers conformed, but this split the episcopalians into a loyal abjuring faction which saw its salvation in opposition through English allies, and a non-abjuring wing which looked to jacobitism for relief. The former encouraged William to imagine a compromise could be effected, but the search for compromise merely prolonged instability. Altogether 664 ministers were dismissed in the following decades, although many of these were protected for years by sympathetic landowners like the earl of Panmure in Angus. The adherence of these ministers to divine right views of monarchy, their influence with the nobility, and the concentration of religious dissent north of the

Tay created a dangerous regional opposition to the revolution which exploded in 1715.

William's involvement in war and diplomacy left little time for Scottish affairs. Personal advice came chiefly from two courtiers, William Bentinck, earl of Portland, his Dutch favourite, and William Carstairs, a presbyterian minister and former exile. The king continued the practice of relying on a Scottish secretary, and a high level of delegation to ministers was necessary for his style of government. Thus the management of parliament, and therefore the crucial voting of money to finance the war effort, was left to ministers. Unlike in England where, from 1694 the triennial act intensified party rivalry, the crown did not have to face elections, and the convention of estates simply evolved into a parliament which sat until 1702. Insofar as he had Scottish policies, William endeavoured to ensure the security of the kingdom and the maintenance of the royal prerogative. He also struggled to avoid becoming the hostage to either the whig-presbyterian interest or the episcopalians, but a balanced ministry eluded him. Ultimately his decisions were shaped by the impact of Scottish politics on the unpopular war and on the English parliament which was of much greater importance to his plans.

The damaging activities of the whiggish club during the parliamentary sessions of 1689 and 1690 demonstrated the danger of party and the need for effective court management. Fortunately for the king the club was compromised fatally by Skelmorlie, whose resentment at not being offered office led him to support the exiled James in return for promises on further constitutional concessions. After 1690 the opposition made no lasting inroads on the power of the executive until 1703. When Melville was accused of corruption in 1690, William took the opportunity to weaken the whig-presbyterian wing of the government, but the 'balanced' ministry which followed was inherently unstable. Internal sniping weakened a government hard-pressed to regain the initiative in parliament. The Glencoe massacre revived the faltering jacobite cause, and the report of the inquiry into the affair in 1695 resulted in a threat by parliament to withhold supply. A further resb---

followed, in which Sir John Dalrymple was a casualty, but the real significance of the ministerial changes was the growing influence of the magnates. The recent deaths of Hamilton and Queensberry, the political restoration of the tenth earl of Argyll, and Atholl's delegation of leadership to Lord John Murray left all four of the most important magnate families in the hands of ambitious younger men with large clientages to satisfy. Since the crown could not provide patronage to create a disciplined court party, it was impossible for any one magnate interest to succeed in monopolising the available patronage, especially when ideological issues clouded the political horizon. The result was an intensification of faction.

The British Problem, 1697–1707

The deterioration in Anglo-Scottish relations after 1698 took place against a background of sustained international tension in Europe. King William knew the peace made at Rijswijk in 1697 would not last, and the secret partition treaties of 1698 and 1699 regulating the fate of the Spanish Empire failed to prevent the anticipated crisis which followed Charles II of Spain's death in 1700. England might have accepted Louis XIV's grandson as heir to the Spanish throne had the French not taken such an aggressive attitude towards the Anglo-Spanish trade. Furthermore, on 6 September 1701 James VII and II died, and Louis provocatively recognised his son, James, as King of Great Britain. War was inevitable, and was declared on France by England and her allies in May 1702. The Scottish privy council followed dutifully but illegally, contravening the 1696 security act by failing to consult parliament. The War of the Spanish Succession started with French successes throughout Europe, and it was not until John Churchill, earl of Marlborough's victory at Blenheim in August 1704 that the tide turned. Nevertheless, the long and costly conflict, which dragged on until 1713 created great political tension within Britain. In England there were differences over whether to fight a land or a naval war with colonial objectives, there were criticisms of the cost, and after 1706 war weariness set in. War also made the English sensitive to their northern frontier, while in Scotland the conflict was perceived as an English war.

European war from 1688 created a massive trade slump, and in 1702 the resurgence of war brought further contraction of markets and a rise in priracy, all of which damaged Scotland's tenuous trade in raw materials. Nor did the English relax their own tight protectionism, and in 1696 further damaging restrictions were imposed on Scottish trade with the colonies. Scotland's trade with her major trading partner, amounting to fifty per cent of the value of the total export trade, was limited to cattle and linen, and while industries like salt and coal thrived in the protected domestic market, Scottish manufacturing remained constrained by a lack of capital and technology. The import of luxury and manufacturing goods easily wiped away the earning power of exports, leaving Scotland with a serious balance of trade deficit and no obvious solution to the problem. The economic situation was exacerbated when dreadful harvests struck for seven successive years from 1692, famine was widespread, prices rose steeply from 1695, and unemployment was rife. Underlying these disasters was the failure of the limited agricultural improvements of the previous four decades to keep pace with a rising population, or to cope yet with sustained adverse weather. Not surprisingly, there was no enthusiasm to pay high taxes to fight a war which had little to do with Scotland. The prosperity of recent years evaporated, landlords ran up spiralling debts, companies collapsed, and in 1704 the new Bank of Scotland (founded in 1695) suspended payments. Jacobites pointed the finger at King William's 'Seven Ill Years', at a nation being punished for its disobedience to their king, and linked economic resentment with episcopalian dissatisfaction. Others blamed the regal union and the subordination of Scottish interests to an English controlled executive and an English dominated foreign policy.

The initiative to kick-start the economy came from the financial and trading sectors of the business community, who were over-impressed by mercantalist ideas and had long lobbied for a colonial policy. However, the Company of Scotland w~

established in 1695 to divert parliament's attention away from Glencoe, to buy burgh votes, and to increase customs revenue. The 1693 trade act and the 1695 charter of the Company of Scotland gave the company a monopoly to trade with Africa, Asia and America with attractive government subsidies to stimulate investment. Interest among London Scots and English investors was high, but was thwarted by the East India Company, whose warring whig and tory shareholders were united by the paranoid exaggeration of the threat from the Scots who in fact lacked the investment or shipping capacity to be serious competitors. The English parliament forbade subscription, and city interests pressurised William to discourage foreign investment. However, the Scots persisted in spite of the difficulties facing them in organising and funding the enterprise. Wounded patriotism ensured that the Company of Scotland assumed an importance beyond the real significance of a trading business in an overwhelmingly rural economy. In 1697 the company directors were persuaded by William Paterson, a financial entrepreneur who had been involved in the founding of both the Bank of England in 1694 and the Bank of Scotland a year later, to back a scheme to establish a trading depot at Darien in Panama. Paterson's plan to transport goods across the isthmus, thus establishing a new trade route between the Pacific and Caribean, was visionary but impracticable. The Scots were incapable of sustaining long-term investment, the enterprise was planned and executed with staggering incompetence, and Darien was Spanish territory. Two attempts to establish the colony between 1698 and 1700 ended in miserable failure with some 2,000 of the colonists losing their lives. More worrying for the Scottish government was the squandering of over £1.8 million, a significant proportion of the nation's liquid capital, much of it invested by aggrieved members of parliament.

In the aftermath of the Darien affair criticism was directed at the king, who had undermined the financial strength of the company, and refused to provide naval support on the grounds that he could not afford to alienate Spain. However, most blame was directed at the English, and in an atmosphere of rising popular Anglophobia and economic panic William's ministers struggled to control parliament. Supply again was threatened in the 1700 session, jacobitism gained ground, and pamphlets circulated attacking the regal union. The whiff of revolution was in the air, but while the Edinburgh mob did burn the house of the secretary of state, James Ogilvy, first earl of Seafield, the absence of religious discontent prevented a repeat of 1637 or 1688. Furthermore, the opposition divided and the diffuse country party was incapable of allying with the jacobites. The government retained enough unity and purpose to struggle through the session, but the issues of Scottish sovereignty and compensation for Darien threatened to make the kingdom ungovernable. William concluded that only a parliamentary union would provide the crown with sufficient political control in Scotland for the smooth running of a war-efficient state.

The last year of William's reign was overshadowed by the additional problem of the death in 1701 of Princess Anne's last surviving child, the duke of Gloucester. As Anne was William's only heir this left the succession vulnerable, especially when Louis XIV recognised Anne's jacobite half brother. Consequently, the English parliament passed the act of settlement, regulating the succcession and making Sophia, the elderly dowager electress of Hanover, heir to Princess Anne. Scottish intentions were ignored in making this unilateral decision, which was seen by the Scottish parliament as another example of English arrogance. William's own unexpected death in March 1702 left the crown in the hands of an unhealthy, childless woman, and made a resolution of the succession urgent.

Simmering anger over Darien, and resentment over Eng handling of the dynastic issue made the crown's prem control over the Scottish parliament more difficu of 1698 William increasingly relied on the manager that James Douglas, second duke of Queensberry to lad to control. In addition to ministerial faction, Que ouped contend with a country party opposition whic f disap- since the demise of the club. This rainbo spoused pointed place seekers, episcopalians, an an incoherent mixture of Dutch republicanism and English country principles, opposing the war, the growth of central government and the oligarchic power of the magnates. As in the 1699 session of the English parliament, where the defence budget was slashed, Dutch influence was attacked, William's demands were ignored, and the Scottish ministry found itself on the defensive. In the 1698 session the country party lacked the discipline to prevent the voting of an adequate supply, but by the 1700 session circumstances had changed. Parliament sat against the background of the Darien fiasco, a growing personal challenge to Queensberry emerged in the person of James Hamilton, fourth duke of Hamilton, and tension within the ministry was aroused by Queensberry's monopolistic ambitions. Anti-English populism, presbyterian demands to free the general assembly from any dependence on the crown, and cries for compensation for the Darien investors forced an adjournment until the end of the year when a package of concessions and judicious patronage allowed the crown to struggle through.

Union was the preferred solution favoured by Queen Anne and by Sidney Godolphin, first Lord Godolphin, the English lord treasurer who assumed responsibility for Scottish affairs at court, to the management problem. Union would secure the succession and seal off any French threat to England – jacobites like Patrick Abercromby did advocate the resuscitation of the Auld Alliance with France – through its vulnerable back-door. Queensberry's conversion to union arose out of his difficulty in managing parliament, and from the hope that union would allow him to dominate Scottish affairs from Westminster. But it was at Westminster that Queensberry's power was undermined. junto whigs' commitment to the war made them more rable to union for strategic and diplomatic reasons, and d hopes of increasing their Westminster strength with members of parliament. However, William's death and reion of the tory Queen Anne ensured that the junto enc ozen out of office. Anne wished to avoid depend- and er party, and relied on the earl of Marlborough court managers with whig inclinations, and on

Robert Harley, a tory moderate who controlled the House of Commons. In the summer of 1702 the tories gained a modest majority, allowing them to press a reluctant ministry for greater restrictions on nonconformity. High tory managers like Daniel Finch, second earl of Nottingham saw union as a means of rescuing episcopalianism in Scotland, and while many tory backbenchers preferred to keep a presbyterian Scotland at a distance, it was Nottingham's pressure which resulted in the calling of an election in Scotland in 1702. Queensberry advised against the election, but his influence at court was waning, and Hamilton's country party had a case in arguing that it was unconstitutional to begin the reign without a new parliament. In the first free election since the revolution the crown's tenuous control over parliament was destroyed. Queensberry's predominantly whig-presbyterian court party was punished by the electors for being perceived as an English interest, and its presbyterian bias did it no good in episcopal localities. The court party was left with between ninety and one hundred seats, some sixty seats fell to Hamilton and his loose country alliance, while the jacobites won around seventy seats, confirming the revival they had experienced since Glencoe. In spite of the set-back, the queen insisted that union negotiations begin in November 1702. The English tories' coolness over union with presbyterian Scotland, and the determination of the Scots to have restitution for the losses of the Company of Scotland led to the proceedings being adjourned indefinitely on 3 February 1703. With the Irish parliament petitioning the queen for union in 1703, it appeared possible that Scotland would be the one kingdom left outside of a parliamentary union.

With Anglo-Scottish union a dead issue the more pressing concern was supply for the ailing war effort. In an effort to broaden the government and give it a more tory complexion, Godolphin pressed for ministerial changes, most significantly the appointment of the pragmatic and skillful James Ogilvie, earl of Seafield as chancellor. The result was an unwieldy alliance which ensured that the government collapsed at the first crisis. Appealing to the episcopalian interest in parliament was insufficient to head-off mounting anger over Darien, the act of succession and English influence in Scottish affairs. The crown also had to be careful of offending the powerful presbyterian lobby, and Queensberry's faction was unhappy at power sharing. The opposition set about freeing parliament from ministerial control, forcing through the act of security which placed the royal succession under its control, stipulating only that any successor must be a protestant. The act left open the possibility of deviating from the English succession if guarantees for the future sovereignty of the kingdom were not attained. Popular anger at English influence in Scottish affairs was stirred by jacobite propagandists who attacked the regal union. For the crown the 1703 session was a disaster and the ministry failed even to obtain supply. The passing of the act anent peace and war, asserting parliament's right to decide on these issues, and the failure by only twenty-four votes to include in the act of security Andrew Fletcher of Saltoun's 'limitations' which would have greatly reduced the prerogative, aroused excitable talk of 1641. Without giving royal assent to the act of security, but having promoted the wine act which permitted trade with France, Queensberry adjourned parliament in the autumn. The executive and legislature remained at logger-heads, and Anglo-Scottish tension remained high. A clumsy attempt by Queensberry to smear his enemies in a muddled jacobite plot – the 'Queensberry plot' – brought on his sacking in May 1704.

What became known as the new party now formed a government under John Hay, second marquis of Tweedale, a pro-unionist. The new party's remit from Westminster was to secure the Hanoverian succession in Scotland. Without any magnates in their ranks, and posing as an alternative and reformed court party, the new party's attraction for the queen was their dependence on the English ministry. Although he was honest and competent, Tweedale was hamstrung by the same lack of patronage, the complexity of the conflicting issues, and in addition Queensberry's covert opposition. Control of parliament proved impossible, and in the summer of 1704 Tweedale assented to the act of security in return for modest supply. Marlborough's victory at Blenheim eased the pressure on the court, but the queen was forced increasingly to rely on the junto whigs as the party more committed to the war. However, while the junto now feared that a Scottish presence at Westminster would strengthen the court, they were keen to settle the succession, and irritation at the Scots brought about a predictable English backlash. On 5 February 1705 the English parliament passed the alien act, mixing retaliation with a jacking up of the stakes in the conflict between the court and the Scottish parliament. The alien act demanded that the act of security be repealed and a Hanoverian succession, or a treaty of union, be under negotiation by 25 December 1705. If the Scottish parliament failed to comply, all Scots in England would be treated as foreigners, and the import of all Scottish goods, principally linen and cattle, would be forbidden. Against the background of another trade recession in 1704, the alien act frightened Scottish landowners and merchants who stood to lose trade and assets in England, but it also aroused a good deal of anger. It was a thunderous response to the legislation passed in the Scottish parliament to allow trade in French wine and to facilitate the smuggling of English wool to the continent. England was the only country with whom Scotland had a balance of trade surplus, and the Scots were in no position to fight an economic war. The xenophobia which never was far from the surface in Anglo-Scottish relations was stirred by polemicists like William Atwood who raised the old bogey of English superiority over Scotland. Outrage spread to the lower orders, with ugly results in the scandalous Worcester affair. On 11 April 1705 members of the crew of an English vessel accused of piracy against Scottish shipping were hanged when the government bowed to the hysterical Anglophobia of the mob. In reality, these sailors were victims in a vendetta with the East India Company which had siezed the last remaining ship of the Company of Scotland. The incident broke the floundering new party, and heightened resolve to press for union at court and among the junto whigs who increased their strength in the 1705 election.

The court turned to John Campbell, second duke of Argyll, a young soldier, and a whig with strong English connections and interests. Argyll and his junto allies forced a reluctant queen to re-employ Queensberry as the man most likely to manage parliament. However, Queensberry's party remained in a minority, and the 1705 session was hostile to the court in spite of the threats posed by the alien act. Then, on 1 September, Hamilton succumbed to court pressure and betrayed his party, allowing the crown to carry a measure giving the queen authority to nominate commissioners to negotiate a union. The vote was decisive in destroying the country party's hopes of extracting constitutional reforms in exchange for agreement on the Hanoverian succession. Supply followed shortly afterwards, the objectionable clauses to the alien act were repealed on 15 November, and the union commission was named in February 1706. The Scottish commission was composed almost entirely of Queensberry and his friends, while the English commission too was weighted in favour of the junto whigs, who had overcome their doubts about union as the best route to secure the succession. However, both Queensberry's court party and the junto whigs commenced the talks with one eye on domestic opposition. For the Scots, allegations of a sell-out would be dangerous, a point appreciated by the junto, and in the end the terms were not unreasonable. Negotiations began on 16 April at Whitehall with the 1702 discussions acting as a starting point. The issue of incorporating union was settled quickly, the English conceded compensation for the Company of Scotland and tax concessions for the Scots, and by 23 July 1706 a draft treaty was agreed.

The treaty bargained Scottish political independence for economic dependence, there being no question of the junto whigs or the court accepting anything less than an incorporating parliamentary union. This implied the abolition of the two national parliaments and their replacement with a single parliament of Great Britain, but in reality the Scottish parliament would be swallowed up in that of England. The enlarged English parliament would contain forty-five members of parliament from Scotland (a 12:1 ratio) and sixteen representative peers. This low representation flattered the nation's economic strength (38:1) in a polity which equated wealth with political power, but grossly under-represented the population ratio (5:1) between the two kingdoms. However, fifteen of the twenty-five articles were concerned with economic issues. The Scots were assured of free trade with England and her colonies, fulfilling the ambitions of those who believed an expanded market was the only route to prosperity. In fact, a vigorous and officially tolerated smuggling community already gave the Scots a foothold in English markets. To compensate for the existing English national debt, concessions were made to the Scots over the implementation of the salt and malt taxes, they were to pay a lower rate on the land tax, and were to be exempted from other taxes like that on stamped paper and windows. The equivalent, a sum of almost £398,000 sterling, would be provided to pay off the debts of the crown in Scotland, chiefly to office holders, and to compensate investors in the Company of Scotland. A second, rising equivalent would be made available as a start-up for Scottish industry. A common flag was agreed along with acceptance of English coinage, weights and measures, the English fiscal system and public law. However, the union was not a full incorporation, and retained elements of Scottish federalism. The Scottish privy council continued, while Scottish law, education local government, the heritable jurisdictions, and the rights of the royal burghs were protected.

Selling the treaty to the English parliament was unlikely to be difficult as long as the junto and the court managers retained control over English politics. But in Scotland, where the treaty first was debated, opposition to incorporation was deep seated and widespread. For the first time since the revolution politics moved dangerously close to erupting outside parliament. How far the pamphlet war reflected genuine ideological differences, and how far it was the product of partisan propaganda is difficult to say. Certainly the economic arguments made some impact. Many landowners were influenced by the threat to the lucrative cattle trade. The burghs were divided on the issue, although a slight majority in the convention of royal burghs voted against union. Some, like Montrose, feared the loss of the linen trade if there was no union, while many towns, including Edinburgh and Glasgow, organised denunciatory addresses to parliament, reflecting fear among merchants and craftsmen that English competition in their previously protected markets would be damaging. The powerful protectionist lobby of salt and coal masters had nothing to gain from union, while fears of high unemployment and high taxes incited the hostile, volatile crowds which filled Edinburgh as parliament sat. However, sovereignty and religion were equally important issues. Lord Belhaven's hyperbolic and emotional 'Mother Caledonia' speech was addressed to a wide constituency which did fear the loss of political power and cultural traditions. Political attitudes to union varied depending on the importance attached to the succession, to constitutional reform, or to independence. The greatest threat to union, however, lay in the church, and the clergy in the west did engage in some rabble rousing. Presbyterian grumblings were silenced when a new article was introduced to the treaty guarenteeing the 1690 church settlement. The new British state, therefore, would have two established churches. Deprived of the kind of nationwide organisation which only the church could provide, and with the magnates refusing to give leadership to popular opposition, the campaign against union failed to unite the localities against the court. Aristocratic opposition was substantial and most shire petitions opposing the union came from localities dominated by anti-union noblemen. However, unlike 1637 or 1689 magnates like Hamilton and Atholl were unprepared to take extra-parliamentary action. There were riots in Dumfries and in Glasgow, where the provost was forced to flee, but the opposition remained fragmentary and leaderless. Surprisingly, the jacobites failed to capitalise on the simmering unrest, confining their dissent to parliament. Sovereignty alone was not a sufficiently popular cause to arouse the people to take up arms, and in 1706–7 the great majority even of the political elite did not bother to register their views. Three quarters of the burghs and two-thirds of the shires did not petition at all. Queensberry and his colleagues held their nerves, comforted by the soldiers who surrounded parliament and by the knowledge that English troops had moved to the border and the Irish coast.

Without a majority since 1702 Queensberry's court party could not rely on Seafield's management alone, and needed to buy support. Within parliament there was a hard core on both sides and a large floating vote prepared to be persuaded or induced. Most patronage therefore was used to shore up wavering court supporters. The most seductive prize for the politicians was the prospect of political influence at Westminster, but there were other direct forms of persuasion employed. Unionists like Argyll and his brother were rewarded with a military commission and an earldom, while Godolphin sent Queensberry £20,000 sterling to purchase votes, and this was paid out as salary arrears, £12,325 sterling to Queensberry himself. In contrast to court managers like Queensberry, Argyll and Seafield, the opposition was divided when the parliamentary session began on 3 October. On 4 November the first article of the treaty passed by a majority of 32, a safe if not comfortable margin which the court secured with the adherence of the new party's 25 votes. The new party, or squadrone as they now were known, wanted to reach an accommodation with Godolphin in the hope of displacing Queensberry, while Godolphin wished to cultivate an alternative court party to Queensberry and Argyll, allies of the junto who were detested by the queen. The court's problems also were eased by the opposition's incompetence. Nominally led by Hamilton, this incohesive muddle of disappointed placemen, patriotic reformers like Fletcher of Saltoun, tories and jacobites, lacked either a unified vision to offer as a workable alternative, or the confidence to appeal to the country. With the passing of the 'Act for securing the protestant religion and presbyterian church government' on 12 November the court reduced any liklihood of such an appeal succeeding. The rout of the opposition continued, but not without detailed revision of each article, especially the economic articles. On 16 January 1707 the treaty of union was ratified by a majority of 43, 110 for the union and 67 against. Passage through the English parliament was secured with large majorities, union being perceived by many English members of parliament as a form of conquest. The Scottish parliament was dissolved on 28 April, and four days later the union came into effect.

Postscript: War, Succession and Rebellion, 1707–15

The parliamentary union belongs within the context of the ongoing whig revolution which deposed James VII and II from his British thrones in 1688–9. The Hanoverian succession now was secure in both kingdoms, the war in Europe could be pushed home without fear of French influence being exerted in Scotland, and sovereignty in the new British state was located unambiguously in Westminster. An overwhelming victory for the whiggish Queensberry-Argyll interest in the 1707 election, in which the equally unionist squadrone secured a minority of seats in the Lords and Commons, vindicated the treaty at court. In Scotland the reorganisation of government to meet the demands of the new British state were minimal. The most important change was the abolition of the privy council in February 1708 for reasons which were political rather than administrative. The squadrone and Hamilton's followers united with the junto to destroy what was seen as a source of patronage for Queensberry. The result was to reduce the accountability of government, and to deprive the crown of any effective agency for wielding executive action in Scotland.

The diminishing prospects of the jacobites in Scotland was to some extent offset by the patriotic propaganda deployed in their cause. The undercurrent of resentment against the union, discontent with Marlborough's expensive and bloody strategy in Europe, and the need for the French to open up a new front in Britain led to a Franco-jacobite campaign aimed at Scotland in the spring of 1708. James Stewart's armada with a complement of some 5,000 troops was a serious threat to an under-garrisoned and unsettled country. Bad luck and incompetence dogged the expedition and the French fleet was chased home before James and his soldiers could land. The episode and the little support aroused within Scotland demonstrated the gulf between anti-union sentiment and jacobitism. Scottish ministers treated the affair lightly, and the not proven verdicts in the few resulting trials would have marked the end of the matter had not anti-jacobite hysteria been unleashed in England. The whig campaign was aimed at the tory party in England, but the ministry intervened in Scotland with a heavy hand, brushing aside the treason laws for the more draconian English legislation, and initiating fresh arrests which served only to heighten anti-English feeling. The election in the summer of 1708 threatened to be a difficult test for the whig ministry, but the Queensberry-Argyll alliance won a surprisingly trouble free contest, and continued to back the junto who were bolstered by Marlborough's stunning victory over the French at Oudenarde on 31 July 1708. However, the junto's determination to impose their will on the queen, to meet the demands of their allies in punishing Louis XIV, and Marlborough's pyrrhic victory at Malplaquet in August 1709 undermined their position. A war-weary English public was wooed by the more conciliatory tories, and Harley effectively castigated the whigs as war profiteers. The Queensberry-Argyll party showed their true colours as primarily a court interest, distancing themselves from the beleaguered junto. Whig desperation to find another jacobite plot backfired in the trial in London in 1710 of Dr Sacheverell which looked more like an attack on the anglican church.

The anglican reaction and the queen's distaste for the whigs ensured that the 1710 election was won by the tories posing as the party of peace, the church and of the country against the whig oligarchs. In Scotland the 1710 election saw gains for the episcopal-tory interest, although Harley had no need of Scottish votes at Westminster in order to form his ministry, and it was the weakness of the Scottish tories which forced Harley to introduce direct rule through the treasury. Queensberry remained in government but his power was diminished, and he died in 1711, removing the one Scot with a significant ministerial profile at Whitehall. At Westminster the Scots were fragmented, weak and increasingly disillusioned with the union. In 1709 Queensberry was prevented from voting in the elections for the representative peers because he sat in the House of Lords as duke of Dover. In December 1711 Hamilton was unable to take his seat in the House of Lords as duke of Brandon in the British peerage (as distinct from one of the sixteen representative peers) for partisan party reasons which the Scots interpreted as prejudice. The impotence of the subsequent Scottish boycott of the Lords merely served to spread further the sense of betrayal and outrage. The Brandon case was followed in February 1712 by the rampant tories' decision to introduce toleration for episcopalians into Scotland and to restore lay patronage in the Church of Scotland. These provocative measures were accompanied by demands for the occasional conformity bill which attacked English dissenters, demonstrating that they did not spring from a sense of enlightenment. The effect in Scotland was to arouse the wrath of the presbyterians, and there were riots in Edinburgh and Leith and renewed calls for conventicling. Among politicians the effect was to draw the Scots into the whig-tory conflict with religion forming the essential ingredient. In itself this reduced the likelihood of the Scots acting together at Westminster. However, there was universal outrage at the flagrant violation of the treaty of union in May 1713, when the malt tax was introduced to Scotland as part of a package of measures designed to relieve the tax burden on the English landed community. Only the government's inability to enforce collection of the new tax prevented widespread rioting. Further resentment flowed from the new commercial treaty with France which took no account of Scottish interests, and from disappointment at the failure of union to bring immediate prosperity. A number of native industries were damaged, and the only success, in tobacco, was based on tax evasion. It was the malt tax which stirred former unionists like Argyll and Seafield to combine with the whigs in an effort to overthrow the union in the House of Lords on 1 June 1713. Four proxy votes prevented a major constitutional crisis.

The tories ended the war in 1713 with the treaty of Utrecht, a treaty regarded as a betrayal by the rival court in Hanover because it was too conciliatory to the French. Consequently, Hanover saw the whigs as the party which represented its interests, a development which in itself pushed the tories towards the jacobites. However, it was the tories who won the 1713 election, and in Scotland John Erskine, sixth earl of Mar managed convincing tory victories in the peerage election, although Argyll and the squadrone each maintained a strong whig showing in the House of Commons. The tory triumph was short-lived, as the end of the war exposed divisions within the party which forced Harley, now earl of Oxford, increasingly into the arms of the crypto-jacobite wing of the party which believed that Queen Anne would consent to an agreement with James. Such an eventuality was unlikely given Anne's belief in James's illigitimacy and the latter's refusal to give up his catholic religion. The treaty of Utrecht was also a blow to James, who was obliged to move from St Germain to Lorraine, outside French territory. His remaining hope of recovering the throne lay with the jacobites in the tory party. In fact many tories, including Mar, simply were hedging their bets, and jacobite strength was exaggerated, often by whig propaganda aimed at smearing their enemies. The tory disarray which preceded the death of Queen Anne on 1 August 1714 was in contrast to the whigs, including Argyll, who assumed control of the government until George I arrived in Britain in September. The jacobite failure to act decisively during the summer of 1714, the death of Louis XIV on 1 September, and the decisive whig victory in the elections in February 1715 seemed to bring the months of political instability to an end.

Yet there remained a final episode to be played out. Spurned by George I, who knew of his jacobite associations, Mar raised James's standard at Braemar on 6 September 1715. Mar succeeded in tapping a mixture of genuine jacobite devotion, episcopalian frustration, the regional conservatism of the north-east, hatred of the Campbells, and political adventuring. He also was helped by the decline in the militia since 1707, and the government's unwillingness before 1715 to interfere in jacobite office-holding in church and state. His army of 10,000 men ought to have broken through into the southern lowlands, but he was fought to a standstill by Argyll's smaller force at Sheriffmuir on 13 November. Simultaneous risings in

Lancashire and the south-west of Scotland were mopped up, the jacobite army retreated, and James arrived a month too late, brandishing a manifesto which promised to dissolve the union, protect the freedom of parliament and guarantee the protestant church. As a meaningful political force jacobitism was finished at Sheriffmuir. Scotland's political future belonged to the whigs, to the presbyterians, to the unionists, and to the house of Hanover. And, some also might add, to the English.

BIBLIOGRAPHY

GENERAL SEVENTEENTH CENTURY

Among the general histories of this period the most useful for Scottish politics remain volumes three and four of the *Edinburgh History of Scotland*, G. Donaldson, *Scotland. James V to James VII* (Edinburgh, 1965), and W, Ferguson, *Scotland. 1689 to the Present* (Edinburgh, 1968). M. Lynch, *Scotland. A New History* (London, 1991) is a useful read and is more up to date. R. Mitchison, *Lordship to Patronage. Scotland 1603–1745* (London, 1983) is less satisfactory on political and religious issues. The specific question of Anglo-Scottish relations is addressed in W. Ferguson, *Scotland's Relations with England. A Survey to 1707* (Edinburgh, 1977), and in B. P. Levack, *The Formation of the British State. England, Scotland and the Union 1603–1707* (Oxford, 1987). Still of some value is D. Nobbs, *England and Scotland 1560–1707* (London, 1952). A very quick introduction to the subject is D. Stevenson, 'The century of the three kingdoms', in J. Wormald (ed.), *Scotland revisited* (London, 1991), 107–18. For an old fashioned Anglocentric world view see H. R. Trevor-Roper, 'The union of Britain in the seventeenth century', in H. R. Trevor Roper, *Religion, the Reformation and Social Change* (London, 1967), pp. 445–67.

Scottish politics of the seventeenth century cannot be understood without some idea of what was going on in England and Ireland. Easily accessible general histories of England are D. Hirst, *Authority and Conflict. England 1603–58* (London, 1986), and J. R. Jones, *Country and Court. England 1658–1714* (London, 1986). On Ireland see M. MacCurtain, *Tudor and Stuart Ireland* (Dublin, 1972), and

---

SHR   Scottish Historical Review
RSCHS Records of the Scottish Church History Society

B. Fitzpatrick, *Seventeenth-century Ireland. The Wars of Religion* (Dublin, 1988).

There are very few successful general British histories for this or any other period, but H. Kearney, *The British Isles. A History of Four Nations* (Cambridge, 1989) is the best. Also of some interest is M. Hechter, *Internal Colonialism: the Celtic Fringe in British National Development, 1536–1966* (London, 1975), and R. S. Thompson, *The Atlantic Archipelago. A Political History of the British Isles* (Lewiston/Queenston, 1986).

1 POLITICAL INSTITUTIONS

Most of what is known about Scottish government in the seventeenth century is scattered throughout the political histories of the period, and there is very little in the way of studies of political institutions. One attempt to investigate kingship over the course of the entire period is K. M. Brown, 'The vanishing emperor', in R. Mason (ed.), *Scots and Britons. Political Thought and the Union of 1603* (forthcoming, Cambridge, 1993). Other studies of particular kings can be found in the bibliographies for later chapters. Still of some use is J. A. Lovat-Fraser, 'The constitutional position of the Scottish monarch prior to the union', *Law Quarterly Review*, 17 (1901), 252–7. The best introduction to the political role of the court is N. Cuddy, 'The revival of the entourage: the bedchamber of James VI in administration and politics 1603–1625', in D. Starkey (ed.), *The English Court from the Wars of the Roses to the Civil War* (Harlow, 1987), pp. 173–225. One interesting aspect of absentee administration is discussed in J. Imrie, 'The royal castles and palaces of Scotland, 1616–1650. An aspect of remote administration', in S. Dyrvik, K. Mykland and J. Oldervoll (eds), *The Satellite State* (Bergen, 1979), pp. 141–56.

There is no satisfactory study of the Scottish parliament other than C. S. Terry, *Scottish Parliaments, 1603–1707* (Glasgow, 1905), and R. S. Rait, *The Parliaments of Scotland* (Glasgow, 1924). Remarkably there is no study of the privy council. The business of taxation and crown finance has received some uneven attention, and an idea of how government finances were administered can be gleaned from J. Goodare, 'Parliamentary taxation in Scotland, 1560–1603', *SHR*, 68 (1989), 23–52; A. L. Murray, 'Sir John Skene and the exchequer, 1594–1612', in *Miscellany One, Stair Society* (Edinburgh, 1971), 125–55; D. Stevenson, 'The king's Scottish revenues and the covenanters, 1625–1651', *Historical Journal*, 17 (1974): 17–41;

D. Stevenson, 'Financing the cause of the covenants, 1638–51', *SHR*, 51 (1972): 89–123; A. L. Murray, 'The Scottish treasury, 1667–1708', *SHR*, 45 (1966): 89–104. For the court of session see R. K. Hannay, *The College of Justice* (Glasgow, 1933). Other branches of the system of formal justice are dealt with in S. J. Davies, 'The court and the Scottish legal system 1600–1747: the case of Stirlingshire', in V. A .C. Gatrell, B. Lenman and G. Parker (eds), *Crime and the Law. The Social History of Crime in Western Europe since 1500* (London, 1980), pp. 120–54; and W. R. Foster, 'The operation of presbyteries in Scotland 1600–1638', *RSCHS*, 15 (1966), 21–33. Some discussion of the changes made to Scottish government by the immediate impact of the treaty of union is found in P. W. J. Riley, *The English Ministers and Scotland 1707–1727* (London, 1964).

2 POLITICAL ELITES

For the most useful background to the Scottish aristocracy in the early seventeenth century see J. Wormald, 'Bloodfeud, kindred and government in early modern Scotland', *Past and Present*, 87 (1980), 54–97; J. M. Wormald, *Lords and Men in Scotland. Bonds of Manrent, 1442–1603* (Edinburgh, 1985); K. M. Brown, *Bloodfeud in Scotland 1573–1625. Violence, Justice and Politics in an Early Modern Society* (Edinburgh, 1986); K. M. Brown, 'The nobility of Jacobean Scotland 1567–1625', in J. Wormald (ed.), *Scotland Revisited* (London, 1991), 61–72. For the highlands R. A. Dodgshon, 'Pretense of blude' and 'place of thair dwelling': the nature of Scottish clans, 1500–1745', in R. A. Houston and I. D. Whyte (eds), *Scottish Society 1500–1800* (Cambridge, 1989), pp. 169–98; R. A. Dodgshon, 'West highland chiefdoms, 1500–1745: a study in redistributive exchange', in R. Mitchison and P. Roebuck (eds), *Economy and Society in Scotland and Ireland 1500–1939* (Edinburgh, 1988), pp. 27–37; and L. Leneman, *Living in Atholl 1685–1785* (Edinburgh, 1986). The economics of the nobility in the years before the covenanting revolution are discussed in K. M. Brown, 'Aristocratic finances and the origins of the Scottish revolution', *English Historical Review*, 54 (1989): 46–87, and K. M. Brown, 'Noble indebtedness in Scotland between the reformation and the revolution', *Historical Research*, 62 (1989): 260–75. For the general question of estate management and agricultural developments see I. Whyte, *Agriculture and Society in Seventeenth Century Scotland* (Edinburgh, 1979). The military dimension to aristocratic power is evident in K. M. Brown, 'From

Scottish lords to British officers: state building, elite integration, and the army in the seventeenth century', in N. Macdougall (ed.), *Scotland and War AD79–1918* (Edinburgh, 1991), pp. 133–69; K. M. Brown, 'Gentlemen and thugs in seventeenth century Britain', *History Today*, 40 (1990): 27–32; B. P. Lenman, 'Militia, fencible men, and home defence, 1660–1797', in Macdougall (ed.), *Scotland and War*, pp. 170–92. Aristocratic social mores are the subject of T. Innes, *Scots Heraldry* (Edinburgh, 1956), and D. Stevenson, 'The English devill of keeping state', in N. Macdougall and R. A. Mason (eds), *People and Power in Scotland* (Edinburgh, 1992). J. Macaulay, *The Classical Country House of Scotland* (London, 1987), and R. K. Marshall, *The Days of Duchess Anne. Life in the Household of the Duchess of Hamilton 1656–1716* (London, 1973) describe aristocratic society. The issue of anglicisation is discussed in K. M. Brown, 'Aristocracy, anglicisation and the court, 1603–38', *British Historical Journal*, forthcoming.

Some idea of the social authority of the clergy can be gauged from B. Lenman, 'The limits of godly discipline in the early modern period with particular reference to England and Scotland', in K. von Greyerz (ed.), *Religion and Society in Early Modern Europe 1500–1800* (London, 1984), pp. 124–45; W. Makey, *The Church of the Covenant 1637–1651. Revolution and Social Change in Scotland* (Edinburgh, 1979); L. M. Smith, 'Sackcloth for the sinner or punishment for the crime? Church and secular courts in Cromwellian Scotland', in J. L. Dwyer, R. A. L. Mason and A. Murdoch (eds), *New Perspectives on the Politics and Culture of Early Modern Scotland* (Edinburgh, 1982), pp. 116–32; R. D. Brackenridge, 'The enforcement of Sunday observance in post-revolution Scotland 1689–1733', *RSCHS*, 17 (1969), 33–45.

Urban elites have received a fair amount of attention in recent years. M. Lynch, 'Continuity and change in urban society, 1500–1700', in Houston and Whyte (eds), *Scottish Society*, pp. 85–117, and M. Lynch, 'Introduction: Scottish towns 1500–1700', in M. Lynch (ed.), *The Early Modern Town in Scotland* (London, 1987), pp. 1–35 provide the best introduction. More detailed studies are M. Lynch, 'The crown and the burghs 1500–1625', in Lynch (ed.), *The Early Modern Town*, pp. 55–80; J. J. Brown, 'Merchant princes and mercantile investment in early seventeenth-century Scotland', in Lynch (ed.), *The Early Modern Town*, pp. 125–46; D. Stevenson, 'The burghs and the Scottish revolution', in Lynch (ed.), *The Early Modern Town*, pp. 167–91; W. Coutts, 'Provincial merchants and society: a study of Dumfries based on the registers of testaments 1600–1665', in Lynch (ed.), *The Early Modern Town*, pp. 167–91; K. M. Brown, 'Burghs, lords and feuds in Jacobean Scotland', in Lynch (ed.), *The Early*

Modern Town, pp. 102–24; A. I. Macinnes, 'Covenanting, revolution and municipal enterprise', in Wormald (ed.), *Scotland Revisited*, pp. 97–106; T. C. Smout, 'The Glasgow merchant community in the seventeenth century', *SHR*, 47 (1968), 53–70; T. M. Devine 'The Scottish merchant community, 1680–1740', in R. H. Campbell and A. S. Skinner (eds), *The Origins and Nature of the Scottish Enlightenment* (Edinburgh, 1982), pp. 26–41; T. M. Devine, 'The social composition of the business class in the larger Scottish towns, 1680–1740', in T. M. Devine and D. Dickson (eds), *Ireland and Scotland 1600–1850* (Edinburgh, 1983), pp. 163–76.

For the legal profession G. Donaldson, 'The legal profession in Scottish society in the sixteenth and seventeenth centuries', *Juridical Review*, n.s. 21 (1976): 1–19 is the best introduction. For more specific topics see D. Stevenson, 'The covenanters and the court of session, 1637–1650', *Juridical Review*, n.s. 17 (1972): 227–47; A. Murdoch, 'The advocates, the law and the nation in early modern Scotland', in W. Prest (ed.), *Lawyers in early modern Europe and America* (London, 1981), pp. 147–63; B. P. Levack, 'The proposed union of English law and Scots law in the seventeenth century', *Juridical Review*, n.s. 20 (1975): 97–115; R. Feenstra, 'Scottish-Dutch legal relations in the seventeenth and eighteenth centuries', in T. C. Smout (ed.), *Scotland and Europe 1200–1850* (Edinburgh, 1986), pp. 128–42; and N. Phillipson, 'The social structure of the faculty of advocates in Scotland, 1661–1840', in A. Harding (ed.), *Law Making and Law Makers in British History* (London, 1980), pp. 146–56.

3 POLITICAL IDEAS

A rare study of the sophisticated media employed by royal patrons in seventeenth-century Scotland is S. Bruce and S. Yearly, 'The social construction of tradition: the restoration portraits and the kings of Scotland', in D. McCrone, S. Kendrick and P. Straw (eds), *The Making of Scotland: Nation, Culture and Social Change* (Edinburgh, 1989), pp. 175–88. A sketchy account of royalist iconography can be found in M. G. H. Pittock, *The Invention of Tradition. The Stewart Myth and the Scottish Identity, 1638 to the Present* (London, 1991). For the court see G. Parry, *The Golden Age Restor'd. The Culture of the Stuart Court, 1603–42* (Manchester, 1981), pp. 1–63, and R. M. Smuts, *Court Culture and the Origins of a Royalist Tradition in Early Stuart England* (Philadelphia, 1987). Masonic lodges are the subject of D. Stevenson, *The First Freemasons. Scotland's Early Lodges and their Members* (Aberdeen,

1988). What little is known of the theatre is found in A. Cameron, 'Theatre in Scotland 1660–1800', in A. Hook (ed.), *The History of Scottish Literature, Vol. 2* (Aberdeen, 1989), pp. 191–5. For the political ballad and song, W. Donaldson, *The Jacobite Song: Political Myth and National Identity* (Aberdeen, 1988); W. Gillies, 'Gaelic: the classical tradition', in R. D. Jack (ed.), *The History of Scottish Literature, Vol. 1, Origins to 1660* (Aberdeen, 1988), pp. 245–60. The growth of printing and of literacy is chronicled in H. C. Aldis, *A List of Books Printed in Scotland before 1700* (Edinburgh, 1970), and R. Houston, *Scottish Literacy and the Scottish Identity 1600–1800* (Cambridge, 1985). For censorship see D. Stevenson, 'A revolutionary regime and the press: the covenanters and their printers', *The Library*, 6th series, 7 (1985): 315–37; J. Buckroyd, '*Mercurius Caledonius* and its immediate successors, 1661', *SHR*, 54 (1975): 11–21, and M. Steele, 'Anti-jacobite pamphleteering, 1701–1720', *SHR*, 60 (1981): 140–55.

The underlying conservatism of Scottish political thought before George Buchanan is demonstrated in R. A. Mason, 'Kingship, tyranny and the right to resist in fifteenth century Scotland', *SHR*, 66 (1987): 125–51, and R. A. Mason, 'Covenant and commonweal: the language of politics in Reformation Scotland', in N. Macdougall (ed.), *Church, Politics and Society: Scotland 1408–1929* (Edinburgh, 1983), pp. 97–126. The same author effectively describes the essence of the debate between Buchanan and James VI in R. A. Mason, 'A king by divine right: George Buchanan, James VI and the presbyterians', in Mason (ed.), *Scots and Britons*, forthcoming. James's own political ideas are outlined in J. Wormald, 'James VI and I, *Basilikon doron* and *The trew law of free monarchies*: the Scottish context and the English tradition', in L. L. Peck (ed.), *The Mental World of the Jacobean Court* (Cambridge, 1991), pp. 36–54. The literature on later royalist ideas is very thin, but see D. Reid, 'Royalty and self-absorption in Drummond's poetry', *Studies in Scottish Literature*, 22 (1987): 115–31; I. M. Smart, 'Monarchy and toleration in Drummond of Hawthornden's works', *Scotia*, 4 (1980): 44–50; T. I. Rae, 'The political attitudes of William Drummond of Hawthornden', in G. W. S. Barrow (ed.), *The Scottish Tradition. Essays in Honour of Ronald Cant* (Edinburgh, 1974), pp. 132–46. D. Stevenson, 'The 'Letter on sovereign power' and the influence of Jean Bodin on political thought in Scotland', *Scottish Historical Review*, 61 (1982): 25–43 analyses the royalist reaction to the covenanters. Of some use in describing royalist ideas for this period, albeit from an English perspective is J. P. Sommerville, *Politics and Ideology in England 1603–1640* (Harlow, 1986), pp. 9–56. For the restoration revival of royalist ideas see

H. Ouston, 'York in Edinburgh: James VII and the patronage of learning', in Dwyer, Mason and Murdoch (eds), *New Perspectives*, pp. 133–55, and H. Ouston, 'Cultural life from the restoration to the union', in Hook (ed.), *The History of Scottish Literature, Vol. 2*, pp. 11–32.

Turning to the alternative tradition, George Buchanan's fundamental importance is underlined in J. H. Burns, 'The political ideas of George Buchanan', *SHR*, 30 (1951): 60–8, and R. A. Mason, '*Rex stoicus*: George Buchanan, James VI and the Scottish polity', in Dwyer, Mason and Murdoch (eds), *New Perspectives*, pp. 9–33. The ideas of the covenanters still require comprehensive treatment, but a clear introduction is I. M. Smart, 'The political ideas of the Scottish covenanters, 1638–88', *History of Political Thought*, 1 (1980): 167–93; S. A. Burrell, 'The covenant idea as a revolutionary symbol: Scotland, 1596–1637', *Church History*, 27 (1958): 338–50; S. A. Burrell, 'The apocalyptic vision of the early covenanters', *SHR*, 63 (1964): 1–24. More detail on the national covenant can be found in M. Steele, 'The 'Politick Christian': the theological background to the national covenant', in J. Morrill (ed.), *The Scottish National Covenant in its British Context 1638–1651* (Edinburgh, 1990), pp. 31–67, and E. J. Cowan, 'The making of the national covenant', in J. Morrill (ed.), *The Scottish National Covenant*, pp. 68–89. On Rutherford see W. M. Campbell, '*Lex rex* and its author', *RSCHS*, 7 (1941): 204–28, and J. D. Ford, '*Lex rex justo posita*: Samuel Rutherford on the origins of government', in Mason (ed.), *Scots and Britons*, forthcoming . For the later covenanters see the idiosyncratic V. G. Kiernan, 'A banner with a strange device: the later covenanters', in T. Brotherstone (ed.), *Covenant, Charter and Party. Traditions of Revolt and Protest in Modern Scottish History* (Aberdeen, 1989), pp. 25–49. Very little indeed is known about the political thoughts of the 1688–9 revolutionaries, but a good background to the subject is J. Kenyon, *Revolution Principles. The Politics of Party 1689–1720* (Cambridge, 1977). The one recent attempt to engage the issue has been dismissive of ideology, B. P. Lenman, 'The poverty of political theory in the Scottish revolution 1689–90', in L. Schwoerer (ed.), *The Glorious Revolution 1688–89: Changing Perspectives* (Cambridge, 1992). For some insights into Fletcher, J. Robertson, *The Scottish Enlightenment and the Militia Issue* (Edinburgh, 1985), pp. 1–59 is useful.

Questions about the ideology surrounding the church-state argument again have attracted more interest among historians of the later sixteenth century. Some idea of the religious temperament of the age can be gleaned from G. Donaldson, 'The emergence of schism in seventeenth century Scotland', in G. Donaldson, *Scottish Church*

History (Edinburgh, 1985), pp. 204–19. A good starting point for presbyterian ideas is M. Lynch, 'Calvinism in Scotland, 1559–1638', in M. Prestwich (ed.), *International Calvinism 1541–1715* (Oxford, 1985), pp. 225–55. There is little presbyterian literature distinctly dealing with this issue which is not already cited above. On the whole episcopal ideas have been more thoroughly researched in recent years. See D. G. Mullan, *Episcopacy in Scotland. The History of an Idea 1560–1638* (Edinburgh, 1986); D. Stewart, 'The "Aberdeen Doctors" and the covenanters', *RSCHS*, 22 (1984): 35–44; and B. P. Lenman, 'The Scottish episcopal clergy and the ideology of jacobitism', in E. Cruickshanks (ed.), *Ideology and Conspiracy: Aspects of Jacobitism 1689–1759* (Edinburgh, 1982), pp. 36–48.

On the sixteenth century background to the British debate R. A. Mason, 'Scotching the Brut: politics, history and national myth in sixteenth century Britain', in R. A. Mason (ed.), *Scotland and England 1286–1815* (Edinburgh, 1987), pp. 60–84 is the best introduction. The early seventeenth century is well covered by A. H. Williamson, *Scottish National Consciousness in the Age of James VI* (Edinburgh, 1979), and B. Galloway, The Union of England and Scotland 1603–1608 (Edinburgh, 1986). Also of use is A. H. Williamson, 'Scotland, antichrist and the invention of Great Britain', in Dwyer, Mason and Murdoch (eds), *New Perspectives* (Edinburgh, 1980), pp. 34–58. On the early unionist propagandists see B. Macgregor, 'The propagandists and the union of 1603', *Scottish Tradition*, 15 (1989): 24–30, and B. R. Galloway and B. P. Levack (eds), *The Jacobean Union. Six Tracts of 1604* (Scottish History Society, Edinburgh, 1985). For the later seventeenth century see W. Ferguson, 'Imperial crowns: a neglected facet of the background to the treaty of union of 1707', *SHR*, 53 (1974): 22–44, and J. Robertson, 'Andrew Fletcher's vision of union', in Mason (ed.), *Scotland and England*, pp. 203–25. More generally B. P. Levack, 'Toward a more perfect union: England, Scotland and the constitution', in B. C. Malament (ed.), *After the Reformation: Essays in Honor of J. H. Hexter* (Manchester, 1980), pp. 57–74 lays out some of the main arguments throughout the century. Royalist propaganda encouraging British ideas can be detected from S. T. Bindoff, 'The Stuarts and their style', *English Historical Review*, 40 (1945): 192–216; J. W. Bennet, 'Britain among the fortunate isles', *Studies in Philology*, 3 (1956): 114–40; G. Parry, *The Seventeenth Century. The Intellectual and Cultural Context of English Literature, 1603–1700* (Harlow, 1989), pp. 9–27; R. Strong, *Britannia Triumphans: Inigo Jones, Rubens and Whitehall Palace* (London, 1980); D. J. Gordon, *Hymenai; Ben Johnson's Masque of Union* (Berkley and Los

Angeles, 1980); M. J. Enright, 'King James and his island: an archaic kingship belief', *SHR*, 55 (1976): 29–40. The English reaction to the idea of Britain can be uncovered in H. A. Macdougall, *Racial Myth in English History. Trojans, Teutons and Anglo Saxons* (Monreal, 1982); S. J. Piggott, *Ancient Britons and the Antiquarian Tradition. Ideas from the Renaissance to the Regency* (London, 1989).

4 THE IMPERIAL EXPERIMENT, 1603–37

A good introduction to the politics of James VI's reign is J. M. Brown, 'Scottish politics 1567–1625', in A. G. R. Smith (ed.), *The Reign of James VI and I* (London, 1973). The best political narrative for the latter half of the reign is M. Lee, *Government by Pen. Scotland under James VI and I* (Urbana, 1980). However, essential reading for understanding how James operated after 1603 is J. Wormald, 'James VI and I: two kings or one?', *History* 68 (1983): 187–209. Also useful is M. Lee, *Great Britain's Solomon. James VI and I in his Three Kingdoms* (Urbana, 1990). An interesting, if uncritical, discussion of James's privy council is M. Lee, 'James VI's government of Scotland after 1603', *SHR*, 55 (1976): 41–53. The same author also argues that James sought to undercut aristocratic power in government, M. Lee, 'James VI and the aristocracy', *Scotia*, 1 (1977): 18–23. For the union there is, in addition to what is cited above, D. H. Willson, 'James I and Anglo-Scottish unity', in W. A. Aiken and B. D. Hennings (eds), *Conflict in Stuart England* (London, 1960), 41–55. A useful study of a Jacobean unionist is M. Perceval-Maxwell, 'Sir William Alexander of Menstrie, 1567–1640', *Scottish Tradition* 11 (1981): 14–25. Union and colonisation is the subject of M. Perceval-Maxwell, *The Scottish Migration to Ulster in the Reign of James I* (London, 1973). The economic context is found in S. G. E. Lythe, *The Economy of Scotland in its European Setting 1550–1625* (Edinburgh, 1960); S. G. E. Lythe, 'The union of the crowns in 1603 and the debate on economic integration', *Scottish Journal of Political Economy*, 5 (1958): 219–28; T. M. Devine and S. G. E. Lythe, 'The economy of Scotland under James VI: a revision article', *SHR*, 50 (1971): 91–106.

For Charles I the best political narrative is M. Lee, *The Road to Revolution. Scotland under Charles I 1625–37* (Urbana, 1985). See too Professor Lee's provocative 'Scotland and the 'General Crisis' of the seventeenth century', *SHR*, 63 (1984): 136–54, and his 'Charles I and the end of conciliar government in Scotland', *Albion* 12 (1980): 315–36. However, for a different interpretation see

A. I. Macinnes, *Charles I and the Making of the Covenanting Movement 1625–1641* (Edinburgh, 1991). Of limited use is C. Carleton, *Charles I. The Personal Monarch* (London, 1983), and D. Mathew, *Scotland under Charles I* (London, 1955).

On the development of church administration see W. R. Foster, *The Church Before the Covenants. The Church of Scotland 1596–1638* (Edinburgh, 1975), and G. I. R. McMahon, 'The Scottish courts of high commission 1610–1638', *RSCHS,,* 15 (1966): 193–209. The important career of John Spottiswoode is the subject of J. Kirk, *Archbishop Spottiswoode and the See of Glasgow* (Glasgow, 1988), and A. B. Bircher, 'Archbishop John Spottiswoode, chancellor of Scotland, 1635–1638', *Church History* 39 (1970): 317–26. A useful insight into James's developing religious ideas is K. Fincham and P. Lake, 'The ecclesiastical policy of James I', *Journal of British Studies,* 24 (1985), 169–207. English influences in Scotland are discussed in G. Donaldson, 'The attitude of Whitgift and Bancroft to the Scottish church', *TRHS*, 4th series, 24 (1942): 95–115; H. Watt, 'William Laud and Scotland', *RSCHS,* 7 (1941): 171–90; and C. Carlton, *Archbishop Laud* (London and New York, 1987), pp. 154–61. On the liturgical reforms see I. B. Cowan, 'The five articles of Perth', in D. Shaw (ed.), *Reformation and Revolution* (Edinburgh, 1967), pp. 160–77; P. H. R. Mackay, 'The reception given to the five articles of Perth', *RSCHS,,* 19 (1977): 185–201; G. Donaldson, *The Making of the Scottish Prayer Book* (Edinburgh, 1954). For early dissent D. Stevenson, 'Conventicles in the kirk, 1619–37', *RSCHS,* 18 (1972–4): 99–114. The existence of a catholic plot at court is the subject of C. M. Hibbard, *Charles I and the Popish Plot* (Chapel Hill, 1983), pp. 3–89.

5 REVOLUTION, WAR AND CONQUEST, 1637–60

D. Stevenson, *The Scottish Revolution 1637–44. The Triumph of the Covenanters* (Newton Abbot, 1973), and D. Stevenson, *Revolution and Counter Revolution in Scotland 1644–1651* (London, 1977) provide the best narrative framework to the covenanting era. A very useful summary is found in D. Stevenson, *The Covenanters. The National Covenant and Scotland* (The Saltire Society, 1988).

The constitutional crisis of the early seventeenth century is outlined in E. J. Cowan, 'The union of the crowns and the crisis of the constitution in 17th century Scotland', in Dysvik, Mykland and Oldervoll (eds), *The Satellite State*, pp. 121–40. The British dimension to the covenanting era is dealt with more fully in P. Donald, *An Uncounselled King. Charles I and the Scottish Troubles 1637–1641* (Cambridge, 1990), and C. Russell, *The Fall of the British Monarchies 1637–1642* (Oxford 1991). Further elucidation of the covenanters concern with British issues can be found in P. Donald, 'The Scottish national covenant and British politics, 1638–1640', in Morrill (ed.), *The Scottish National Covenant,* pp. 90–105; P. H. Donald, 'New light on the Anglo-Scottish contacts of 1640', *Historical Research,* 62 (1989): 221–31; D. Stevenson, 'The early covenanters and the federal union of Britain', in Mason (ed.), *Scotland and England,* pp. 163–81; L. Kaplan, 'Steps to war: the Scots and the parliament, 1642–1643', *Journal of British Studies,* 9 (1970): 50–70; C. V. Wedgewood, 'The covenanters and the first civil war', *SHR,* 39 (1960): 1–15; C. Russell, 'The British problem and the English civil war', *History,* 72 (1987): 395–415. On the solemn league and covenant period see L. Kaplan, *Politics and Religion During the English Revolution. The Scots and the Long Parliament, 1643–1645* (New York, 1976); E. J. Cowan, 'The solemn league and covenant', in Mason (ed.), *Scotland and England,* pp. 182–202; and L. Mulligan, 'The Scottish alliance and the committee of both kingdoms, 1644–46', *Historical Studies,* 14 (1970): 173–88. For the older interpretation which stressed the covenanters' obsession with religion see Trevor-Roper, 'Scotland and the puritan revolution', in Trevor-Roper, *Religion, the Reformation and Social Change,* pp. 392–444. The best introduction to Ireland's position in the constitutional tangle is M. Perceval-Maxwell, 'Ireland and the monarchy in the early Stuart multiple kingdom', in *Historical Journal,* 34 (1991): 279–95. The connection with events in Britain is explored in C. Russell, 'The British background to the Irish rebellion of 1641', *Historical Research,* 61 (1988): 166–82; M. Perceval-Maxwell, 'Ireland and Scotland 1638–1648', in Morrill (ed.), *The Scottish National Covenant,* pp. 193–211; and D. Stevenson, *Scottish Covenanters and Irish Confederates* (Belfast, 1981). More specific topics are discussed in M. Perceval-Maxwell, 'Strafford, the Ulster Scots and the covenanters', *Irish Historical Studies,* 18 (1973): 524–51; M. Perceval-Maxwell, 'The adoption of the solemn league and covenant by the Scots in Ulster', *Scotia,* 2 (1978): 3–18; and R. Gillespie, 'An army sent from God: Scots at war in Ireland, 1642–9', in Macdougall (ed.), *Scotland and War,* pp. 113–32.

On the government of the covenanters see A. I. Macinnes, 'The Scottish constitution 1638–51: the rise and fall of oligarchic centralism', in Morrill (ed.), *The Scottish National Covenant,* pp. 106–33, and D. Stevenson (ed.), *Government under the Covenanters 1637–1651* (Scottish History Society, Edinburgh, 1982), pp. vii–l. The covenanting army is the subject of E. Furgol, 'Scotland turned Sweden, 1638–1651', in Morrill (ed.), *The Scottish National Covenant,* pp. 134–54, and

E. M. Furgol, 'The military and ministers as agents of presbyterian imperialism in England and Ireland, 1640–1648', in Dwyer, Mason and Murdoch (eds), *New Perspectives*, pp. 95–115. Religious topics are the subject of D. Stevenson, 'The radical party in the kirk, 1637–45', *Journal of Ecclesiastical History*, 25 (1974): 135–65; D. Stevenson, 'The general assembly and the commisssion of the kirk, 1638–51', *RSCHS*, 19 (1977): 59–80; W. Makey, 'Presbyterians and canterburians in the Scottish revolution', in Macdougall (ed.), *Church, Politics and Society*, pp. 151–66; and R. A. Mason, *The Glasgow Assembly, 1638* (Glasgow, 1988). Some explanations for support are offered in R. Mason, 'The aristocracy, episcopacy and the revolution of 1638', in Brotherstone (ed.), *Covenant, Charter and Party*, pp. 7–24. Prominent royalists are the subjects of E. J. Cowan, *Montrose. For Covenant and King* (London, 1977); H. L. Rubinstein, *Captain Luckless. James, First Duke of Hamilton* (New Jersey, 1976); and D. Stevenson, *Alasdair MacColla and the Highland Problem of the Seventeenth Century* (Edinburgh, 1980). A more general analysis of royalist support is K. M. Brown, 'Courtiers and cavaliers: service, Anglicisation and loyalty among the royalist nobility', in Morrill (ed.), *The Scottish National Covenant*, pp. 155–92. For the wider highland attitude to the covenants see A. I. Macinnes, 'Scottish Gaeldom, 1638–1651: the vernacular response to the covenanting dynamic', in Dwyer, Mason and Murdoch (eds), *New Perspectives*, pp. 59–94; A. I. Macinnes, 'The first Scottish tories', *SHR*, 67 (1988): 56–66; A. I. Macinnes, 'The impact of the civil wars and interregnum: political disruption and social change within Scottish Gaeldom', in Mitchison and Roebuck (eds), *Economy and Society in Scotland and Ireland*, pp. 58–69.

The 1650s is very exhaustively detailed in F. Dow, *Cromwellian Scotland 1651–1660* (Edinburgh, 1979). Much more accessible is D. Stevenson, 'Cromwell, Scotland and Ireland', in J. Morrill (ed.), *Oliver Cromwell and the English Revolution* (Harlow, 1990), pp. 149–80. R. Hutton, *The British Republic 1649–1660* (Basingstoke, 1990) does not really live up to its title. More specialised topics are dealt with in P. J. Pinckney, 'The Scottish representation in the Cromwellian parliament of 1656', *SHR*, 46 (1967): 95–114; J. A. Casada, 'The Scottish representation in Richard Cromwell's parliament', *SHR*, 51 (1972): 124–47; R. Gillespie, 'Landed society and the interregnum in Ireland and Scotland', in Mitchison and Roebuck (eds), *Economy and Society in Scotland and Ireland*, pp. 38–57; T. M. Devine, 'The Cromwellian union and the Scottish burghs: the case of Aberdeen and Glasgow, 1652–60', in J. Butt and J. T. Ward (eds), *Scottish Themes. Essays in Honour of Professor S. G. E. Lythe* (Edinburgh, 1976), pp. 1–16;

J. Buckroyd, 'Lord Broghill and the Scottish church 1655–1656', *SHR*, 27 (1976): 359–68.

6   RESTORING THE KINGDOM, 1660–88

The restoration period still awaits a good political history. However, R. Hutton, *Charles II King of England, Scotland, and Ireland* (Oxford, 1989) is a fine example of British history. Less impressive, but worth a look is J. Miller, *James II. A Study in Kingship* (London, 1978), pp. 210–16. Also on high politics, specifically on Lauderdale, is M. Lee, *The Cabal* (Urbana, 1965), pp. 28–69. Lauderdale's more domestic affairs are the subject of J. Patrick, 'The origins of opposition to Lauderdale in the Scottish parliament of 1673', *SHR*, 53 (1974): 1–21. Useful narratives of the religious problem in Scotland are J. Buckroyd, *Church and State in Scotland 1660–1681* (Edinburgh, 1980); I. B. Cowan, *The Scottish Covenanters, 1660–88* (London, 1976); J. M. Buckroyd, *The Life of James Sharp Archbishop of St Andrews 1618–1679* (Edinburgh, 1987). See too J. M. Buckroyd, 'Bridging the gap: Scotland 1659–1660', *SHR*, 46 (1987): 1–25; J. M. Buckroyd, 'Anti-clericalism in Scotland during the restoration', in Macdougall (ed.), *Church and Society*, pp. 167–85; J. A. Lamb, 'Archbishop Alexander Burnet: 1614–1684', *RSCHS*, 11 (1951–3): 133–48; J. M. Buckroyd, 'The dismissal of Archbishop Alexander Burnet, 1669', *RSCHS*, 18 (1973): 149–55. The government of the highlands is refreshingly analysed in A. I. Macinnes, 'Repression and conciliation: the highland dimension 1660–1688', *SHR*, 66 (1986): 153–74. For the union and economic relations see J. Patrick, 'A union broken? Restoration politics in Scotland', in Wormald (ed.), *Scotland Revisited*, pp. 119–28; D. Woodward, 'Anglo-Scottish trade and English commercial policy during the 1660s', *SHR*, 56 (1977): 153–74, and E. Hughes, 'The negotiations for a commercial union between England and Scotland in 1668', *SHR*, 24 (1926–7): 30–47.

7   SCOTLAND AND THE BRITISH REVOLUTION, 1688–1715

The history of the revolution of 1688–9 in Scotland has yet to be written. A useful starting point for the events which made up the revolution is H. B. Van der Zee, *Revolution in the Family* (London, 1988). W. A. Speck, *Reluctant Revolutionaries. Englishmen and the Revolution of 1688* (Oxford, 1988) is not only helpful for the

English background, but shares a common theme with I. B. Cowan, 'The reluctant revolutionaries: Scotland in 1688', in E. Cruickshanks (ed.), *By force or Default? The Revolution of 1688–1689* (Edinburgh, 1989), pp. 65–81. On the revolution settlement, I. B. Cown, 'Church and State Reformed? The Revolution of 1688–9 in Scotland' in J. I. Israel (ed.), *The Anglo-Dutch Moment* (Cambridge University Press, 1991), 163–84. A solid political history of Scotland during William's reign is provided by P. W. J. Riley, *King William and the Scottish Politicians* (Edinburgh, 1979). More detail on the revolutionary settlement can be found in B. P. Lenman, 'The Scottish nobility and the revolution of 1688–1690', in R. Beddard (ed.), *The Revolutions of 1688* (Oxford, 1991), 137–62; and J. Halliday, 'The Club and the revolution in Scotland 1689–90', *SHR*, 45 (1966): 143–59. For the military dimension to the revolt in Scotland and the origins of jacobitism see P. Hopkins, *Glencoe and the End of the Highland War* (Edinburgh, 1986); B. P. Lenman, The Jacobite Risings in Britain 1689–1746 (London, 1980); and B. Lenman, *The Jacobite Clans of the Great Glen 1650–1784* (London, 1984). A concise survey of jacobitism is B. Lenman, *The Jacobite Cause* (Glasgow, 1986). Claverhouse's inflated career is examined in A. M. Scott, *Bonnie Dundee. John Grahame of Claverhouse Viscount Dundee* (Edinburgh, 1989), and M. Linklater and C. Hesketh, *For King and Conscience. John Graham of Claverhouse, Viscount Dundee* (London, 1990), but both biographies are disappointing on wider issues. Later jacobite issues are discussed in J. Gibson, *Playing the Scottish Card. The Franco-jacobite Invasion of 1708* (Edinburgh, 1988); E. K. Carmichael, 'Jacobitism in the Scottish commission of the peace, 1707–1760', *SHR*, (1978): 58–69; E. Gregg, 'Was Queen Anne a jacobite?', *History* 57 (1972): 358–75.

The on-going religious dispute of the post-revolutionary years is surveyed in A. L. Drummond and J. Bulloch, *The Scottish Church 1688–1843* (Edinburgh, 1973). More detailed studies are L. K. Glassey, 'William II and the settlement of religion in Scotland 1688–1690', *RSCHS*, 23 (1989): 317–29; T. Clarke, 'The Williamite episcopalians and the glorious revolution in Scotland', *RSCHS*, 24 (1990): 35–51; R. B. Knox, 'Establishment and toleration during the reigns of William, Mary and Anne', *RSCHS*, 23 (1989): 330–47, and D. Szechi, 'The politics of 'persecution': Scots episcopalian toleration and the Harley ministry, 1710–12', *Studies in Church History*, 21 (1984): 275–87. Of more limited interest are T. Maxwell, 'William III and the Scots presbyterians. Part I – The crisis in Whitehall' *RSCHS*, 15 (1966): 117–40: T. Maxwell, 'William III and the Scots presbyterians. Part II', *RSCHS*, 15 (1966): 169–91;

D. H. Whiteford, 'Jacobitism as a factor in presbyterian episcopalian relationships in Scotland 1689–90. I – James by divine right', *RSCHS*, 16 (1967): 129–49; and D. H. Whiteford, 'Jacobitism as a factor in presbyterian episcopalian relationships in Scotland 1689–1714. II – The afflicted church', *RSCHS*, 16 (1967): 185–201.

For the economic background to the treaty of union see T. C. Smout, *Scottish Trade on the Eve of Union* (Edinburgh, 1963); T. C. Smout, 'The road to union?' in J. Holmes (ed.), *Britain after the Glorious Revolution 1689–1714* (London, 1969), pp. 176–96; T. C. Smout, 'The Anglo-Scottish union of 1707 I. The economic background', *Economic History Review*, 16 (1963–4): 455–67; T. C. Smout, 'Scotland in the seventeenth century: a satellite economy?', in Dyrvik, Mykland and Oldervoll (eds), *The Satellite State*, pp. 9–35; C. A. Whatley, 'Salt, coal and the union of 1707: a revision article', *SHR*, 66 (1987): 26–45; C. A. Whatley, 'Economic causes and consequencies of the union of 1707. A survey', *SHR*, 68 (1989): 150–81. The Darien issue is in need of revision, but still of use is G. P. Insh, *The Company of Scotland trading to Africa and the Indies* (London, 1932), and for some colour see J. Prebble, *The Darien Disaster* (London, 1968).

The politics of Queen Anne's reign and the treaty of union is well covered by P. W. J. Riley, *The Union of Scotland and England* (Manchester, 1978). There is also some value in reading separately P. W. J. Riley, 'The formation of the Scottish ministry of 1703', *SHR*, 44 (1965): 112–34; P. W. J. Riley, 'The Scottish parliament of 1703', *SHR*, 47 (1968): 129–50; P. W. J. Riley, 'The making of the treaty of union of 1706', *SHR*, 43 (1964): 89–110. Something of the queen's attitude to the Scots can be picked up in E. Gregg, *Queen Anne* (London, 1980). Post-union politics is surveyed in P. W. J. Riley, 'The structure of Scottish politics and the union of 1707', in T. I. Rae (ed.), *The Union of 1707. Its impact on Scotland* (Glasgow, 1974). Details of the Scots at Westminster can be found in G. Holmes, *British Politics in the Age of Anne* (London, 1987), pp. 337–9, 393–5; C. Jones, 'Godolphin, the whig junto and the Scots: a new Lords division list from 1709', *SHR*, 58 (1979): 158–74; C. Jones, 'The scheme lords, the necessityous lords, and the Scots lords': the earl of Oxford's management and the 'party of the crown', in the house of lords, 1711–14', in C. Jones (ed.), *Party and Management in Parliament 1660–1784* (Leicester, 1984), pp. 123–51; D. Szechi, 'Some insights on the Scottish MPs and peers returned in the 1710 election', *SHR*, 40 (1981): 61–75; G. S. Holmes, 'The Hamilton affair of 1711–12: a crisis in Anglo-Scottish relations', *English Historical Review*, 77 (1962): 257–82.

INDEX